IMAGES
of America

BIBB COUNTY

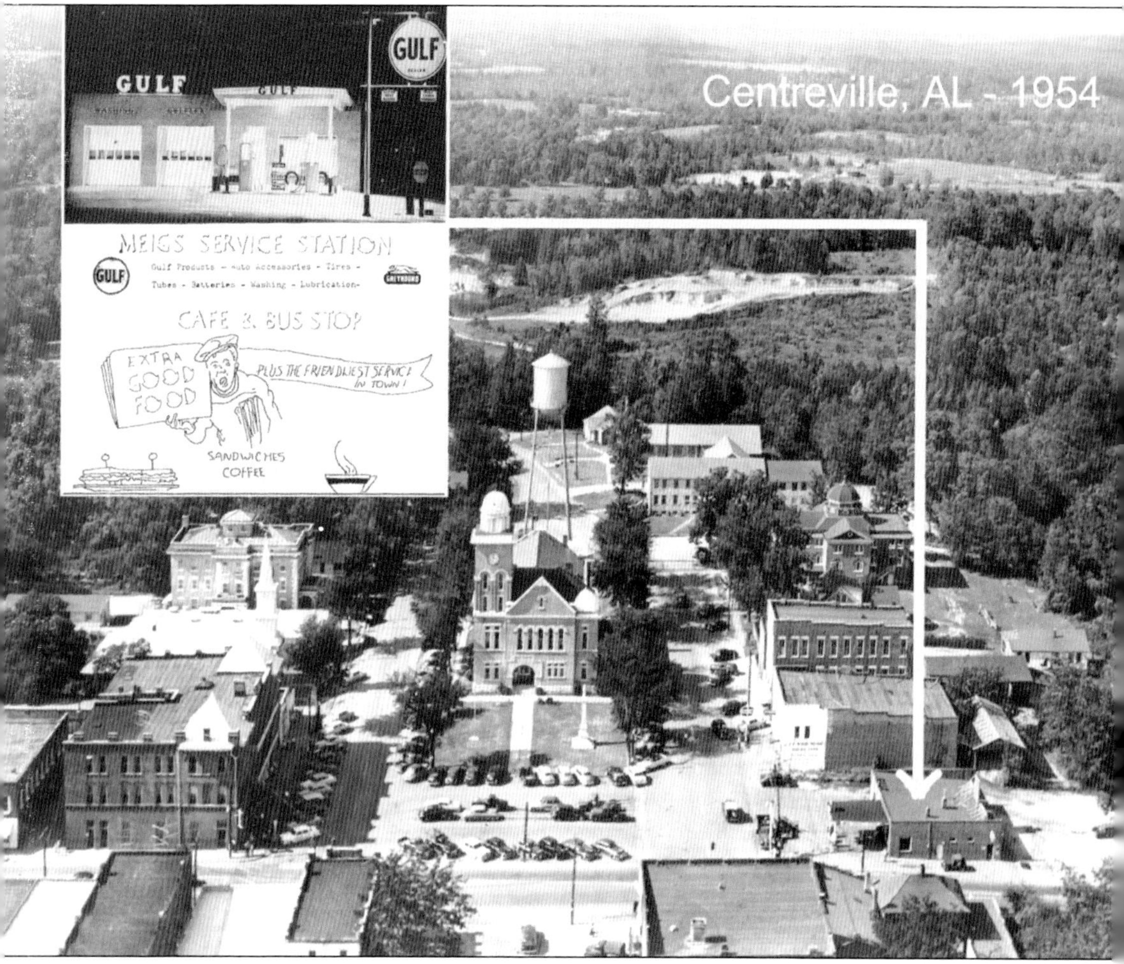

This aerial photograph was taken in the mid-20th century by a photographer who traveled from town to town taking pictures that he would then sell to local businesses and individuals. This particular photograph was sold to Dozier Meigs, who ran the gas station located in the bottom right corner of the image. It shows the way Centreville Historic Town Square looked in 1954. Little has changed in the way the historic square has looked in the past 100 years, and Bibb County is fortunate to have one that still possesses the look, charm, and character of a small, traditional Alabama town. (Courtesy of Dozier Meigs.)

ON THE COVER: Mariana and O. P. Dailey Mercantile store, c. 1939, can also be seen in the above aerial photograph between the Centreville Presbyterian Church and the bank building, which is the largest one in town. The store is where all the cars are located on the left side of the image. As was typical of Alabama in the "Pre-Mega-Mart" days, a general mercantile was a place where a shopper could generally find anything needed. Among the things for sale were Corn Flakes for 8¢, boxes of ABC and Liberty Bell Soda Crackers, brooms, beans, pots, pans, pickles, hoop cheese, washtubs, McCormick Tea, Pure Princess ice cream, apple juice, bread, Hershey's chocolate bars, tobacco, butter churns, Rainbow washing detergent, work hats, school supplies, boys' dress shirts for 49¢, ties, ladies dresses for 98¢, clocks, boots, shoes, cloth, Keen Kutter razor blades, Golden Flake potato chips, and even chamber pots. Also Dailey's would deliver right to the front door. (Courtesy of Betty Burt.)

IMAGES
of America

BIBB COUNTY

Vicky Clemmons and David Daniel
on behalf of the
Centreville Historic
Preservation Commission

ARCADIA
PUBLISHING

ISBN 978-0-7385-6729-7

Published by Arcadia Publishing
Charleston, South Carolina

Printed in the United States of America

Library of Congress Catalog Card Number: 2008926857

For all general information contact Arcadia Publishing at:
Telephone 843-853-2070
Fax 843-853-0044
E-mail sales@arcadiapublishing.com
For customer service and orders:
Toll-Free 1-888-313-2665

Visit us on the Internet at www.arcadiapublishing.com

Contents

ACKNOWLEDGMENTS

The Centreville Historic Preservation Commission members wish to express gratitude to all who have assisted us in the preparation and completion of this book. To all who have submitted photographs, provided research, donated their time, and helped in so many other ways, we say a heartfelt thank you! Thank you also to those who have gone before us in this effort to preserve and document our treasured Bibb County history and heritage. We would be amiss if we did not acknowledge your hard work and your contribution. It helps us to better understand who we are. Your work will also help thinking persons of future generations in their efforts to understand who they are and where they have come in this sacred and shared journey of life.

From David Daniel: I want to thank my wife, Karen Reynolds Daniel, not just for your hard work on this book—I know that is standard fare with you. Karen, getting to know you through the years we have shared means I have a better vision of the Father of all life, because I have seen you allow Him to have His way with the gifts He has given you. You light up my life.

From Vicky Lynn Patton Clemmons: I personally dedicate this book to my husband, Cliff Clemmons—the love of my life, my support system, my complaint department, my therapist, my partner in crime, and the other part of my heart. I also thank him for my new pretty pink laptop. And to my daughter Catie Perry, you are my best friend and my own personal gift from God.

INTRODUCTION

The Choctaw people referred to this area as Cahawba, which means "the river above." This meaning is probably derived from the fact that it is at this location in the namesake Cahaba River where it rises from the coastal plains of Alabama to meet the Piedmont Plateau. Early settlers picked up this name from the original inhabitants, and the name "Falls of the Cahaba," or "Cahaba Falls," came into common use. It was here, within three weeks of territorial governor William Wyatt Bibb's appointment of officers, that the County of Cahawba was formed, and by so doing Bibb County enjoys the distinction of being a county that is actually older than the State of Alabama itself, which was formed later in 1819.

In the pages of this book, the authors believe that individuals living both within and outside the county will be able to find photographic records of family homes, places, and people they may have heard about from ancestors or relatives but never had the opportunity to see. We hope that by seeing these images each person will come to better understand and appreciate those who have lived before us in this beautiful land we call Bibb County Alabama.

While many of the photographs and pictures in this book have been previously published, we have made a distinct effort to use, within the limits of this particular publication, as many unpublished pictures as possible. We wish people to know that, at the time of publication, we have accumulated more than 1,500 additional photographs that are not in this book. These photographs and documents have been made available to the Centreville Historic Preservation Commission by both local citizens and county individuals. These gracious folk have allowed us to scan and copy their family and historic photographs in order that you may see them and benefit from their generosity. We hope you take advantage of this offer and use them for family, historic, or genealogical research.

All of us have, or know of, photographs that we treasure and wish to preserve. Readers of this book will see a number of images that have deteriorated over time, and some images have become almost indiscernible. Since this deterioration continues because of paper acidity, handling, and other detriments, even with excellent care by the owner, it is recommended that every person who has such treasured photographs makes a concentrated effort to preserve them.

Today one of the best and most economical means of preservation is to have any valuable photographs or other paper-based historic records digitized in a professional manner with master copies to be stored in a safe place. One of the goals of the Centreville Historic Preservation Commission is the preservation of the photographs, letters, and documents that reflect the history of Bibb County. It is our goal to preserve a digital database of these records and make them available to the public for personal, family, historic, or genealogical research.

This is why we now offer to any individual or group free digital copying of any historically significant photograph or document related to Bibb County. This allows the owner of the item to retain the original and receive a free-of-charge, professional, digital master copy for safekeeping. By doing this, we hope to create a database of rapidly deteriorating, gelatin-based photographs and acid-based paper records so that these valuable historic resources may be preserved for future generations.

If you have, or know of someone who has, photographs, letters, or documents relevant to the history of Bibb County, its people, places, or industry, we gladly offer this service free of charge in exchange that your records be entered into our historic database for the public to see.

Toward this end, we at the Centreville Historic Preservation Commission hope that those who have an interest in further discovery will avail themselves of our new historic preservation project by visiting our new Web site at www.HistoricBibb.org. This Web site will be used to disseminate and gather information about Bibb County's history, with a special focus on photographs and letters. It includes the images gathered for this book and other documents that have not been available to the public before. On this site, users will be able to communicate information about each item and exchange photographs and documents placed on the site by other users. We hope this leads to the discovery of additional content for this online historic database and helps preserve more of Bibb County's history.

We ask that you help us support this ongoing effort with a donation, which may be made on the Web site or by mail to Centreville Historic Preservation Commission / 1270 Walnut Street / Centreville, Alabama, 35042.

People wishing to have their historic photographs and documents considered for preservation, please contact David Daniel by telephone at (205) 316-9331 or by e-mail at ddaniel@HistoricBibb.org.

All proceeds from the sale of this book and from the digital historic database located at www.HistoricBibb.org will be used by the Centreville Historic Preservation Commission for preservation projects in Bibb County, Alabama.

The Centreville Historic Preservation Commission wishes to acknowledge that there may be incorrect information in the content of our book, such as misspellings, incorrect dates, inaccurate information, or other errors. We have attempted to avoid such problems but this book is based on material submitted by individuals and obtained from other historical records, family genealogy, and legend. It is therefore impossible to guarantee total accuracy.

The greatest treasure to be found in Bibb County is its people. We hope you enjoy this photographic glimpse back into the county's history, and we hope you come and see what makes Bibb County such a special place. Welcome to beautiful and historic Bibb County, Alabama. Thank you for your purchase of this book.

One

Early Families and Homes

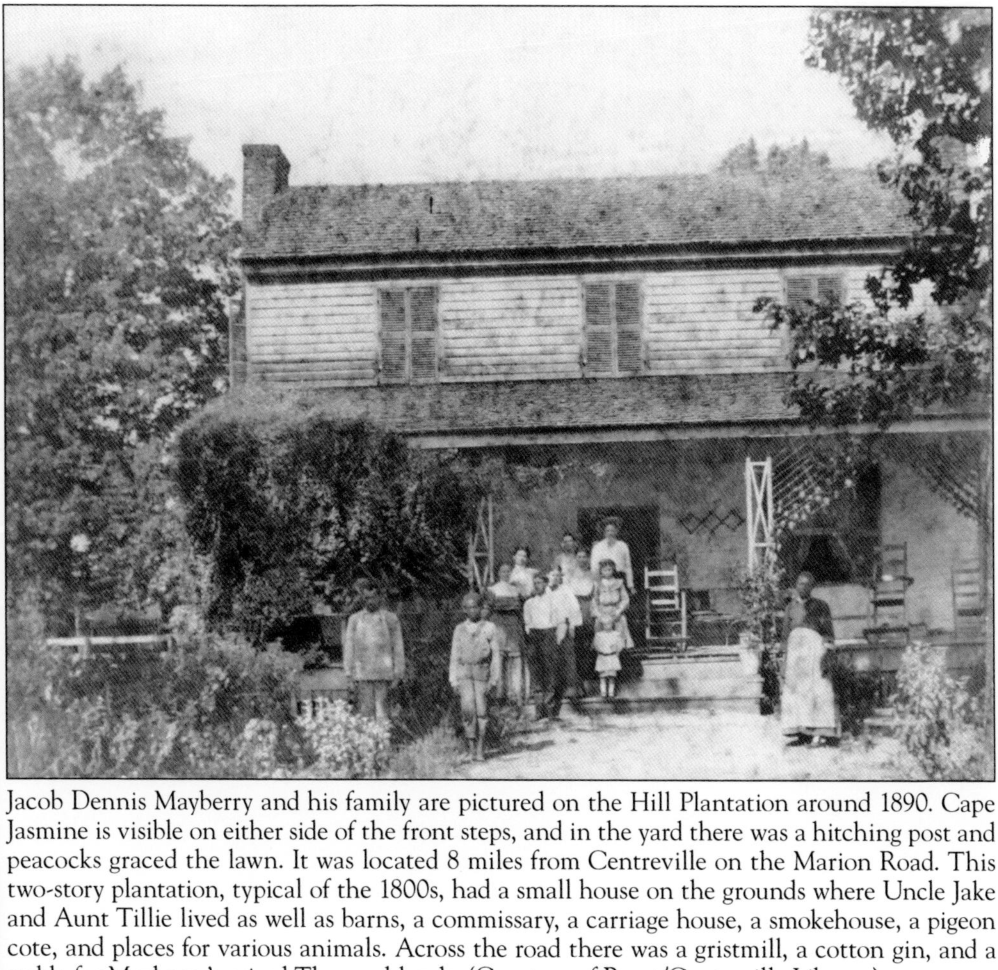

Jacob Dennis Mayberry and his family are pictured on the Hill Plantation around 1890. Cape Jasmine is visible on either side of the front steps, and in the yard there was a hitching post and peacocks graced the lawn. It was located 8 miles from Centreville on the Marion Road. This two-story plantation, typical of the 1800s, had a small house on the grounds where Uncle Jake and Aunt Tillie lived as well as barns, a commissary, a carriage house, a smokehouse, a pigeon cote, and places for various animals. Across the road there was a gristmill, a cotton gin, and a stable for Mayberry's prized Thoroughbreds. (Courtesy of Brent/Centreville Library.)

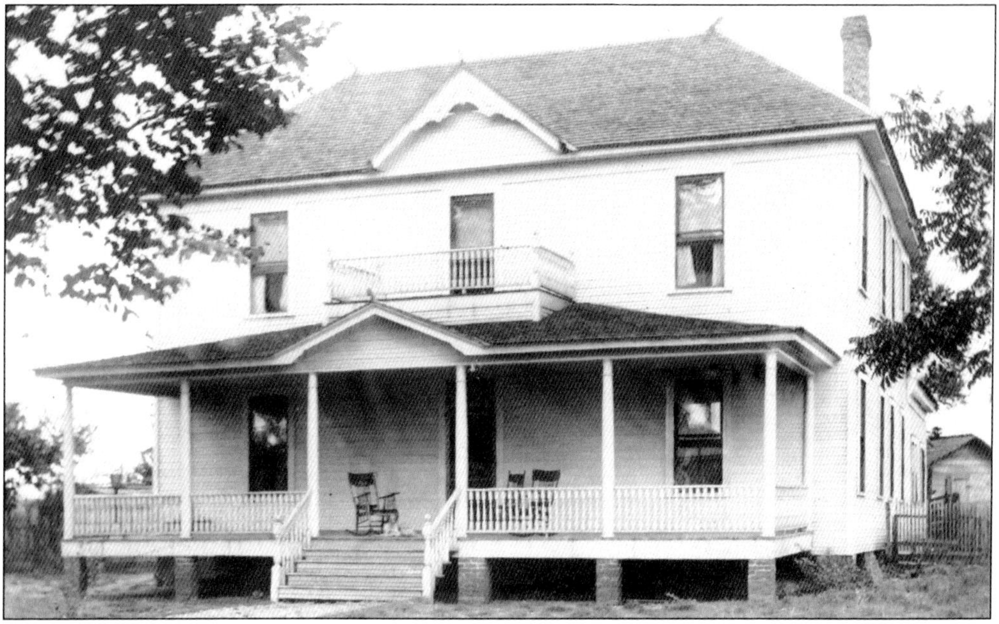

This was the home of the Avery family. Built in the late 1800s, the house was considered the family's plantation home and was sold in the early 1900s when the Averys decided to move to Centreville and build a home near the Centreville Historic Town Square. This earlier house is still a family residence. (Courtesy of Dalton and Anne Murphy.)

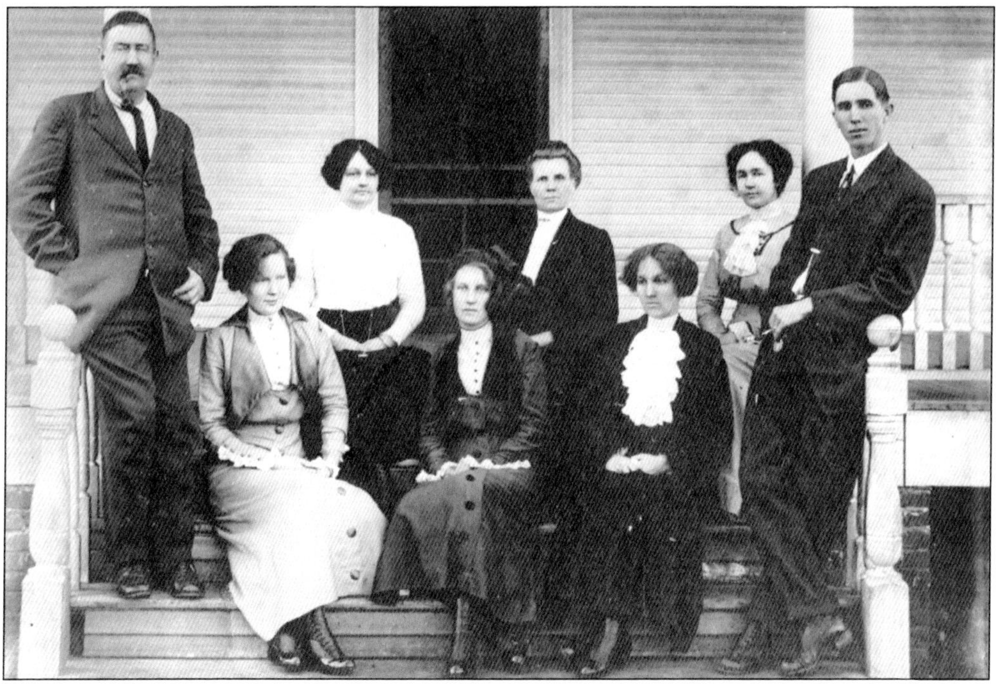

The Avery family poses on the steps of its home on Christmas Day in 1912. The family members are, from left to right, Alec, Grace, Stella, Christine, Ola, Josie Mae, Birdie, and Henry. This home is located at the junction of Alabama State Route 219 and Highway 82, just north of Centreville. (Courtesy of Dalton and Ann Murphy.)

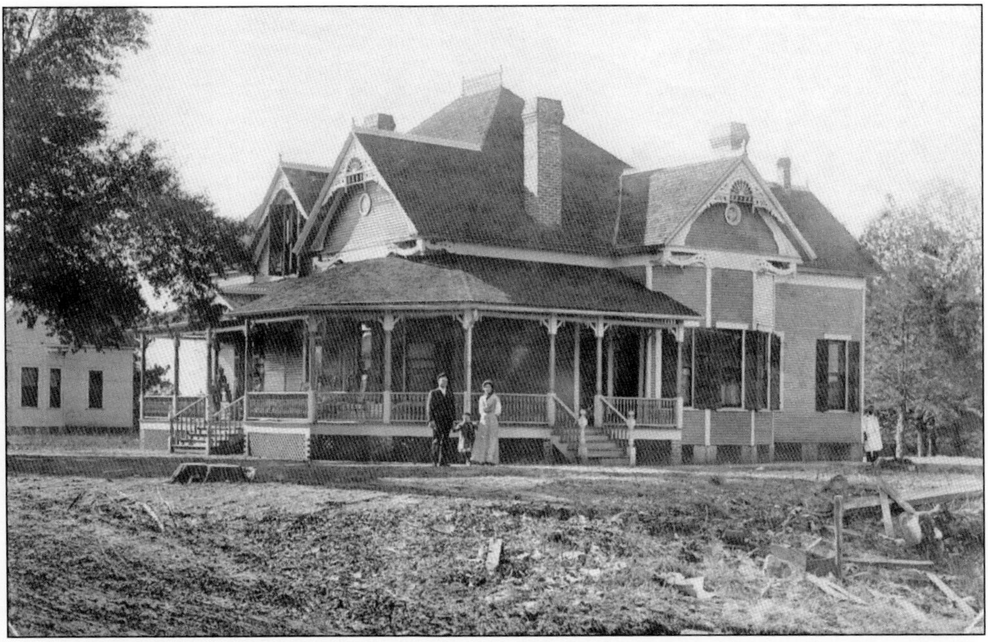

The home of the R. S. Avery family was built in 1909. It was later owned by the Alex Avery family. This house is currently the home of Mayor Dalton Murphy and his wife, Anne. It is located on 119 Cedar Street in Centreville. (Courtesy of Dalton and Anne Murphy.)

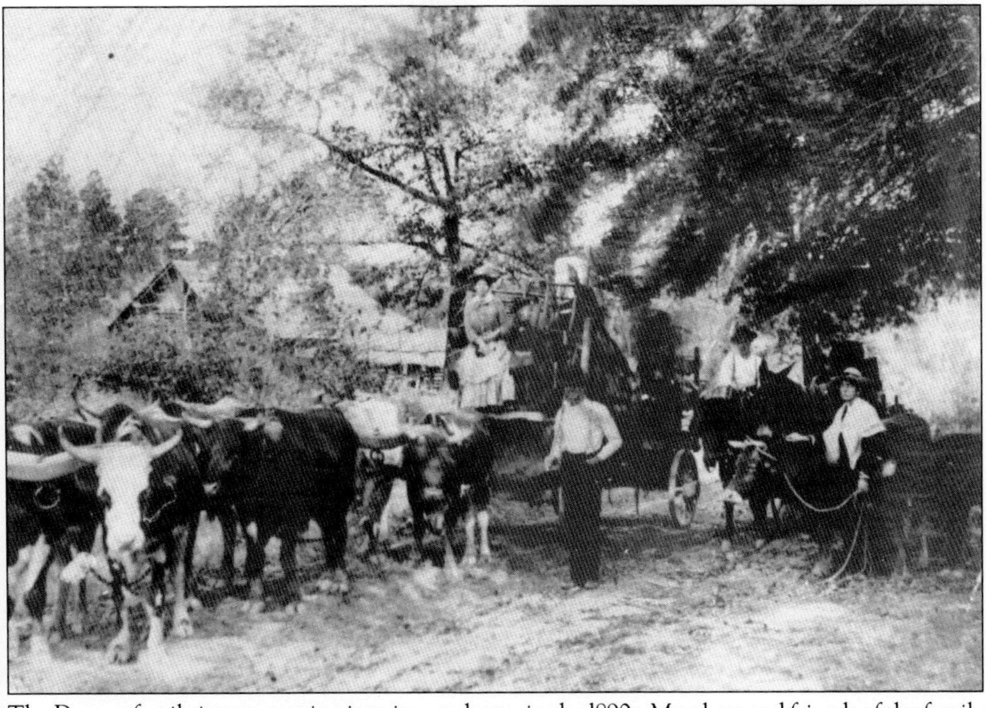

The Deason family is seen moving into its new home in the 1890s. Members and friends of the family are, from left to right, Magnolia Deason and unidentified on the wagon; John Owens in charge of the three-team of steers; and Mary Jean Deason tending her cows with two neighbors, Melford and Rufus Kornegay mounted on mules, helping. (Courtesy of Brent/ Centreville Library.)

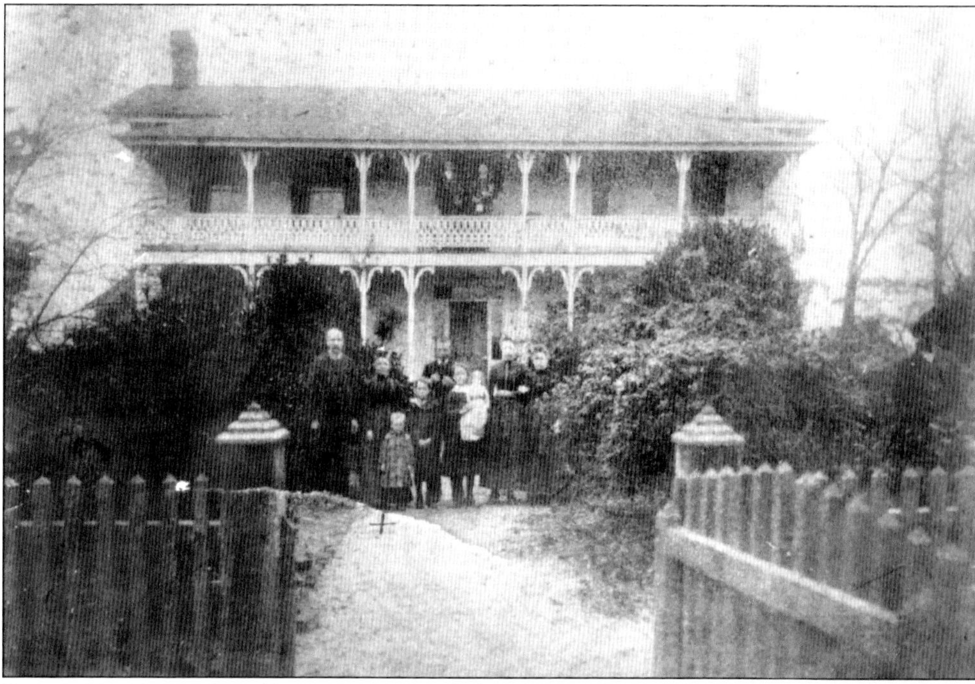

Pictured in 1890 is Jesse Dean Cooper with family members and students that boarded with the family. Cooper was a schoolmaster in the area, and Cooper Street in Centreville near the residence was named after him. He was instrumental in early education for Centreville and the surrounding communities. The present owners are Randy and Jennifer Ford. (Courtesy of Harold Cottingham.)

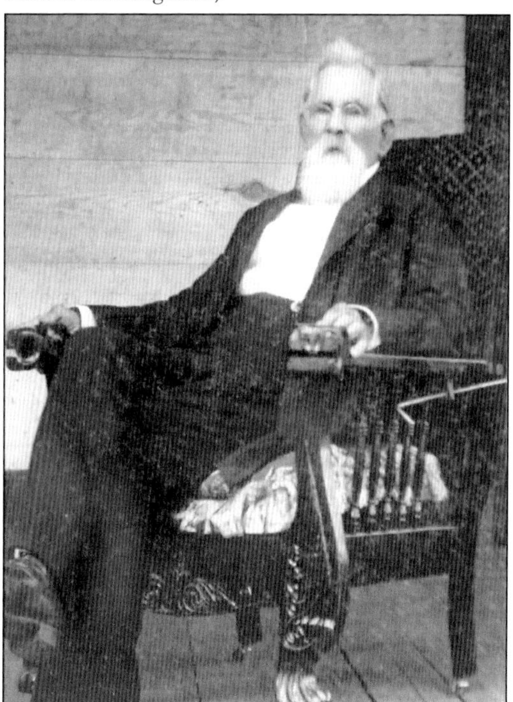

Richard Hopkins Pratt (1828–1908) graduated from the University of Alabama with a degree in teaching. His parents were Absalom and Mary Dickerson Pratt from River Bend. In 1861, Richard entered the service of the Confederacy as a captain in Company D of the 20th Alabama Regiment. He devoted his life to education in the classroom, and he was the superintendent of education until his death. He was known for his contributions to education at Sandy Chapel and later for the Six Mile Male and Female Academy. (Courtesy of Mary McCord Garner.)

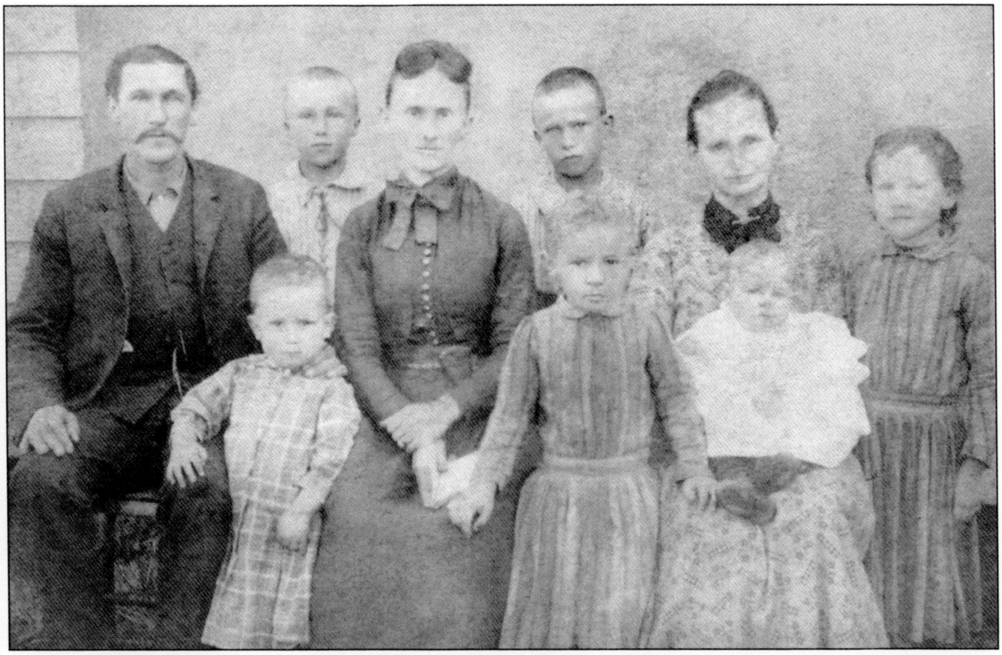

C. H. "Doc" Cleveland is pictured with his wife, Mollie, and their children. Doc was from the community of Trio, which was located on the buggy route from Montevallo to Selma. Trio had its own blacksmith shop and general store/post office. (Courtesy of Mary McCord Garner.)

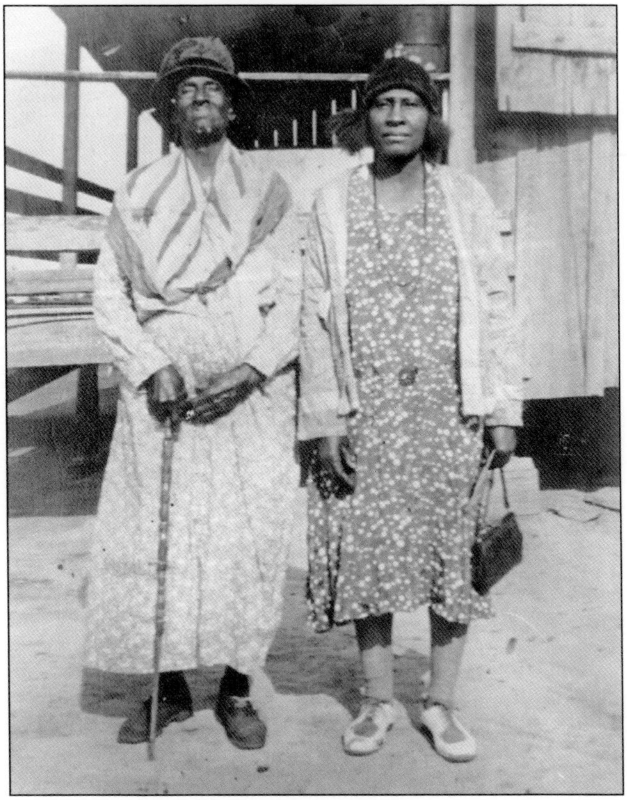

Easter Clark (left) and her daughter Rosie Clark Underwood are photographed here at their home on Bear Creek Road. (Courtesy of Gwendolyn Valentine.)

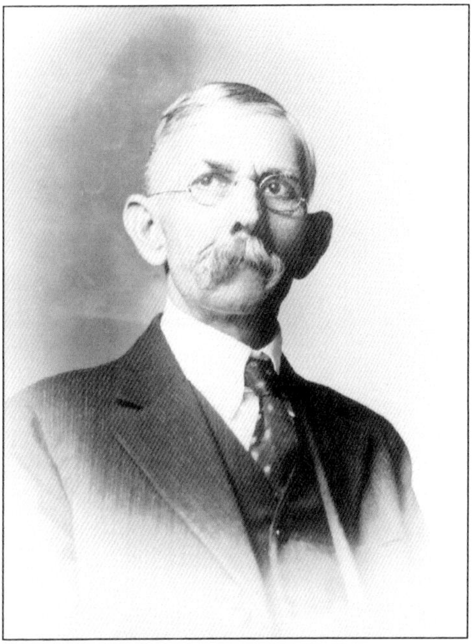

A mining supervisor and resident of Hargrove, James Morgan Turner was the son of Henry Clay and Leila Bailey Turner. He was born in Mason City, West Virginia. James married Margaret Lucinda Ollie Morrison in 1896. He died in May 1944 and was buried at Mount Carmel Cemetery in West Blocton. (Courtesy of Paula Fancher.)

This is a photograph of Susanne "Sudie" Fancher (1871–1947). She was the wife of William J. Martin (1869–1930), who was a lawyer and author. They were married in 1896 and lived in Six Mile, a community located 8 miles northeast of Centreville. (Courtesy of Paula Fancher.)

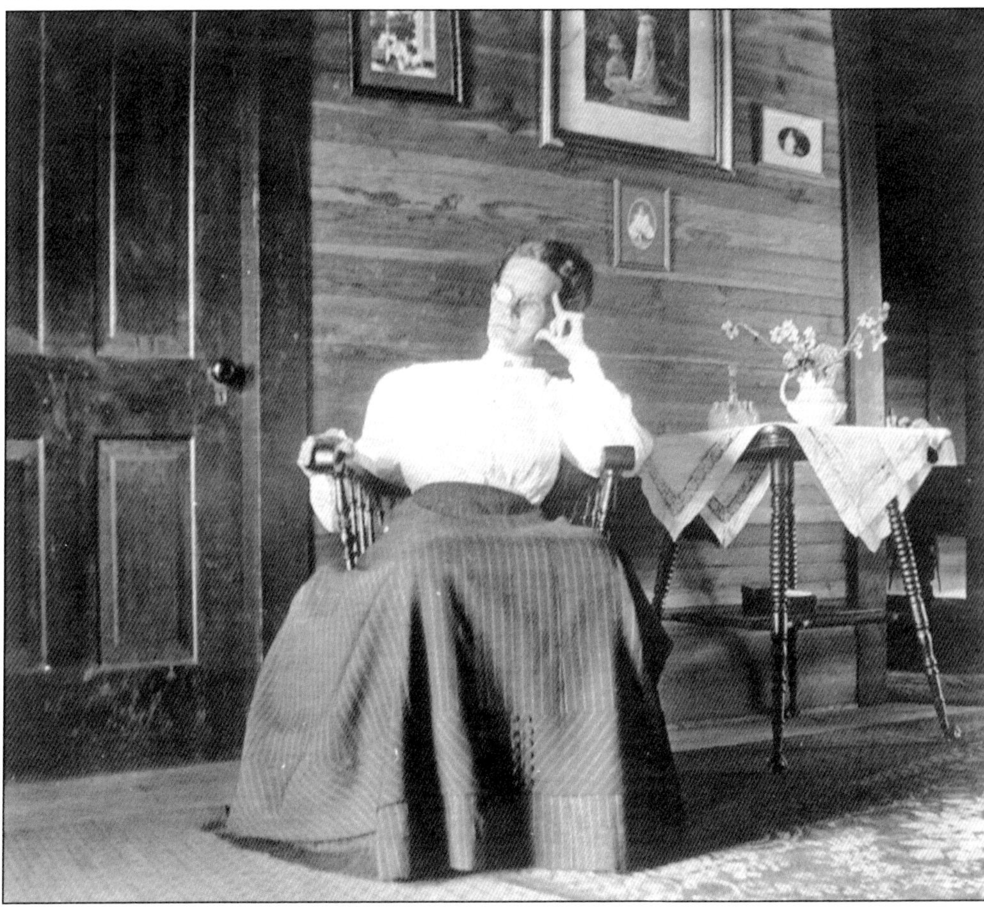

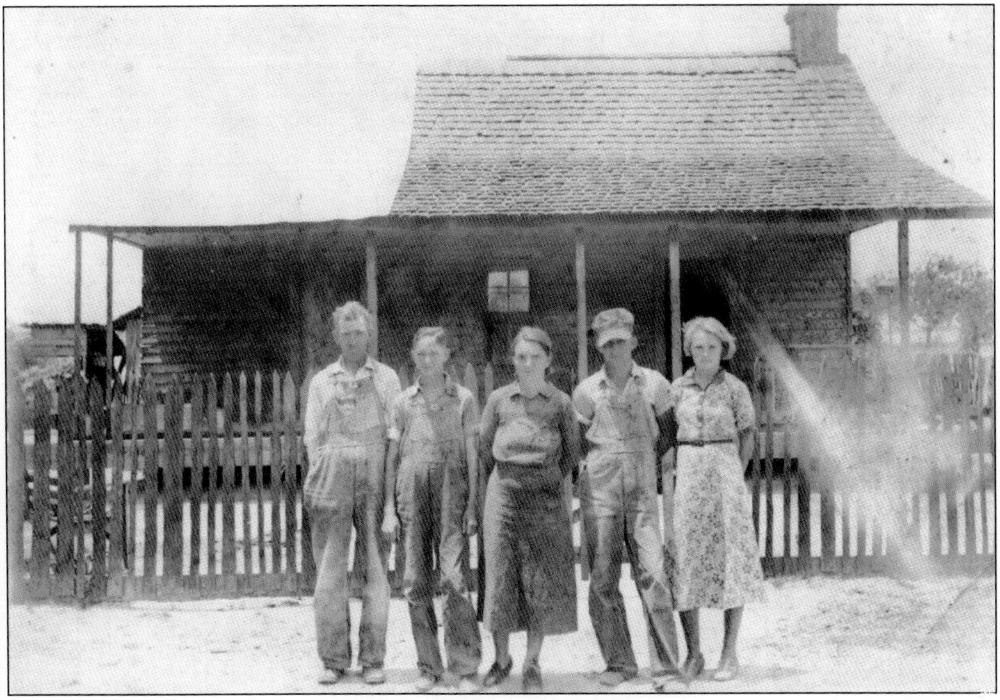

The Wallace family is seen at their home in the Liberty community. Family members are (from left to right) Willie Wallace, Pitt Wallace, unidentified, Sam Wallace (father of Rayford Wallace), and Roberta Foster Wallace (mother of Rayford Wallace). Sam and Roberta Wallace had four children: Rayford Delton, Raymond Hoyt, Samuel Kager, and Mattie Ree. (Courtesy of Rayford Wallace.)

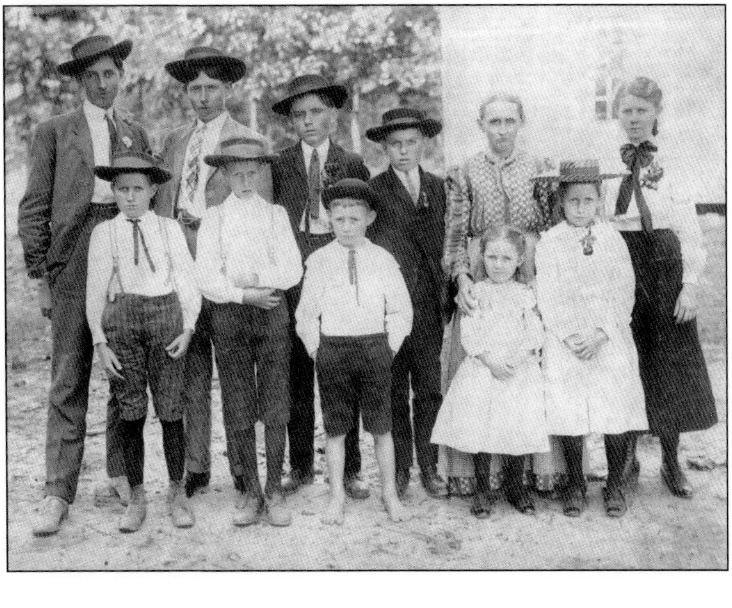

Pictured is the Wallace family from the community of Liberty in southeast Bibb County. From left to right are (first row) Felix Wallace, Lum Wallace, Vandon Wallace, Ruth Wallace, and Idell Wallace; (second row) Tommy Wallace, Henry Wallace, Decator Wallace, Willie Wallace, Mollie Wallace, and Becky Wallace. (Courtesy of Rayford Wallace.)

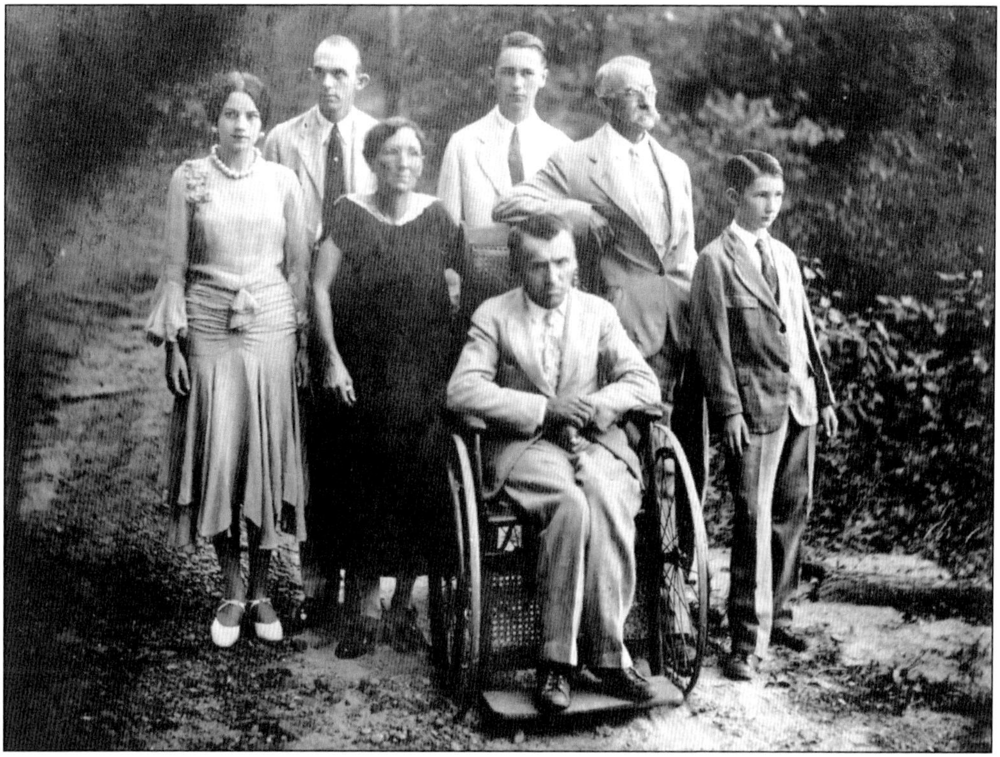

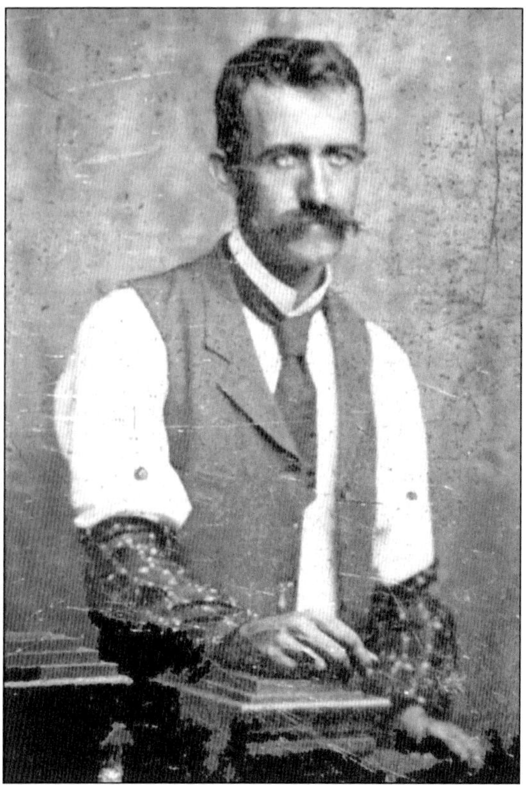

A prominent photographer in Bibb County, John Timothy Weeks is shown here with his family. Pictured from left to right are Hortense Weeks (the wife of Vernon Weeks), Vernon Weeks, Belle Spinks Weeks (the wife of J. T Weeks), Barney Hudson Weeks, Clifford Paul Weeks, John Timothy Morgan Weeks, and Ben Ollan Weeks. The John Weeks family lived in the community of Sand Mountain in south Bibb County, near the Chilton County line, before moving south to the Prattville area. (Courtesy of Beverly Weeks Beasley.)

John Timothy Morgan Weeks, a noted photographer, poses here in his work attire. Weeks lived near Randolph in the community of Sand Mountain and operated a photography business in the county. He was known for photographing local scenes and selling printed postcards. (Courtesy of Beverly Weeks Beasley.)

These are children of John Weeks at Christmas time. The names of these kids are unknown, and the exact year is not identified. Take note of the useful gifts of the era and how simple the tree was decorated. (Courtesy of Beverly Weeks Beasley.)

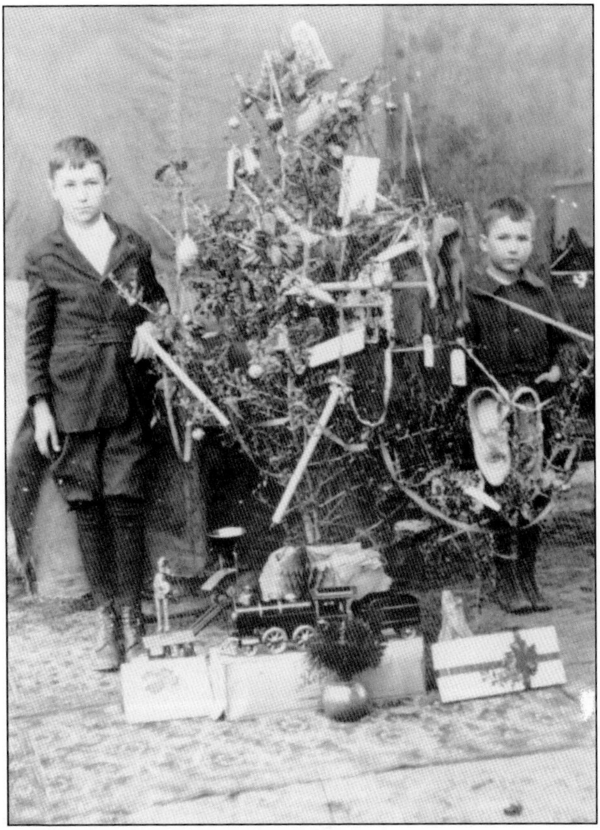

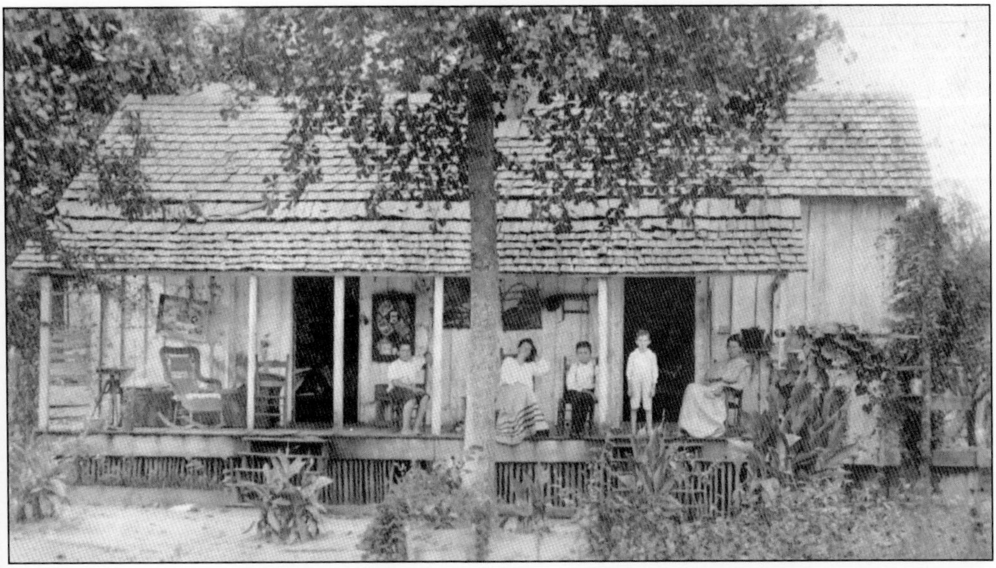

Pictured is the home of John Timothy Morgan Weeks in the Sand Mountain community. The family is shown relaxing on the porch on a summer afternoon. All that is left of this house is a few bricks from the foundations and pleasant memories. (Courtesy of Beverly Weeks Beasley.)

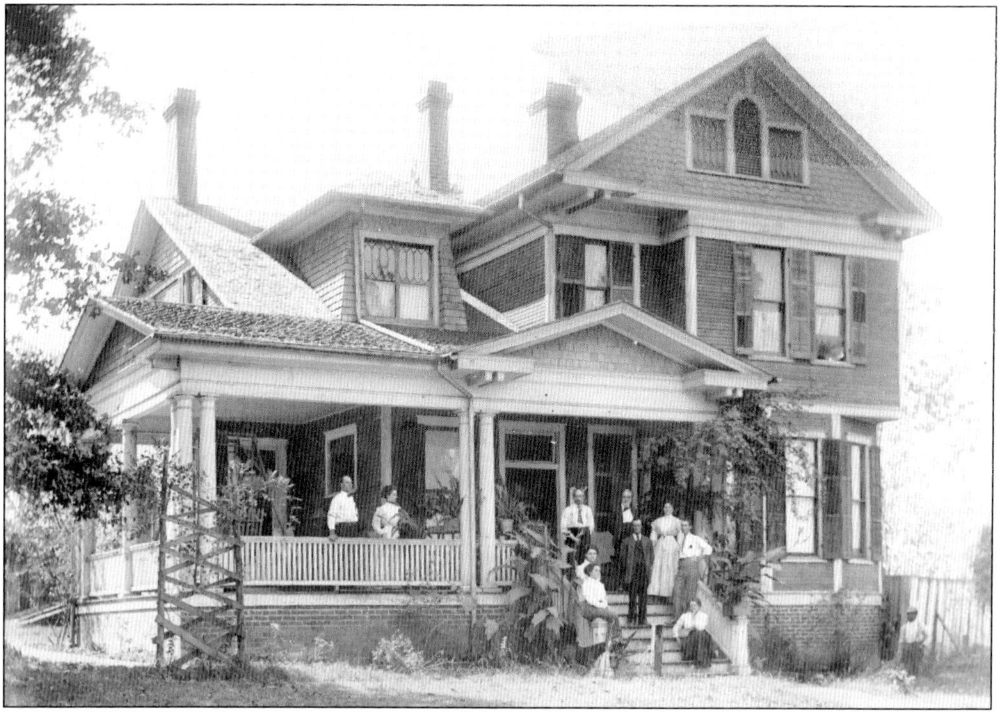

This is the A. D. Smith home in 1910, which was located in the settlement of Smith Hill in West Blocton. (Courtesy of Caroline Horton.)

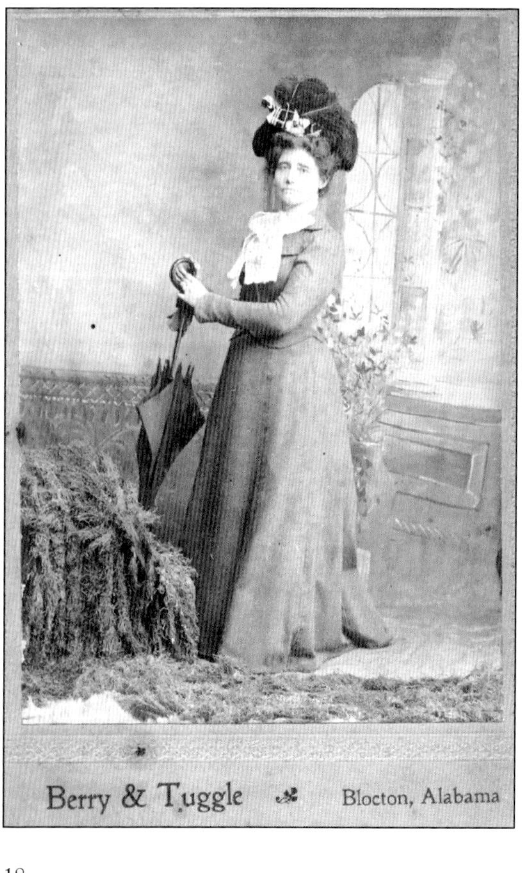

Seen in dress attire is Lula E. Smith (1863–1946) of West Blocton around 1900. She was from the Smith Hill community and was an ancestor of Caroline Horton from Prattville. This image was taken by well-known photographer T. C. Tuggle. (Courtesy of Caroline Horton.)

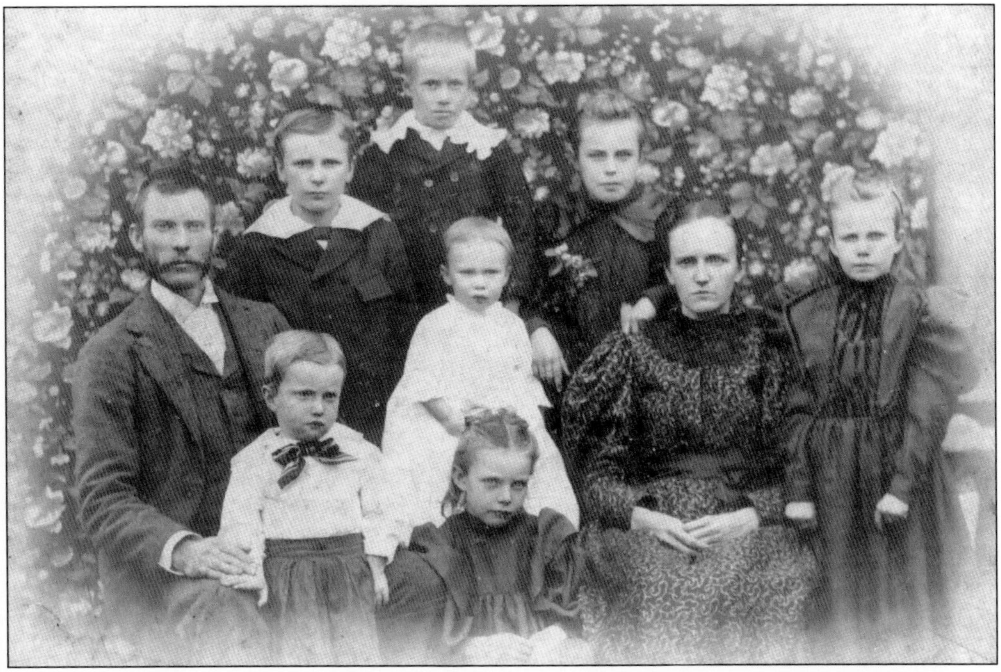

This is the family of Gustavos Adolphus and Josephine Jones Parker of Antioch. Gus is the son of R. C. and Harriet Sessions Parker and the brother of Reese Coleman Parker of Brierfield and West Blocton. Family members from left to right are (first row) Fred H. Parker (with bow tie) and Adelaide Parker Smitherman; (second row) Gustavos, RC Parker, Ida Parker Hendricks, and Ethel Parker Hunter; (third row) Moultrie Parker, Harley Parker, and Pruitt Parker. (Courtesy of Paula Fancher.)

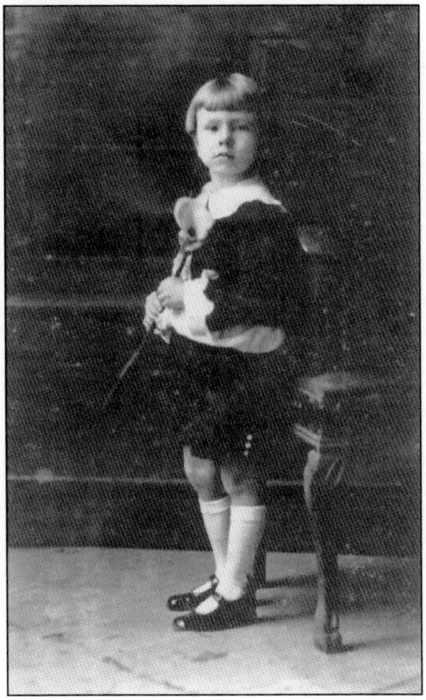

James Coleman Parker (1919–2003) was the son of Coleman and Lelia Turner Parker. This picture was taken in 1924, when he was a member of his cousin's (Edward Leverette) wedding party in Dallas County, Alabama. (Courtesy of Paula Fancher.)

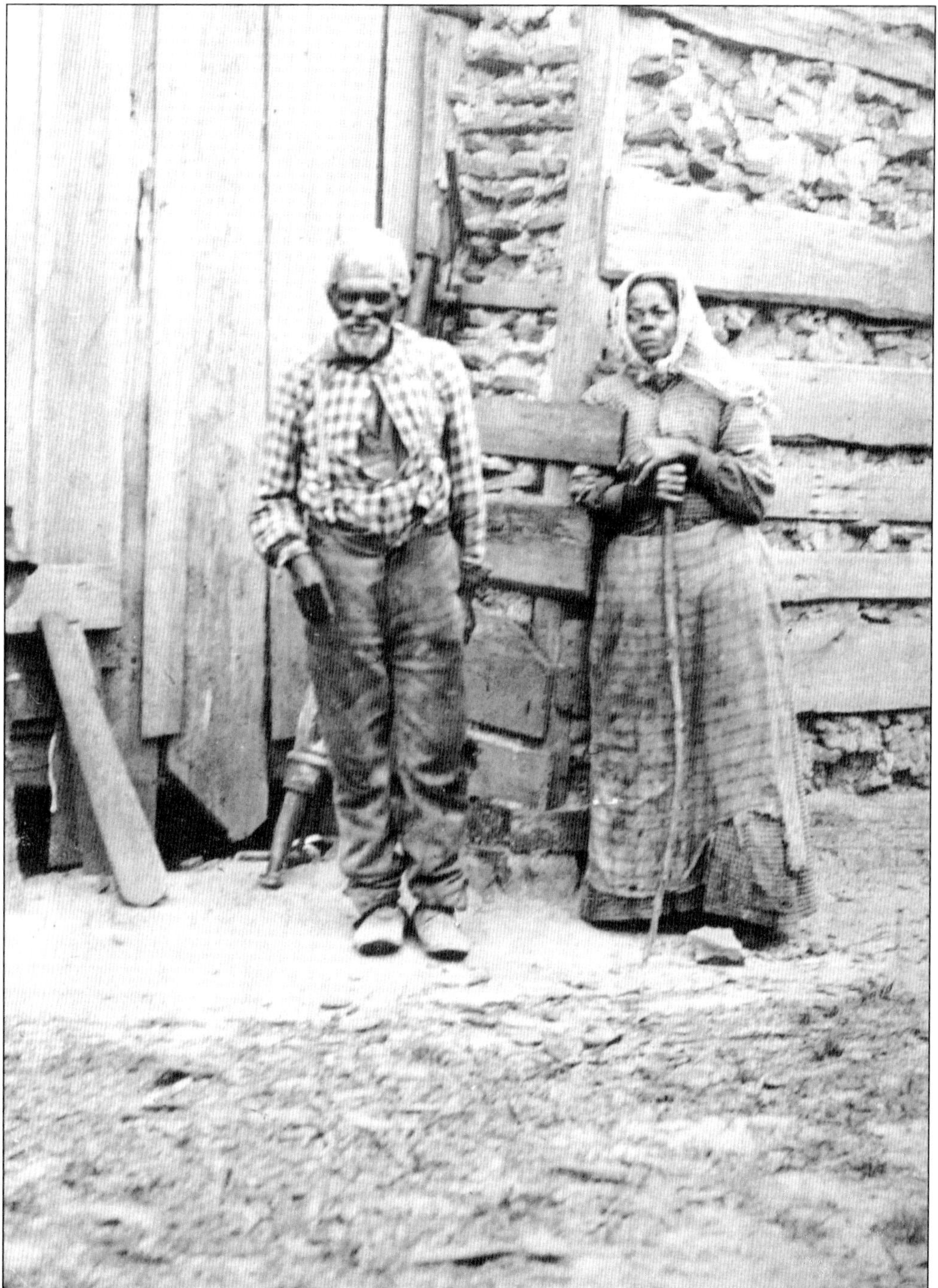

Edmund and Julie Lightsey lived 6 miles from Centreville. Edmund claimed to be 109 years old in a newspaper article before he died. He was brought here from Richmond, Virginia, as a small child and remembered Centreville as a mostly wooded area with a small town across the river. Julie Lightsey (age unknown) died six months before Edmund. They are buried at Sandy Cemetery, located just north of Lightsey's pond, south of Centreville. (Courtesy of Alice Lightsey.)

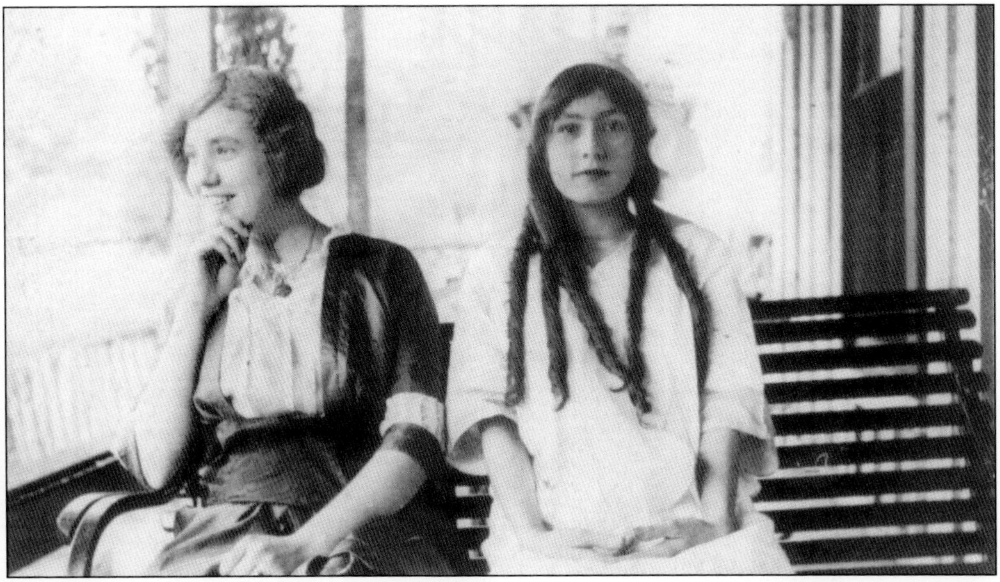

Daughters of James M. and Ollie Morrison Turner, Nancy Virginia Turner (left) and Leila Payne Turner, are pictured at home in Hargrove around 1911. Hargrove was a mining town located 3 miles southeast of West Blocton, but it no longer exists except for a historical marker. (Courtesy of Paula Fancher.)

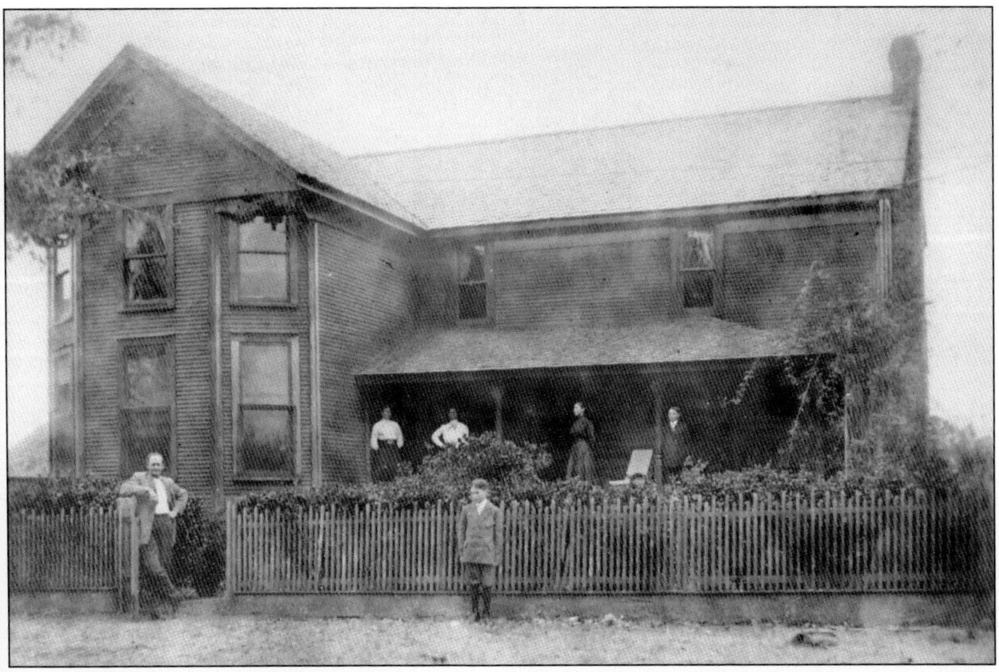

The Walter Ford Faucette home is shown here. Faucette family members are (from left to right) Walter Faucette, unidentified, Mattie Kinnaird Faucette, Bill Faucette (in front of gate), Norvia Faucette, and Floyd Winford Faucette. Walter (1866–1936) married Mattie Alma Kinnaird (1871–1932), and they had three children. (Courtesy of Ruth Dailey.)

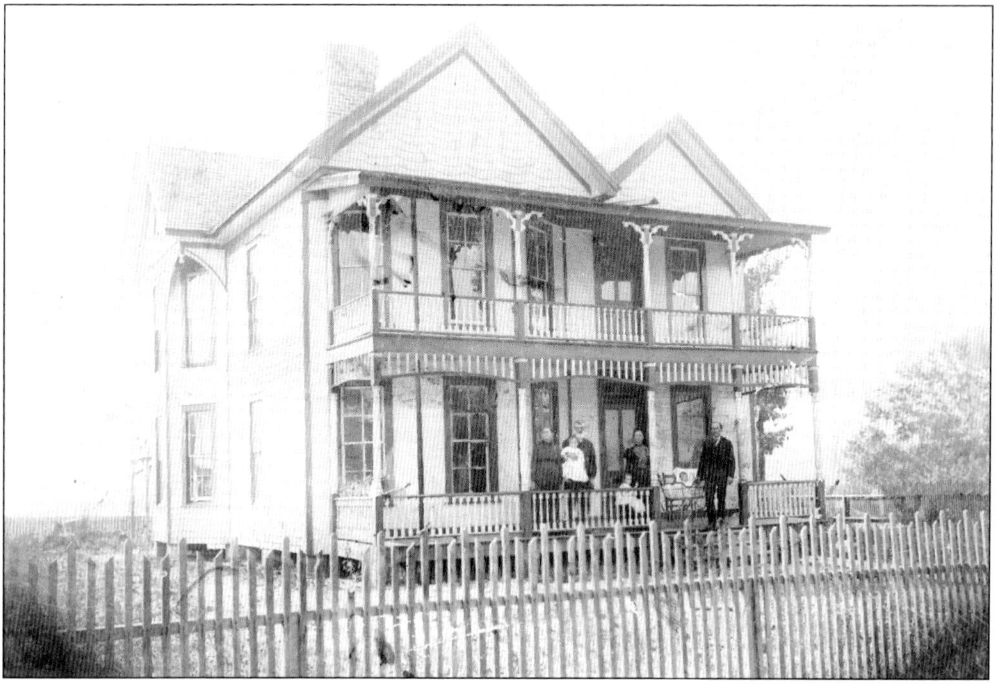

Fielding Oakley is pictured with his family in the 1800s. This home is located on Walnut Street and is the previous home of the Hicks family. Fielding Oakley was the great-grandfather of Jim Oakley Jr. (Courtesy of Jim Oakley Jr.)

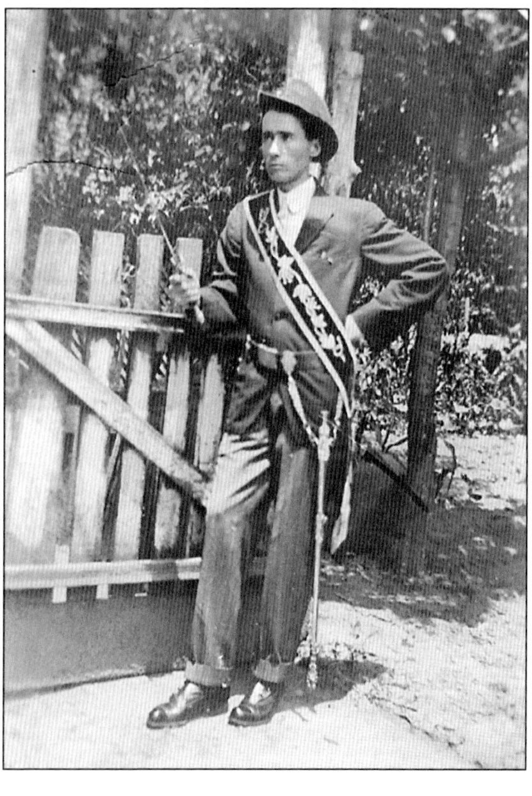

This 1900 photograph is of Morgan T. Smith, who made his home in Scottsville. (Courtesy of Caroline Horton.)

Byrd Belle Smith (1888–1963), from Scottsville, was the daughter of Andrew David Smith (1832–1921) and Joanna Elizabeth Caffee (1832–1905). (Courtesy of Caroline Horton.)

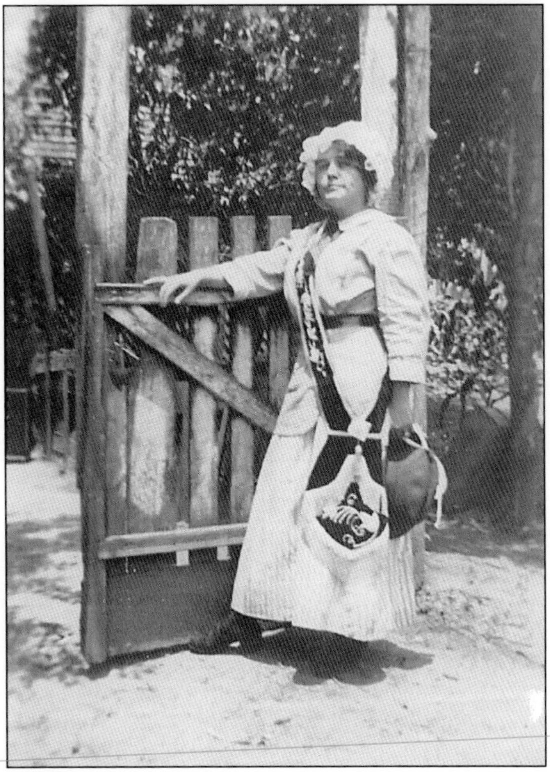

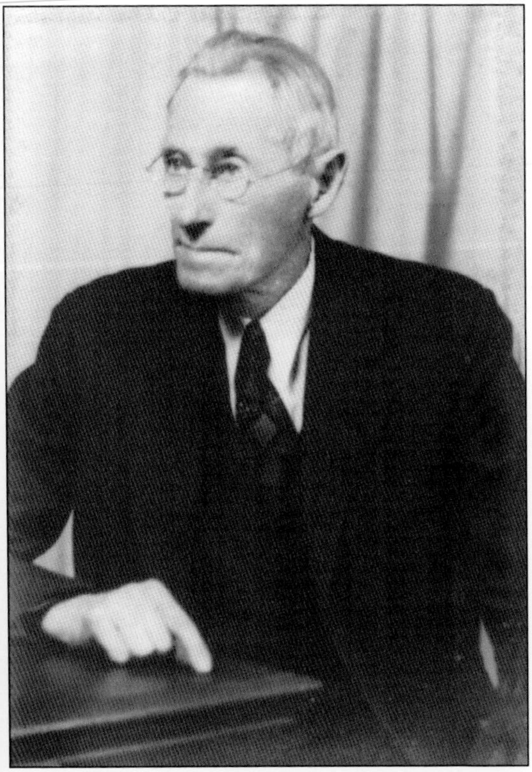

Reese Coleman Parker (1859–1955) married Caroline Childers in Sumerfield in 1887. Parker was raised on a plantation in Tuscaloosa County and attended the University of Kentucky. He served as the town clerk and accountant of West Blocton. In the early 1900s, he owned a store in Brierfield. (Courtesy of Paula Fancher.)

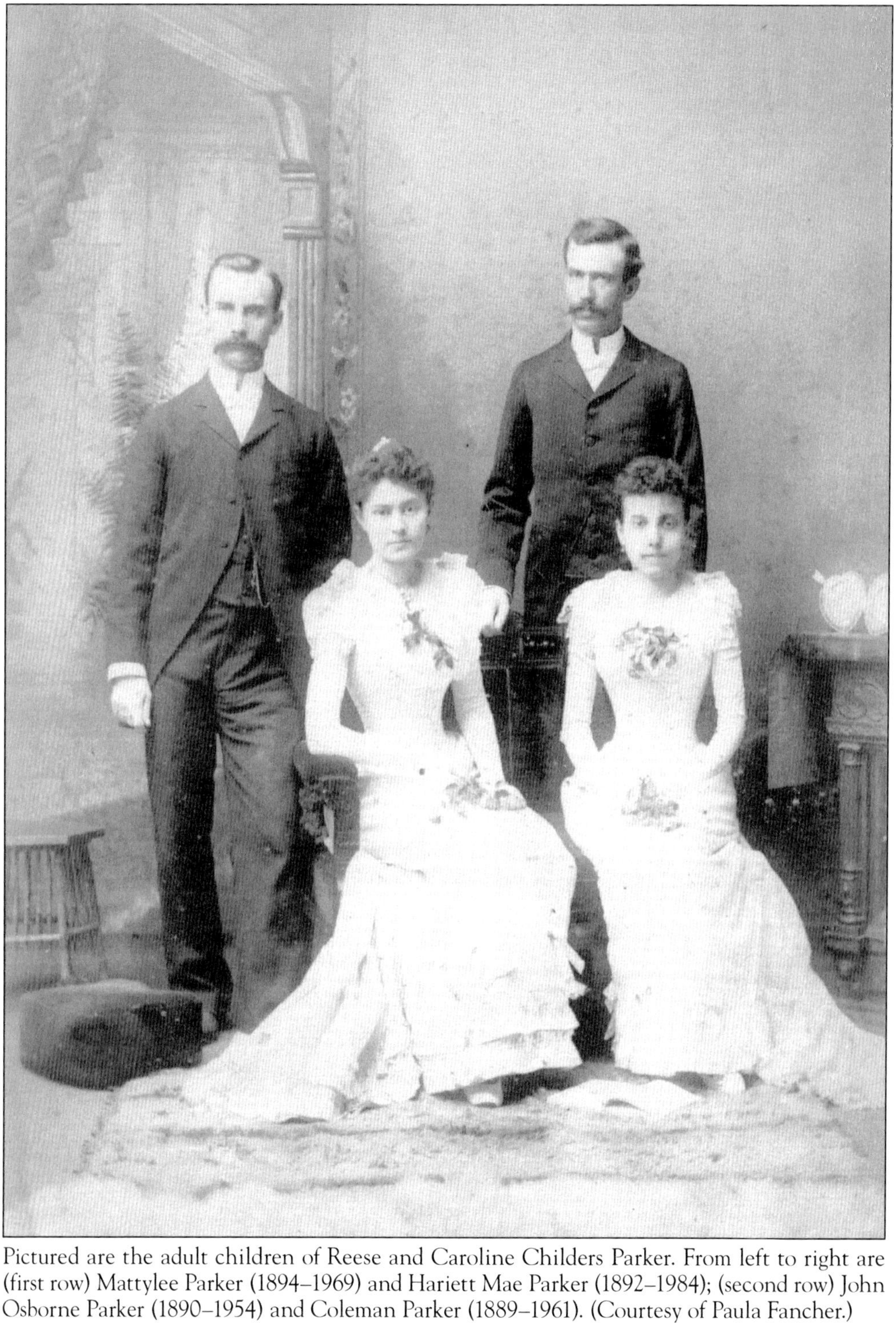

Pictured are the adult children of Reese and Caroline Childers Parker. From left to right are (first row) Mattylee Parker (1894–1969) and Hariett Mae Parker (1892–1984); (second row) John Osborne Parker (1890–1954) and Coleman Parker (1889–1961). (Courtesy of Paula Fancher.)

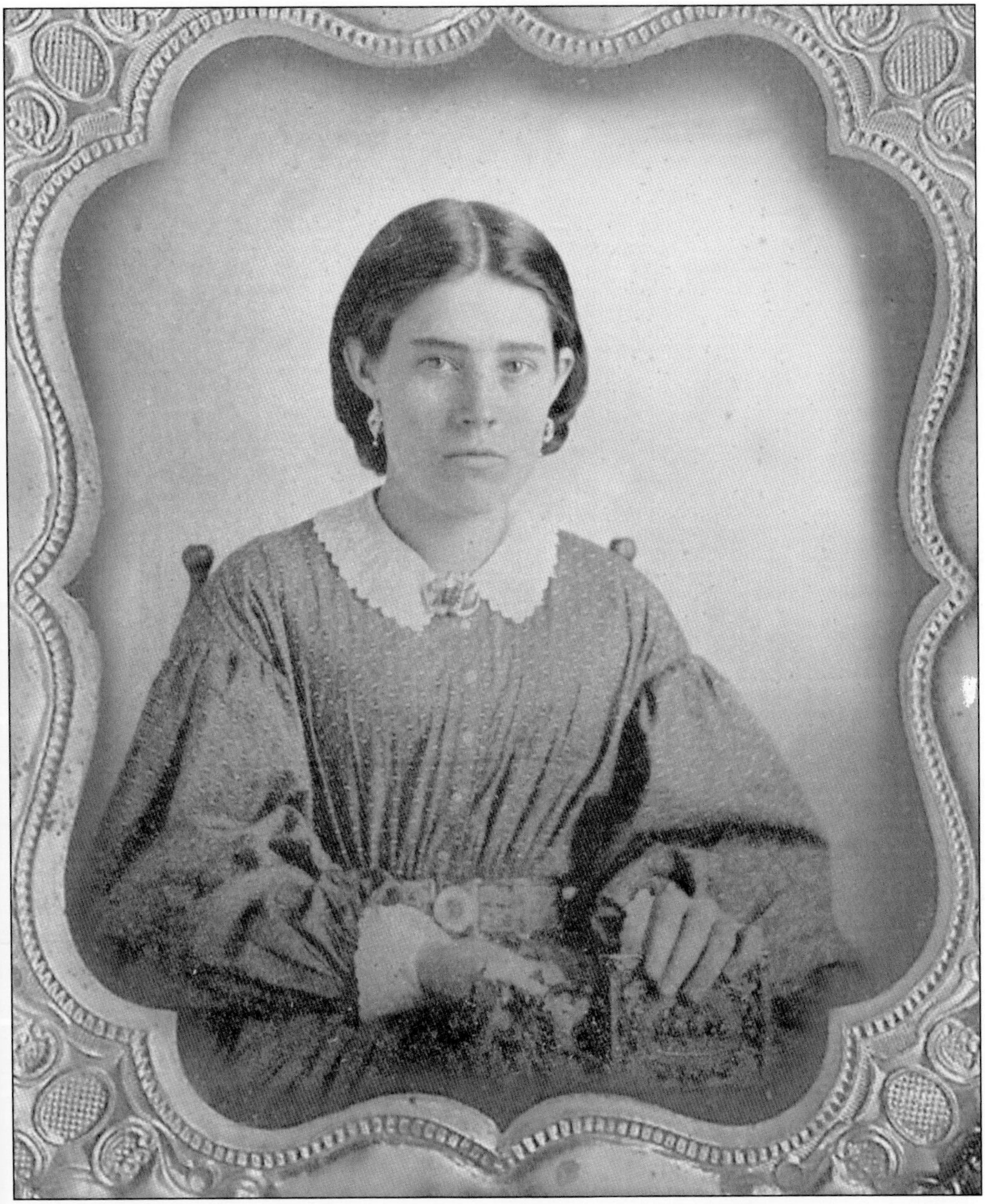

Joanna Elizabeth Caffee was born on October 12, 1837, and died in her home in Scottsville on August 20, 1905. She was the wife of A. D. Smith in 1860, when this picture was taken. She had 12 children and according to relatives lived a consistent Christian life until her death. (Courtesy of Caroline Horton.)

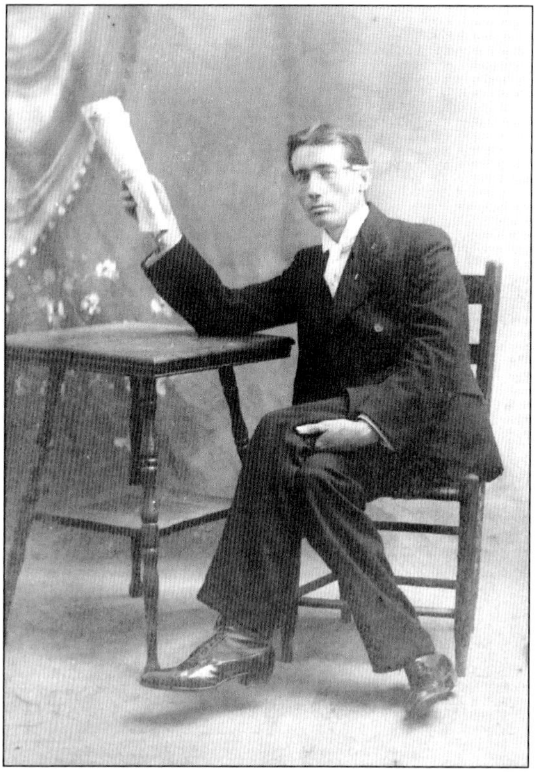

Morgan Truman Smith was a member of the Methodist Church of West Blocton, a member of the Civitan Club, and owned and operated the Smith Hardware Store. (Courtesy of Caroline Horton.)

This is the Smith family at their home in Scottsville. Family members (from left to right) are uncle Vance, Alice, uncle Tom, Lydia, grandfather Smith, Byrd, grandmother Smith, Fannie, Walter, Lula, Arthur, Sallie (MaMaw), Yancy, and Morgan. (Courtesy of Caroline Horton.)

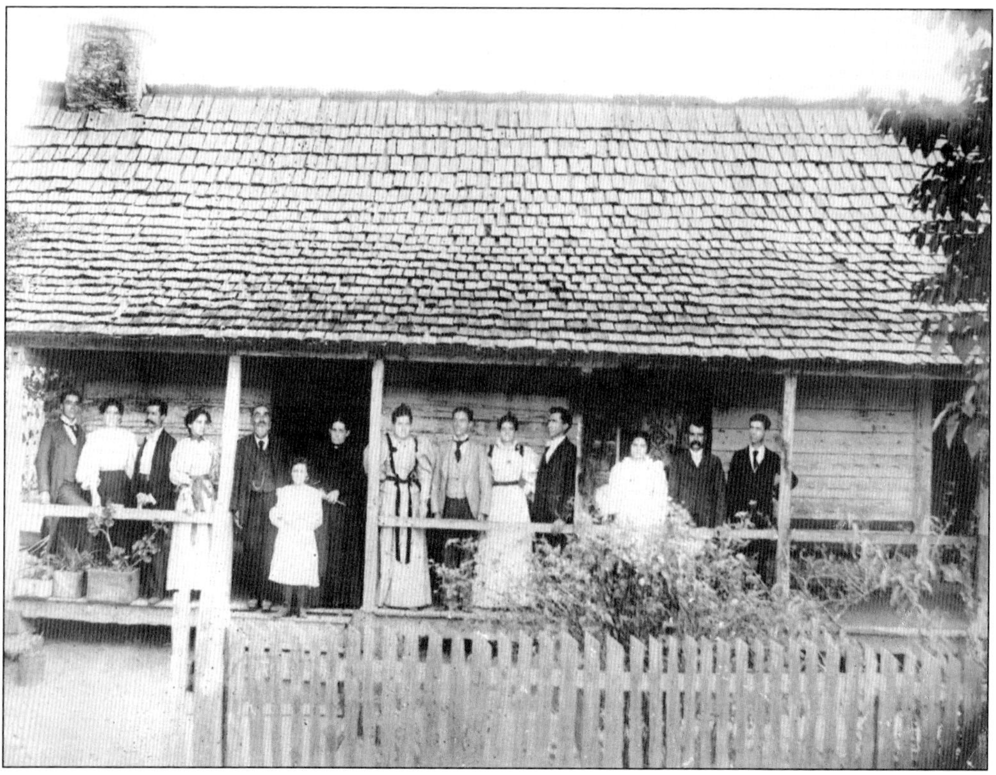

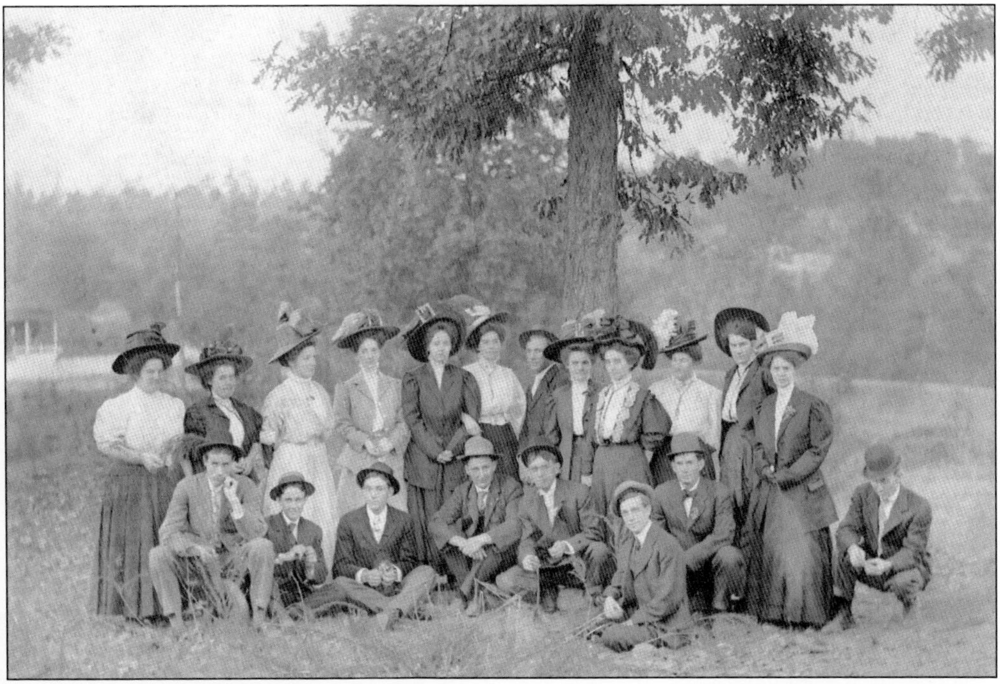

Pictured is a gathering of the Smith family in the settlement of Smith Hill, which members established in the 1800s. (Courtesy of Caroline Horton.)

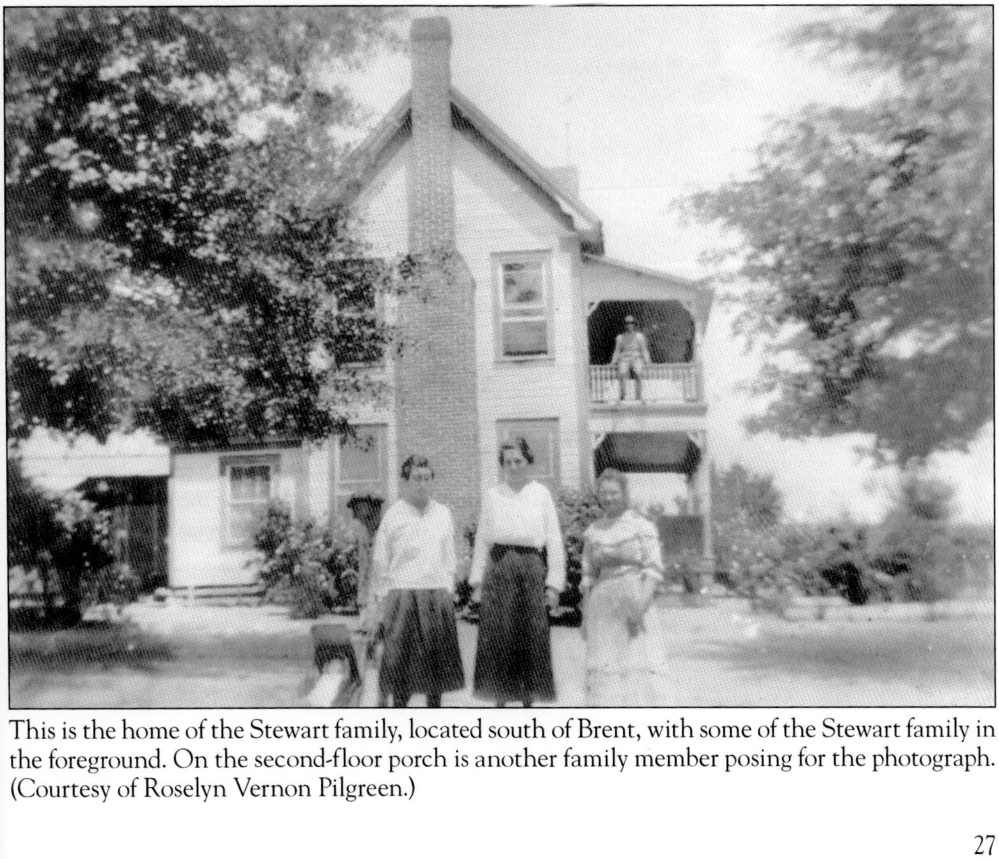

This is the home of the Stewart family, located south of Brent, with some of the Stewart family in the foreground. On the second-floor porch is another family member posing for the photograph. (Courtesy of Roselyn Vernon Pilgreen.)

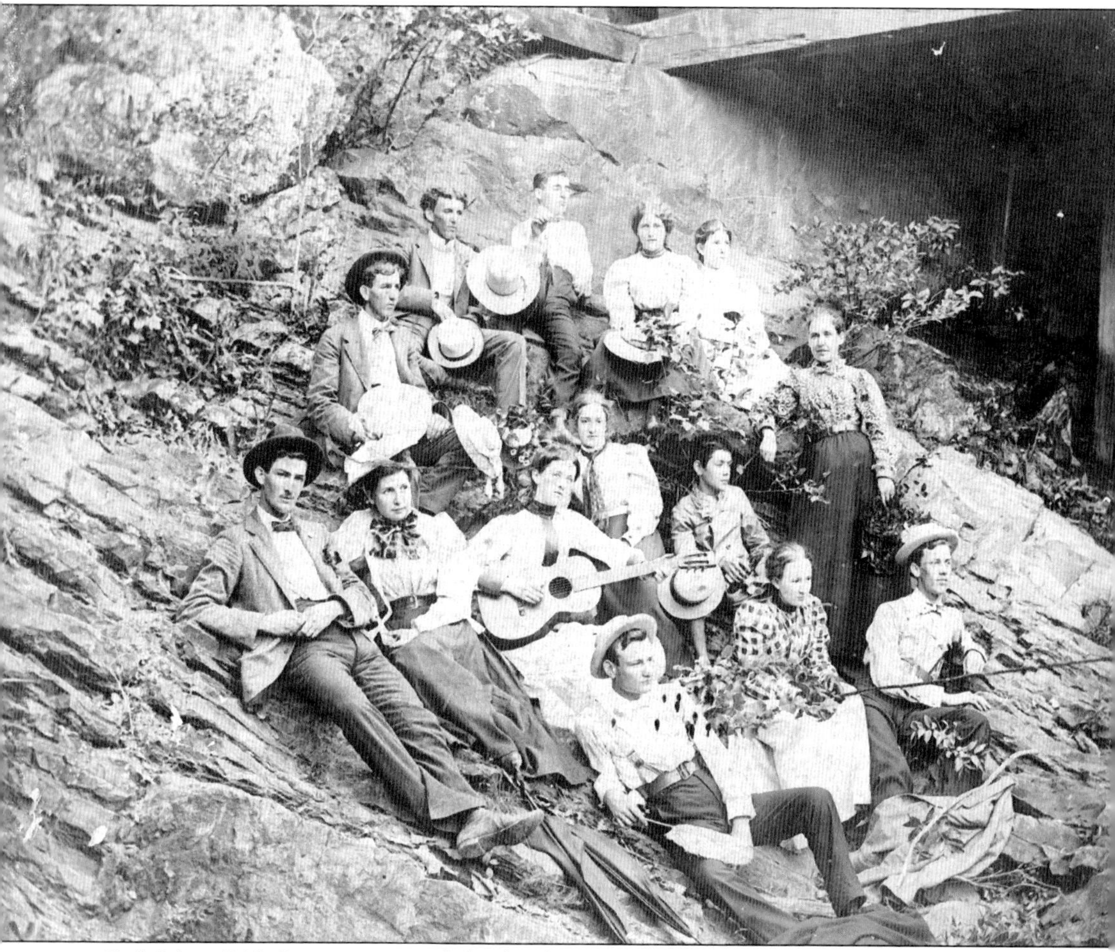

Early life in Bibb County was simple but hard. Most settlers were farmers, mill workers, blacksmiths, and wagon builders. In this photograph, the Avery family is shown spending a day on the Cahaba River with friends. Entertainment of that day would have been music, fishing, picnics, and storytelling. This image was most likely made under the Gulf Mobile and Ohio Railroad trestle over the Cahaba River near Centreville. (Courtesy of Dalton and Anne Murphy.)

Two

Churches and Congregations

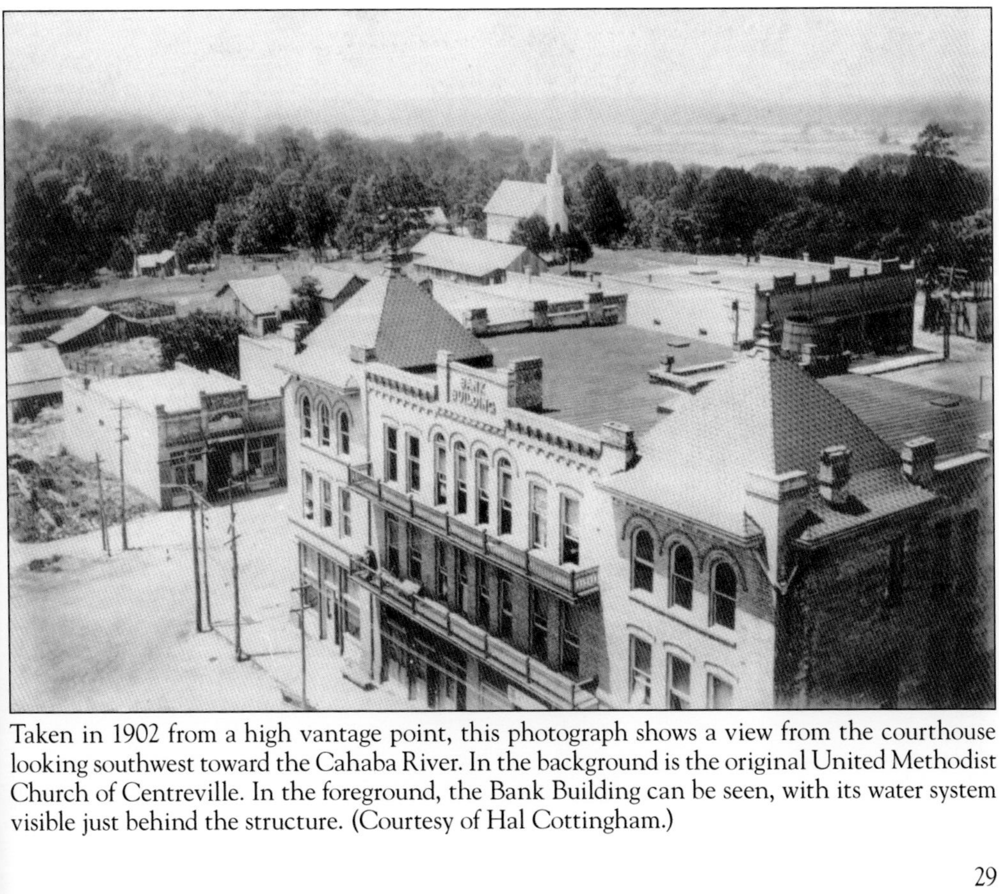

Taken in 1902 from a high vantage point, this photograph shows a view from the courthouse looking southwest toward the Cahaba River. In the background is the original United Methodist Church of Centreville. In the foreground, the Bank Building can be seen, with its water system visible just behind the structure. (Courtesy of Hal Cottingham.)

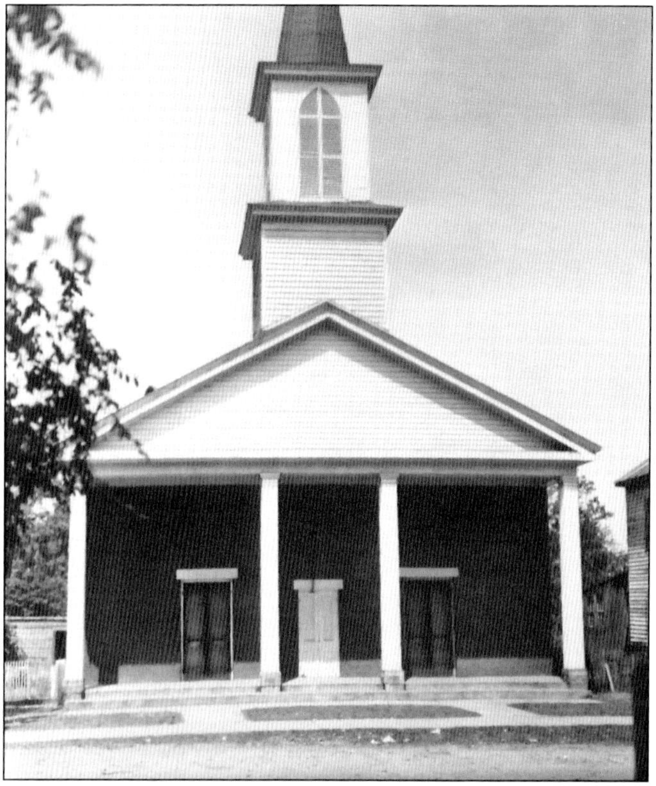

The Centreville Presbyterian Church, located on the Court Square, is listed on the National Register of Historic Places. It was established in 1824, but this building was constructed in 1859 with bricks made from clay taken from the grounds. It is the oldest continuous church in Centreville and is in the top 50 nationwide in the Presbyterian Church (PCA). The sanctuary has a central pulpit signifying the centrality of the Word of God, a pipe organ, and beautiful stained-glass windows. Locals and visitors alike can hear the Schulmerich Carillion Chimes that ring out the time, as well as melodious gospel songs 365 days a year. (Courtesy of Birmingham Public Library.)

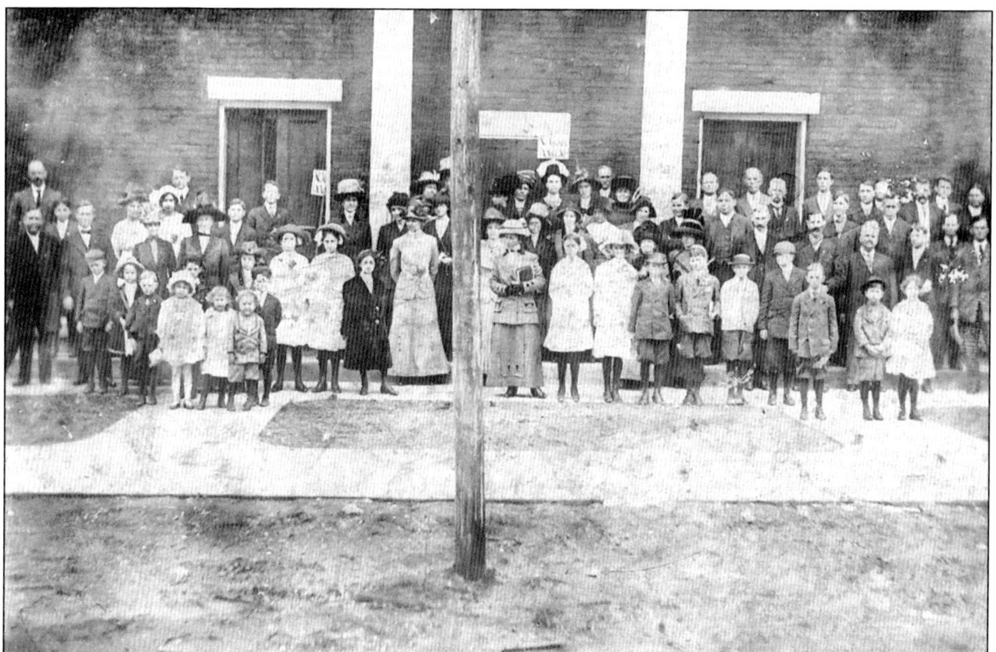

Centreville First Presbyterian Church is located on Court Square. In this c. 1915 picture of Sunday school classes, two of the members are holding signs stating, "Class One" and "Class Two." (Courtesy of Centreville First Presbyterian Church.)

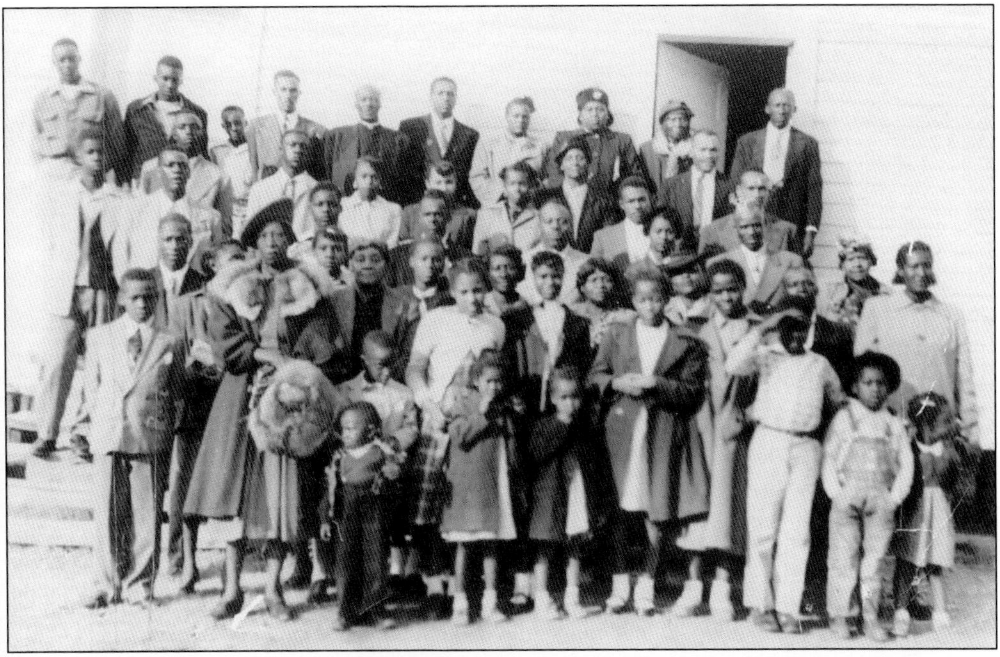

The congregation of Hopewell Methodist Church poses for a group picture in front of the church. It is located on Bear Creek Road just south of Brent and is active today. (Courtesy of Gwendolyn Valentine.)

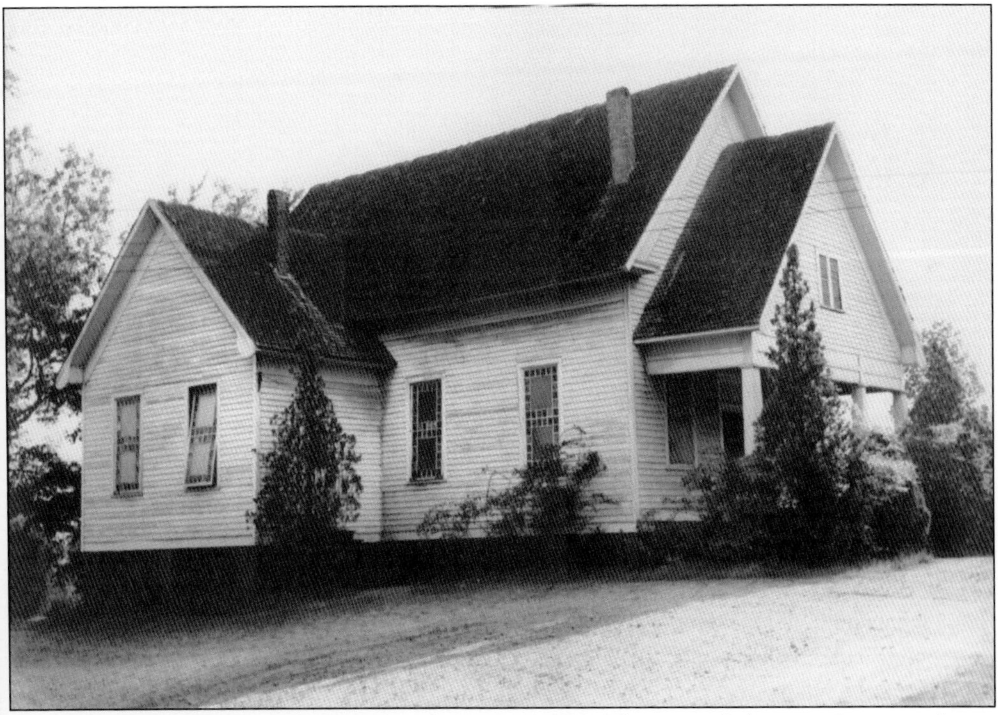

Pictured is Centreville Methodist Church prior to 1948. The stained-glass windows are almost exact replicas of the Centreville First Presbyterian Church's windows. (Courtesy of Centreville Methodist Church.)

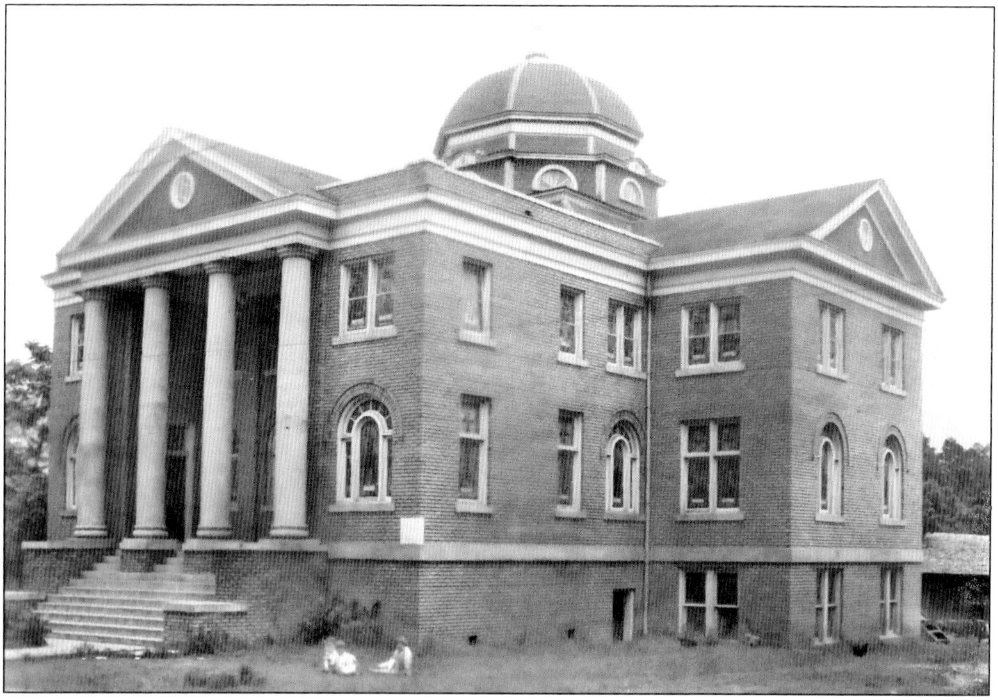

This beautiful church was the Centreville First Baptist Church, located on Court Square, before it burned in 1966. The church prior to this one was a frame building with one room. The church in this photograph was the second one, built in 1922. The current church building was constructed in 1967. Notice the unidentified children sitting on the front lawn. (Courtesy of Birmingham Public Library.)

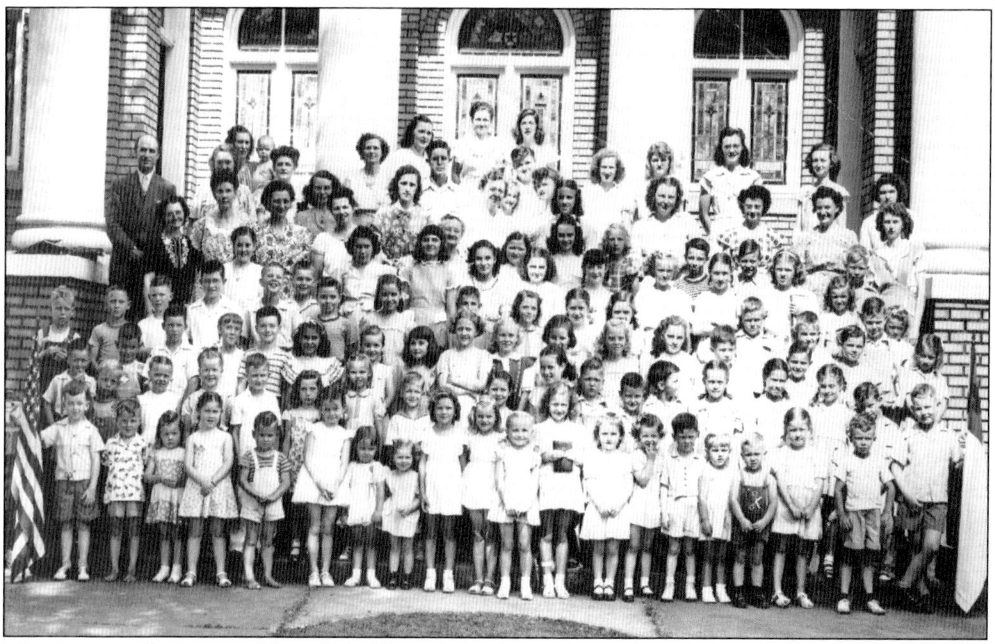

The Centreville Baptist Church held its vacation Bible school in the 1940s. The teachers and students are gathered on the front steps for this picture. (Courtesy of Betty Burt.)

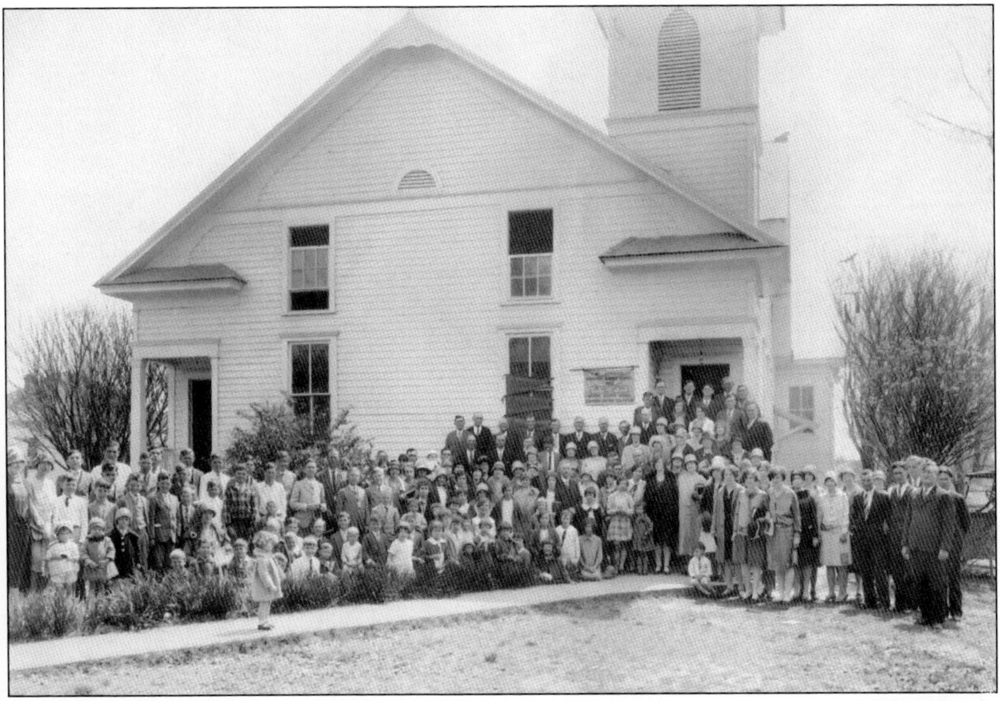

The Brent Baptist Church was built in 1910 and was used for worship until 1966. At that time it was replaced by a new brick structure, which was destroyed by a tornado in May 1973. Pictured is the 1928 Sunday school of Brent Baptist gathered in front of the first church. (Courtesy of Brent Baptist Church.)

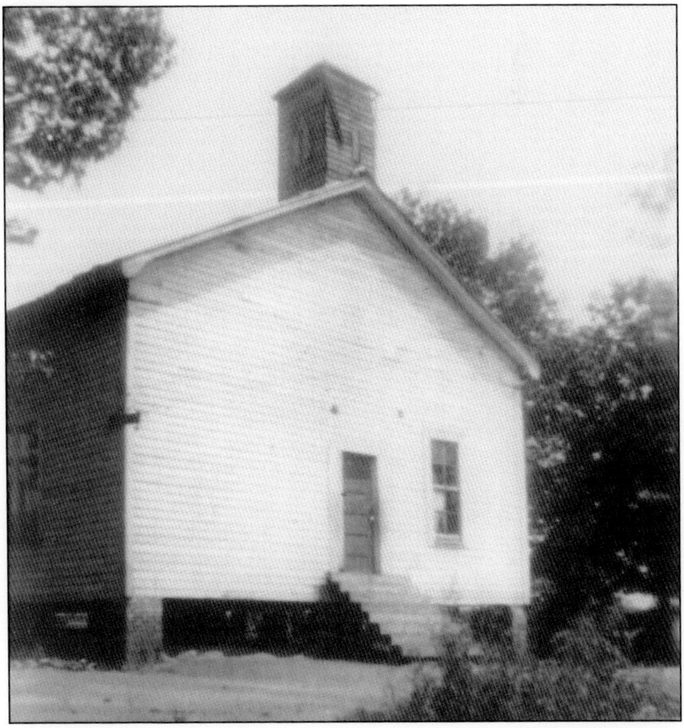

Mount Ebell Baptist Church is located just southwest of the city of Brent and is still in use today. Since this photograph was taken, it has been bricked and remodeled. (Courtesy of Ruth Dailey.)

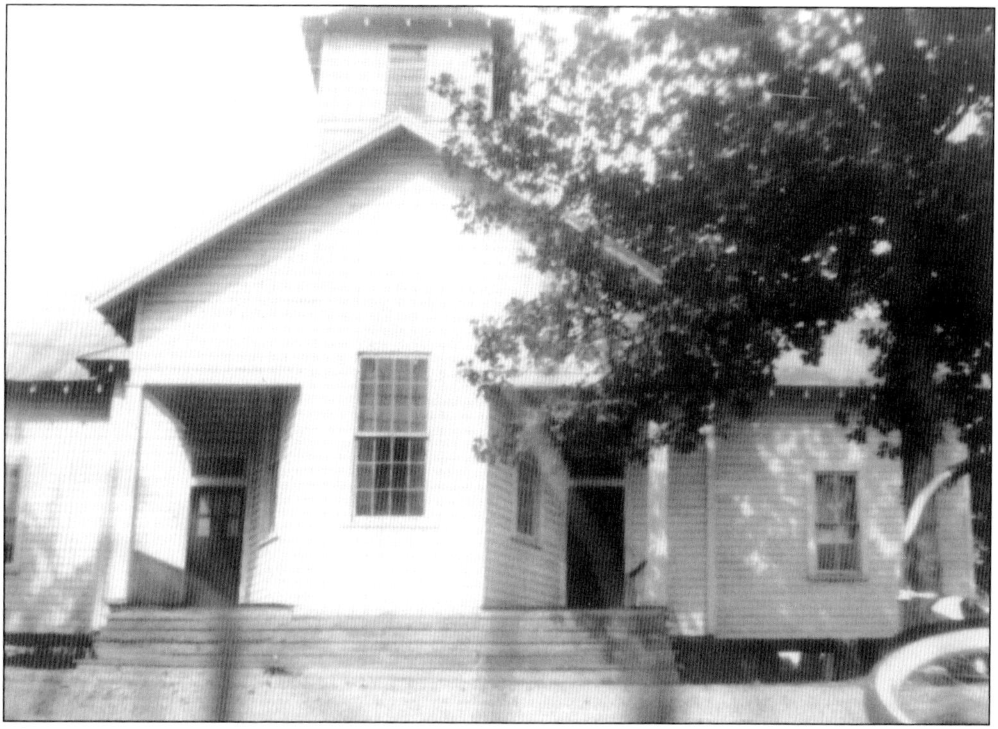

The Brent Methodist Episcopal Church was located just north of the city of Brent. It was later renamed the McDaniel Memorial United Methodist Church and was rebuilt in 1961. (Courtesy of Ruth Dailey.)

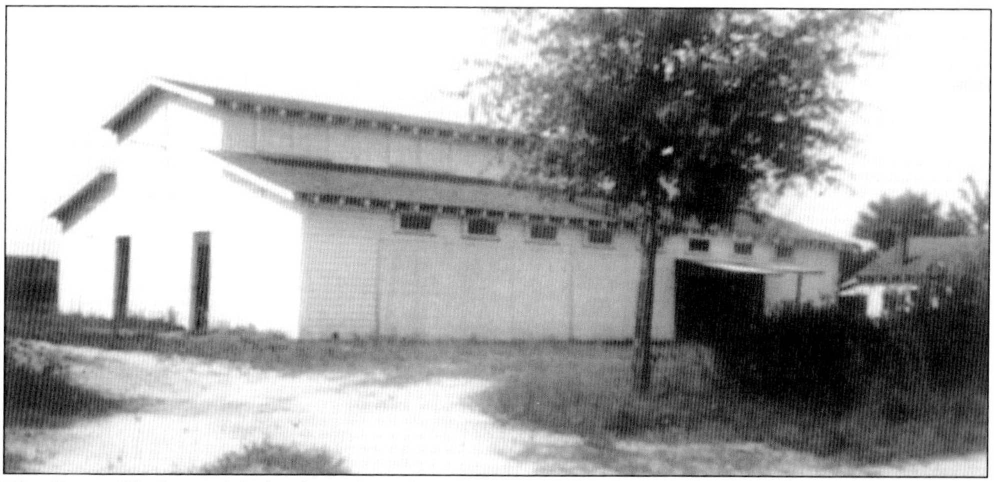

The Brent Wesleyan Methodist Church was built in the fall of 1929. In January 1949, the old tabernacle was torn down, and the present church was constructed. (Courtesy of Ruth Dailey.)

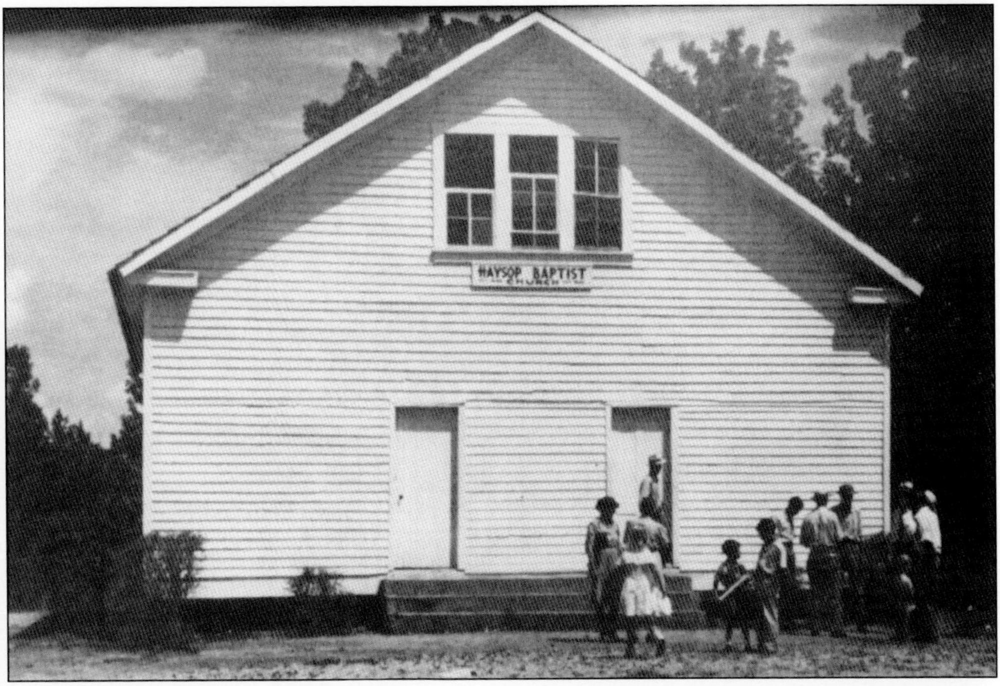

Some time around 1830, a Baptist church was constituted in the settlement along Haysop Creek. At that time, the church was a log structure and was later replaced with a white clapboard church in 1890. The church seen here was used for worship from 1890 to 1952, when it was replaced with a brick sanctuary. Additions were made in the 1970s, and the church is still active today. (Courtesy of Brent/Centreville Library.)

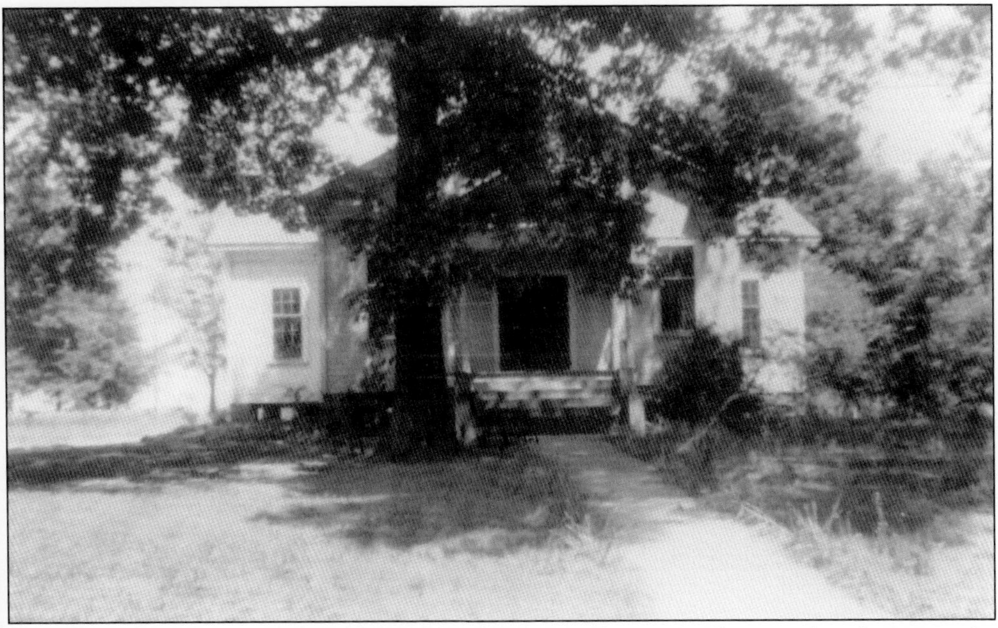

The Brent Presbyterian Church was organized in September 1907. The new church went under construction in 1907 and was finished in 1908. The church shown in this photograph was later destroyed by a tornado in 1973. (Courtesy of Ruth Dailey.)

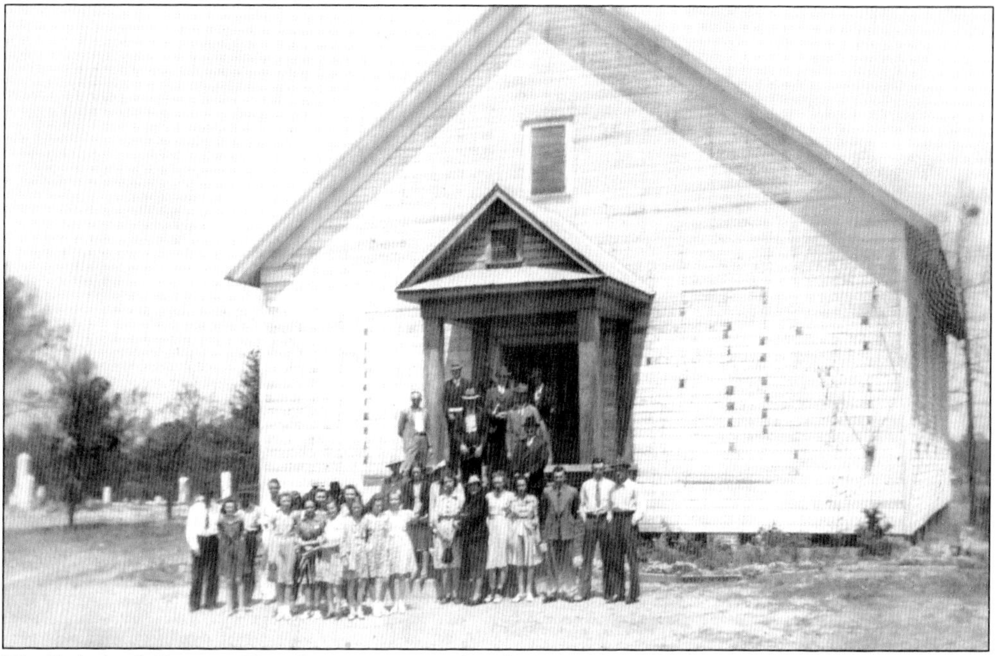

The Rehobeth Baptist Church was organized and admitted to the Cahawba Baptist Association in 1819. The first pastor was Elder Isaac Suttle. This is a 1946 photograph of the church, which was built in 1912, and shows the congregation of Rehobeth Baptist. The church was destroyed by arson in February 2006, making national news. (Courtesy of Frank and Edith Wilson.)

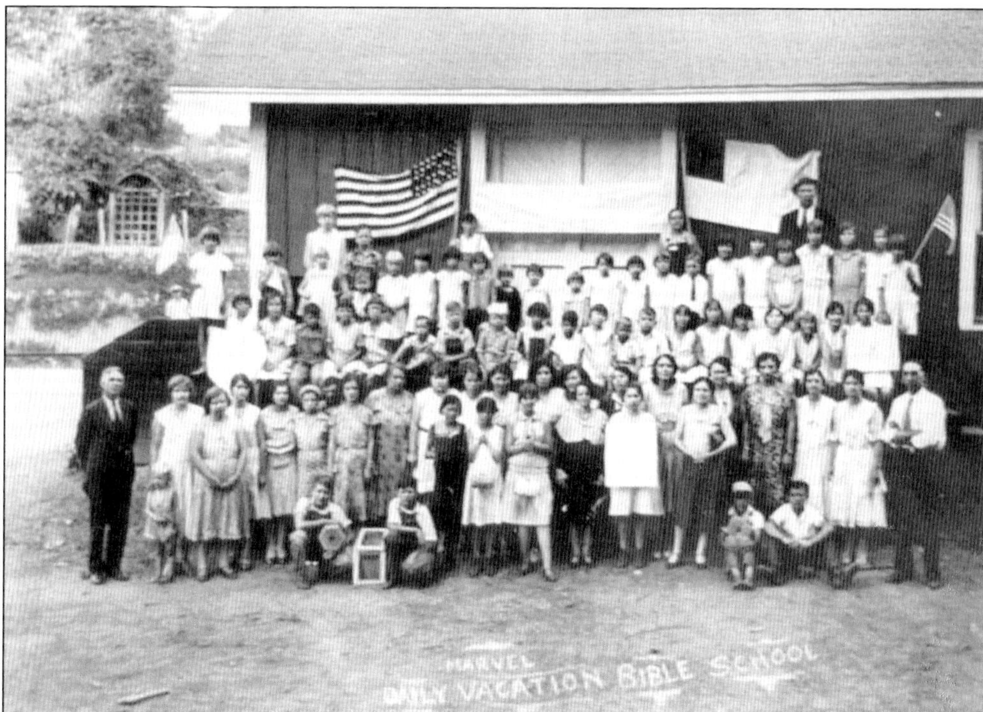

This is a photograph of the Marvel vacation Bible school. (Courtesy of Marshall Goggins.)

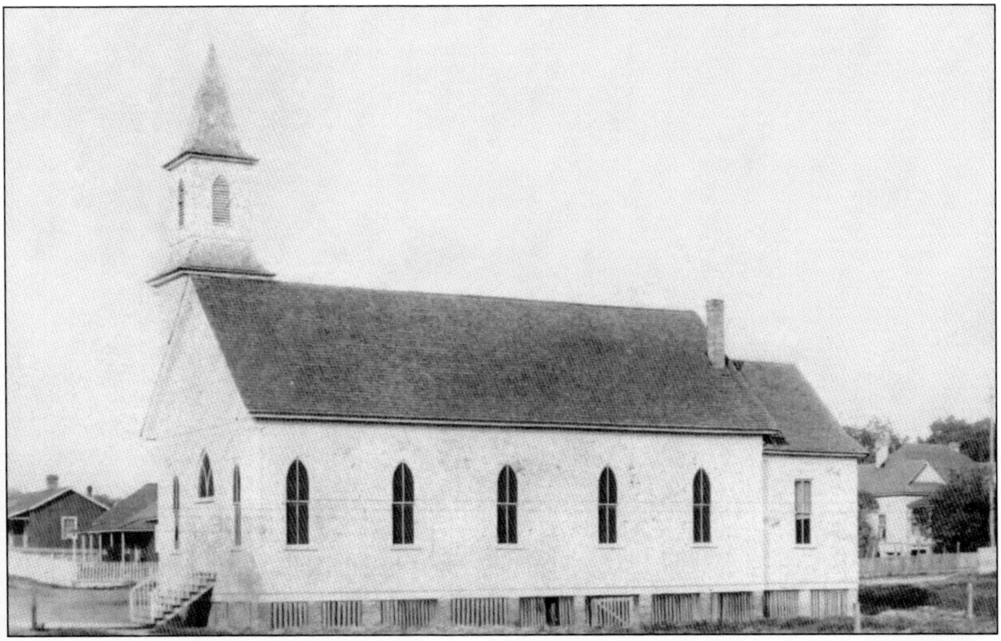

The First Methodist Church formed in Blocton around 1910. The church was built in the Victorian Carpenter Gothic style and served a large congregation for more than 35 years. The photograph was taken by John T. Weeks. (Courtesy of Beverly Weeks Beasley.)

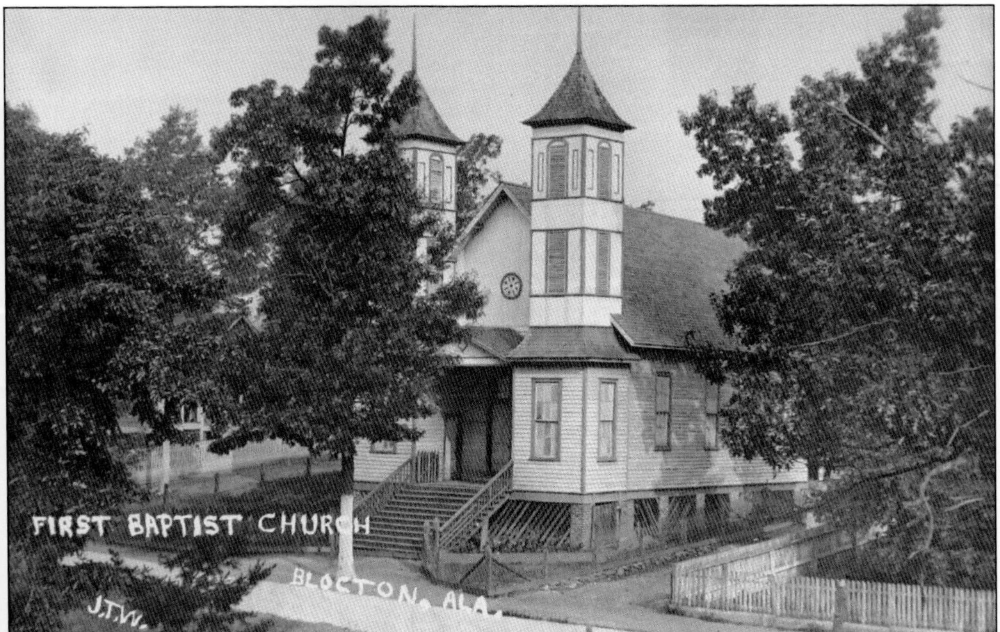

Pictured is the First Baptist Church in Blocton, which had two towers as part of an unusual architectural design. One tower contained the church bell, and the other was simply part of the design. The First Baptist Church in this photograph was started in 1888 and was located on Gun Lock Hill. It burned on August 28, 1922, and its location was moved to the present-day site. (Courtesy of Beverly Weeks Beasely.)

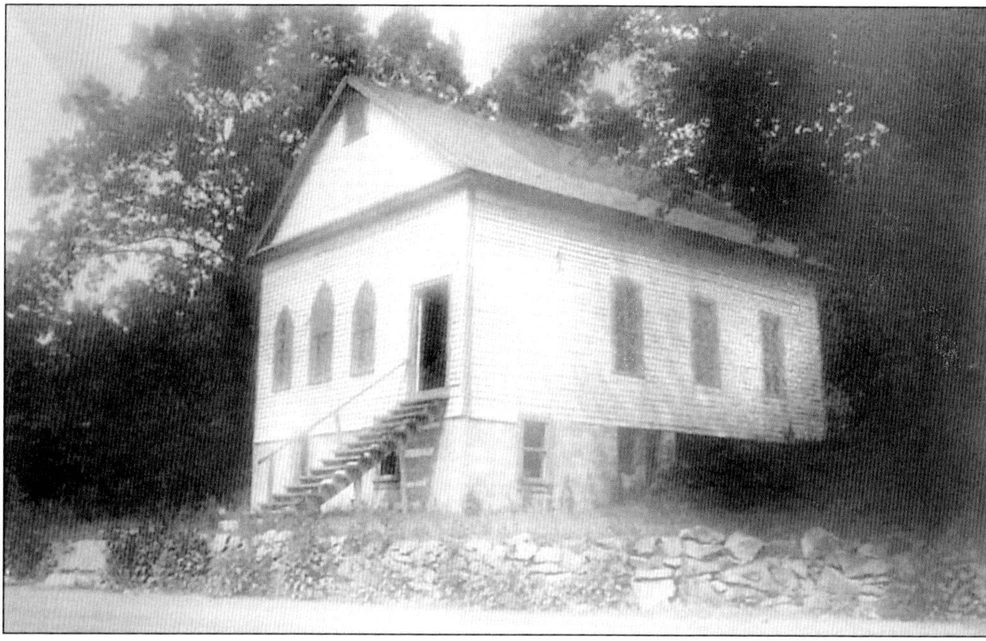

Belle Ellen was a coal mining town located 3 miles east of West Blocton. The community was named after mine owner Henry Debardeleben's wife, Ellen, and his daughter Belle. This church would have served the mining community as a place of worship and as a meeting place. (Courtesy of Cecil Crews.)

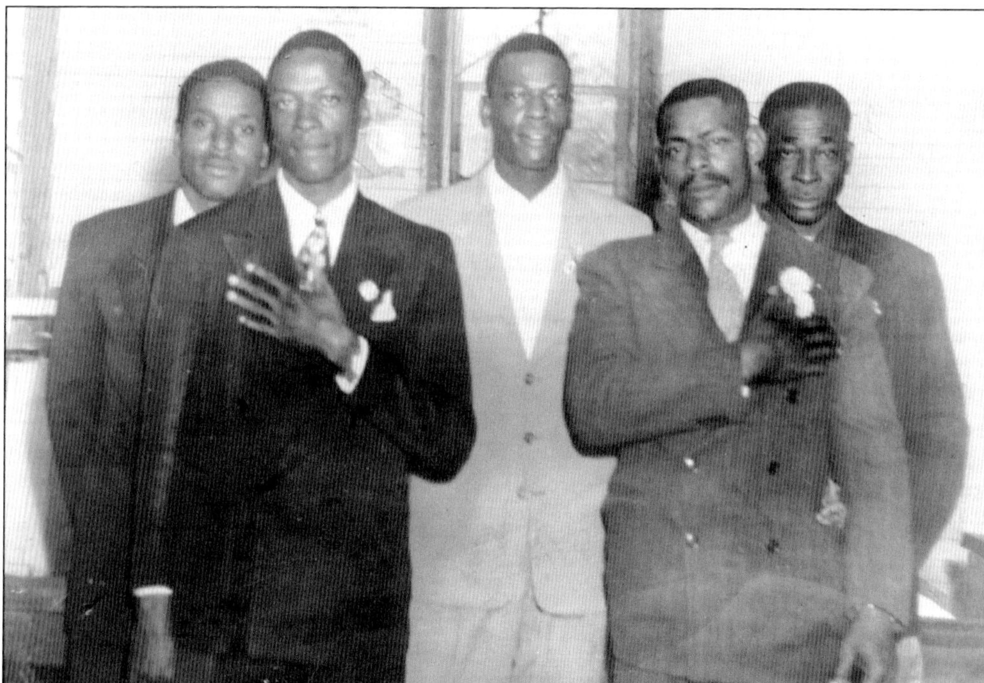

Members of the gospel singing group known as the White Robes from Brent are (from left to right) (first row) Walter Johnson and unidentified; (second row) Raymond Underwood, Joe Johnson, and William Underwood. (Courtesy of Gwendolyn Valentine.)

Three

SCHOOLS AND ACTIVITIES

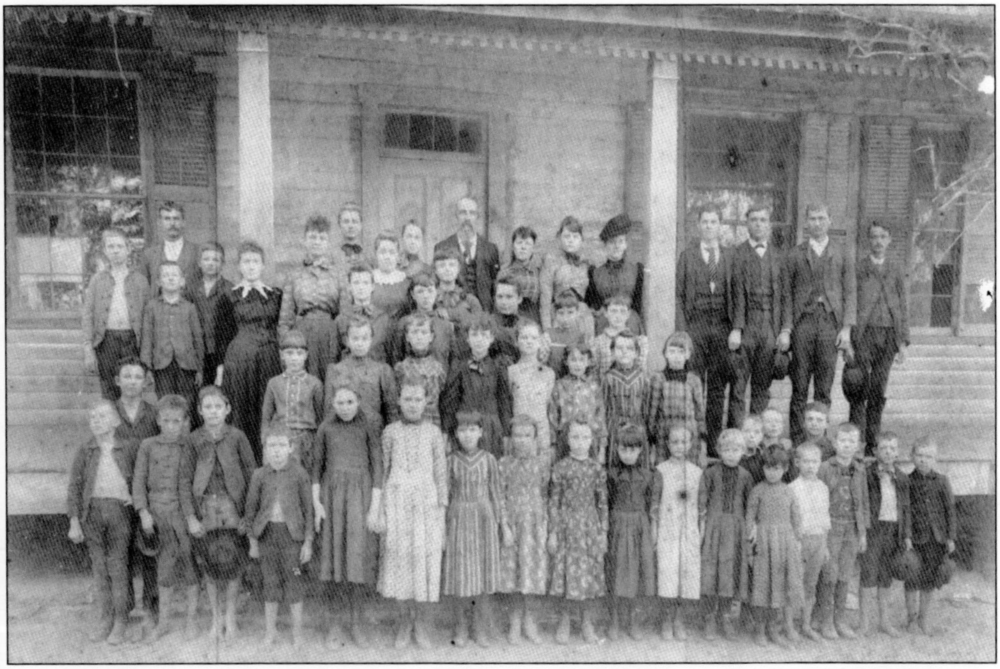

The Centreville Academy opened around 1837 in a small building 40 feet long and 22 feet wide. The school in the picture is not the first Centreville Academy. The academy transferred to the Centreville Masonic Institute (seen here) on November 1, 1852. The land for the Centreville Masonic Institute was purchased from Samuel W. Davidson. It would serve as a school and Masonic Lodge. This school operated as the Centreville Masonic Institute until it was sold to Rev. H. A. Smith of Centreville in 1873, when the name was changed to the Centreville Male and Female Academy. In 1882, the name changed again, this time to the Cahaba Valley Academy after Reverend Smith sold the school to his son Prof. E. K. W. Smith. At that time, some improvements were made, such as classrooms equipped with desk and blackboards on the wall. The Cahaba Valley Academy was incorporated as the Centreville College in February 1885 and continued under this name until 1909, when the school ceased to exist. In February 1894, the Centreville College burned, and its classes were moved to the courthouse. Professor Cooper bought the lot of the Centreville College for $250, and a new school was built. The school was then sold to Prof. H. K. W. Smith. In 1909, Professor Smith sold the school to Prof. J. D. Cooper. This school is now the residence of Wayne and Jonlee Melton, on Walnut Street in Centreville. (Courtesy of Wayne and Jonlee Melton.)

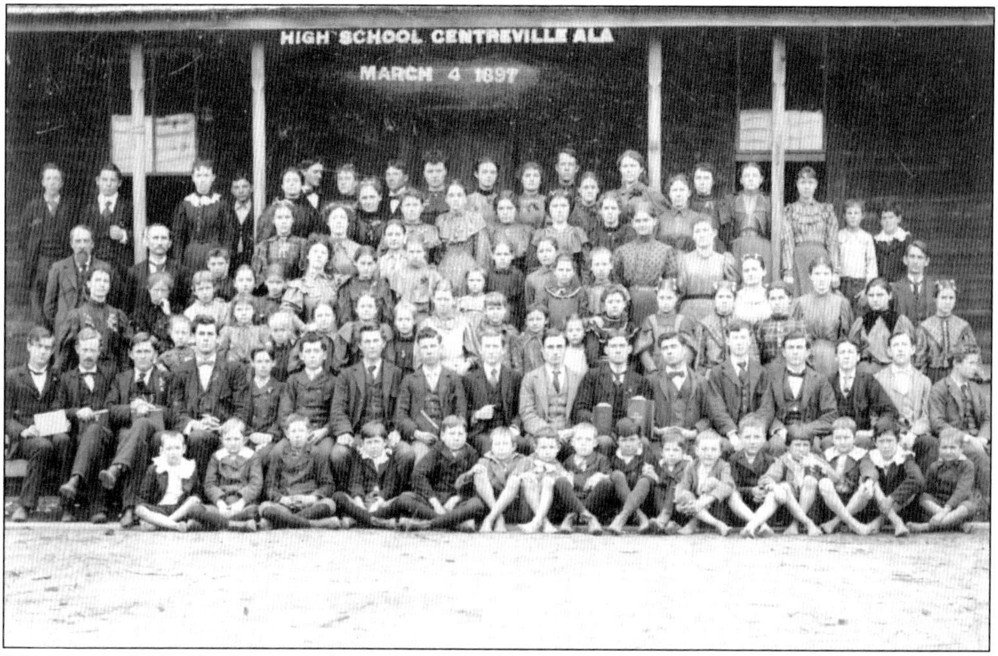

Writing on the back identifies this picture as the front of the O. C. Oakley home at the time of the Centreville School in 1897. (Courtesy of Wayne and Jonlee Melton.)

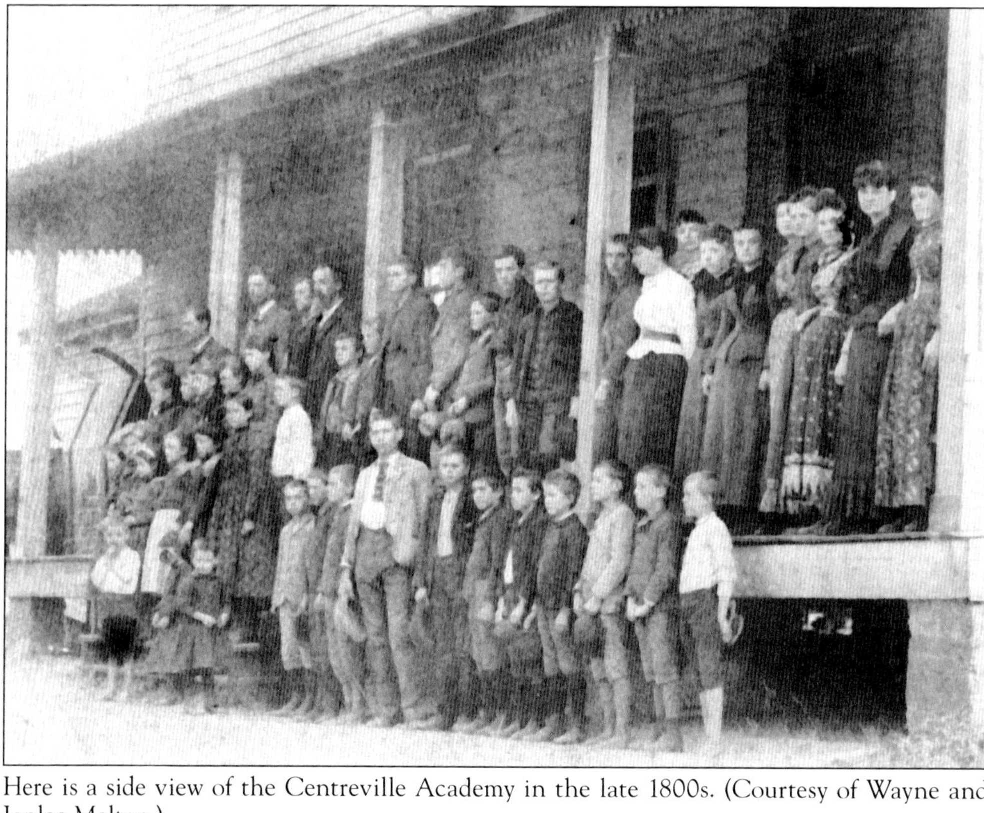

Here is a side view of the Centreville Academy in the late 1800s. (Courtesy of Wayne and Jonlee Melton.)

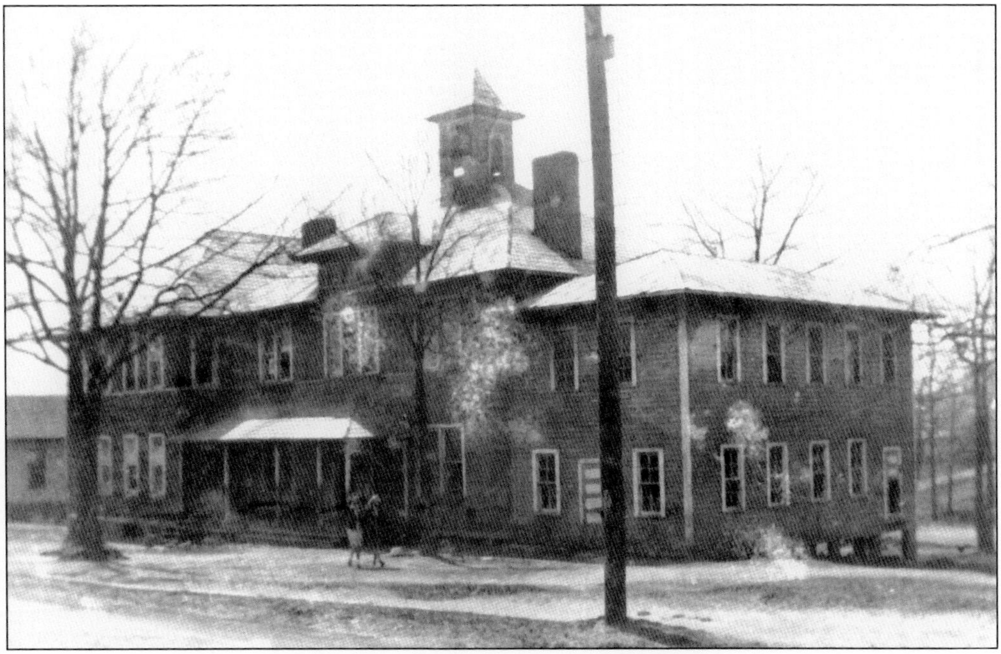

This photograph shows the Blocton No. 1 County School. Writing on the back dates this school to around 1940, which would be four years after the building was abandoned. (Courtesy of Paula Fancher.)

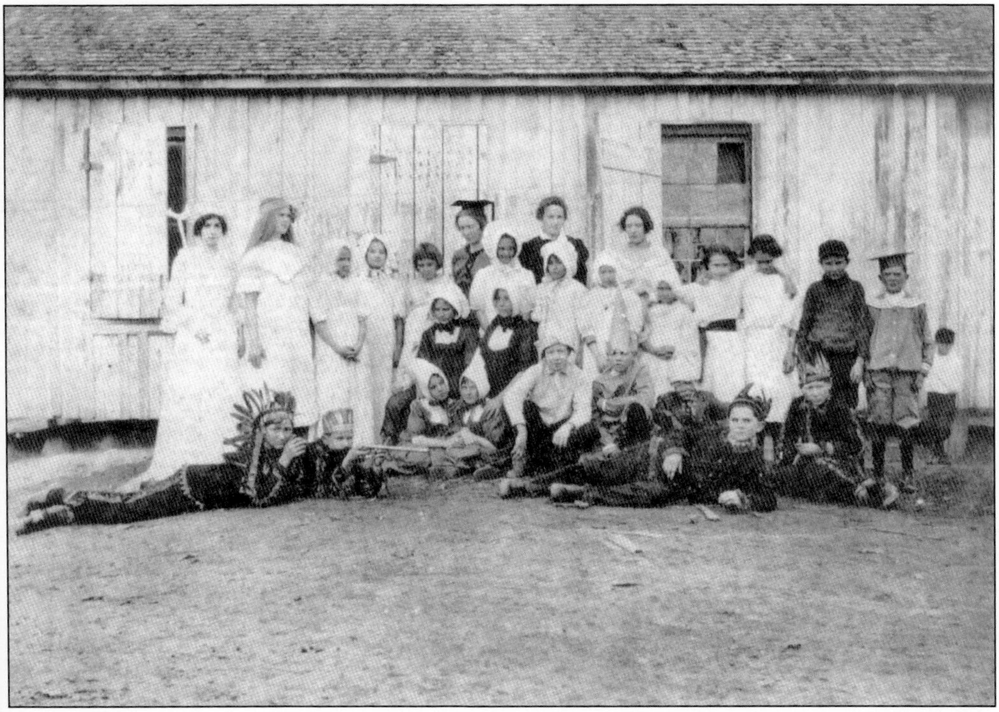

The exact location of this picture is unknown, but it was somewhere in Blocton in 1915. On the back is written that this was a play, and the students were all dressed in their costumes. (Courtesy of Paula Fancher.)

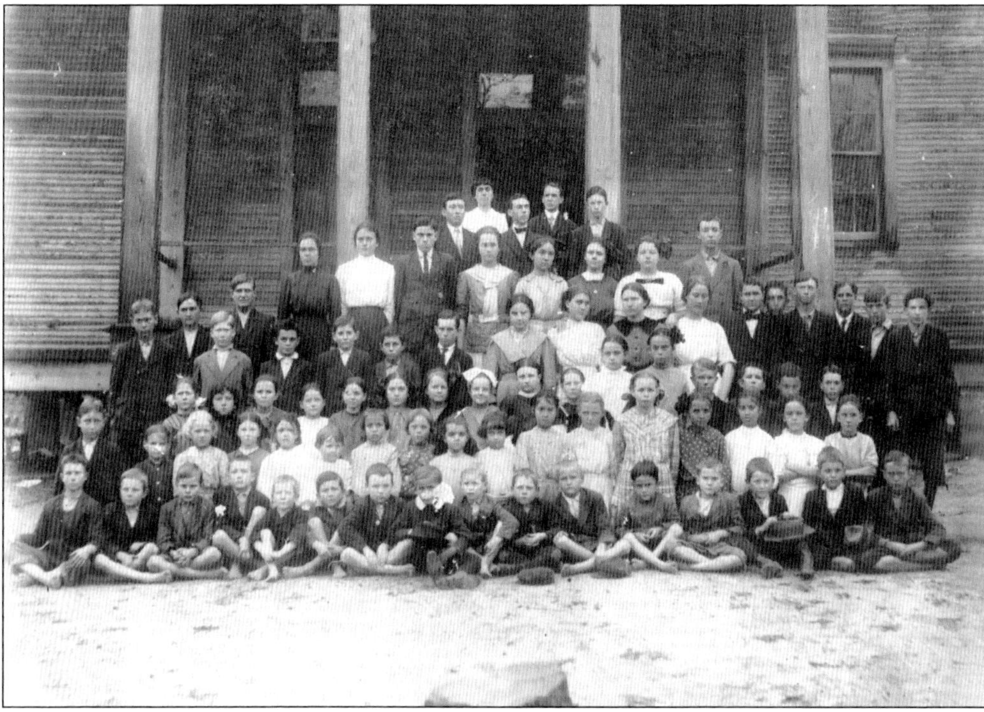

This late-1800s photograph is of the student body of the Lawley School, which was located in the Lawley community south of Centreville. (Courtesy of Frank and Edith Wilson.)

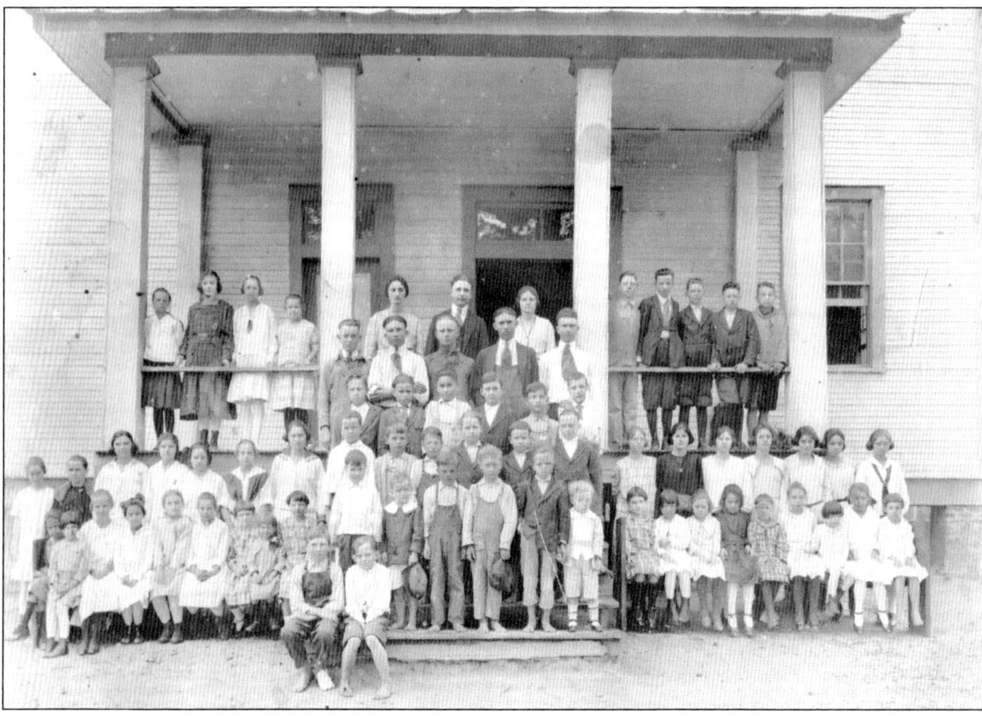

The Lawley School was named for the family of Jackson and Joseph L. Lawley. (Courtesy of Belcher Hobson.)

Henry Damon Davidson (1869–1955) stands in front of the Bibb County Training School in 1950. He was the founder, builder, and principal of this school. Davidson dedicated his life to education and the development of life skills within the African American community. (Courtesy of Jim Oakley Jr.)

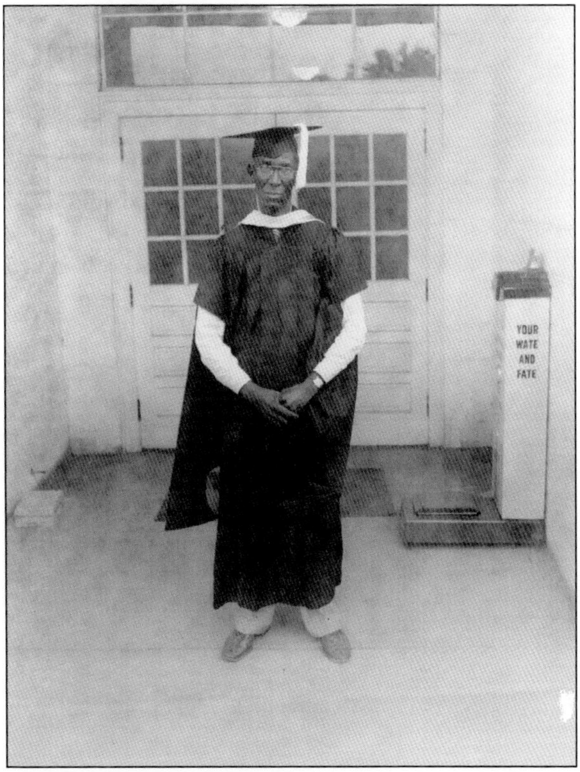

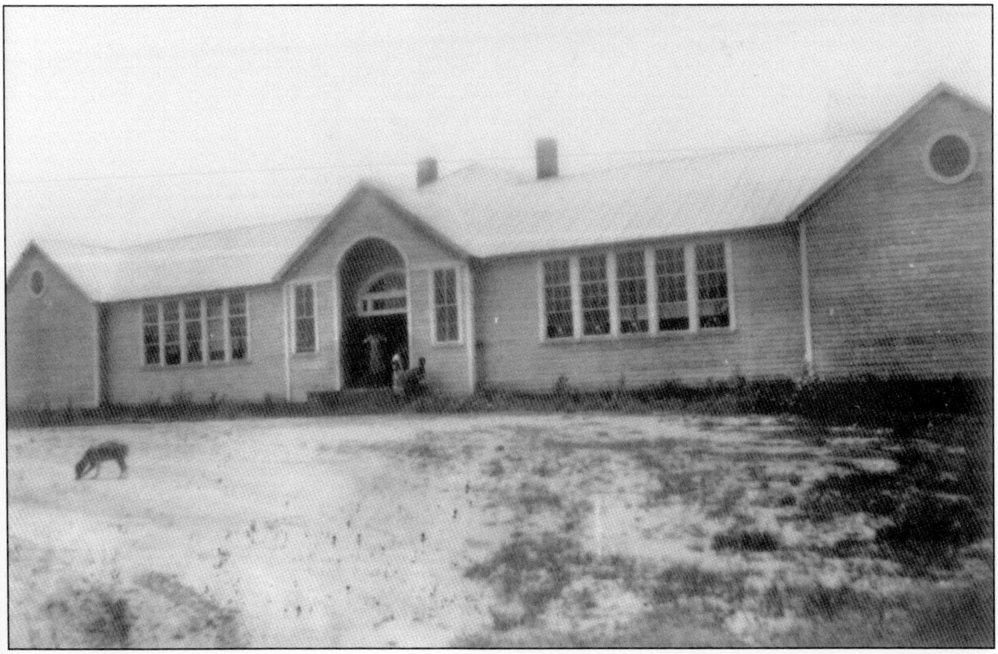

In 1935, the Brent Colored School was located in the Mount Ebell Baptist Church. In 1937, it was moved to a new school building, which was named the Faucett Jr. High School after Henry Von Faucett, who was instrumental in securing the land and building. In July 1956, the school burned, but it was later rebuilt. (Courtesy of Ruth Dailey.)

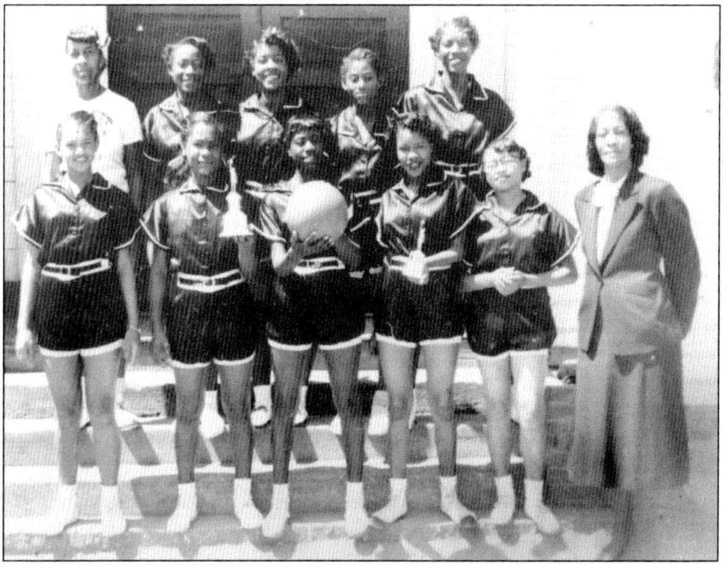

Pictured is the girls basketball team from the Faucett School. From left to right are (first row) Alene Ford, Martha Sanders, Majorie Huff, Esther Thurman, Eljola Ford, and coach Minnie Bochelion; (second row) Stella Cutts, Ruby Crews, Mamie Parker, unidentified, and Hattie Mae Sanders. (Courtesy of Gwendolyn Valentine.)

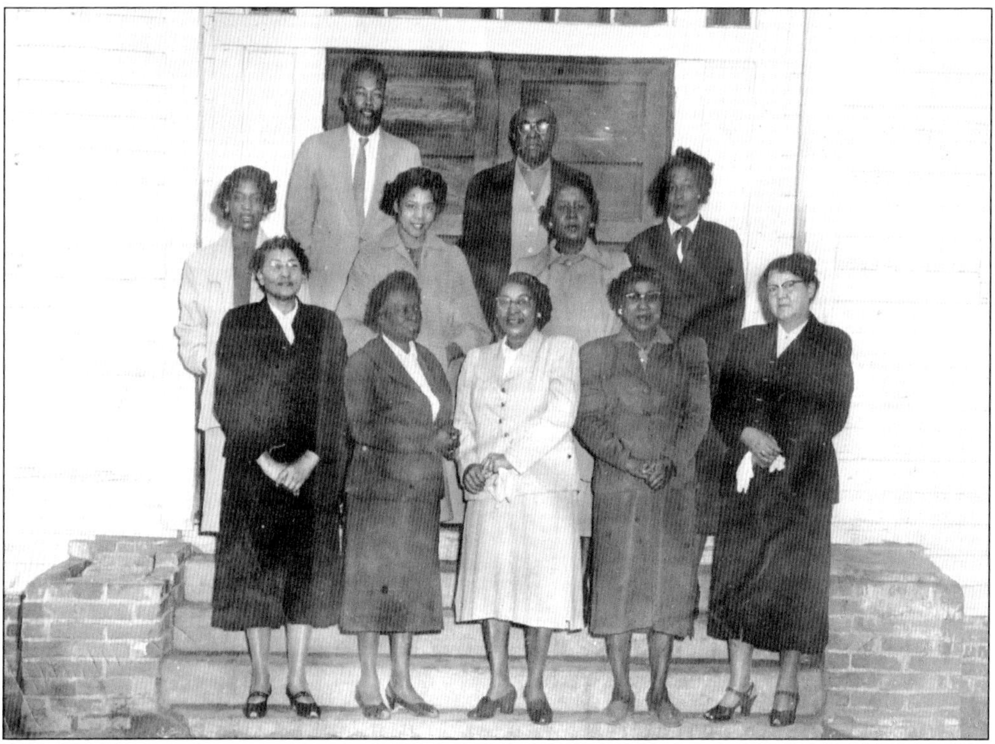

Teachers pose for a group picture in front of the Faucett School in Brent. From left to right are (first row) Bessie Tubbs, Ela Mae Burts, Iola Harris, Irene Hollifield, and ? Avery; (second row) Connie Edward, Lola Cooper, Clara Payne, and Minnie Bochelion; (third row) Charles Cooper and principal David Harris. (Courtesy of Gwendolyn Valentine.)

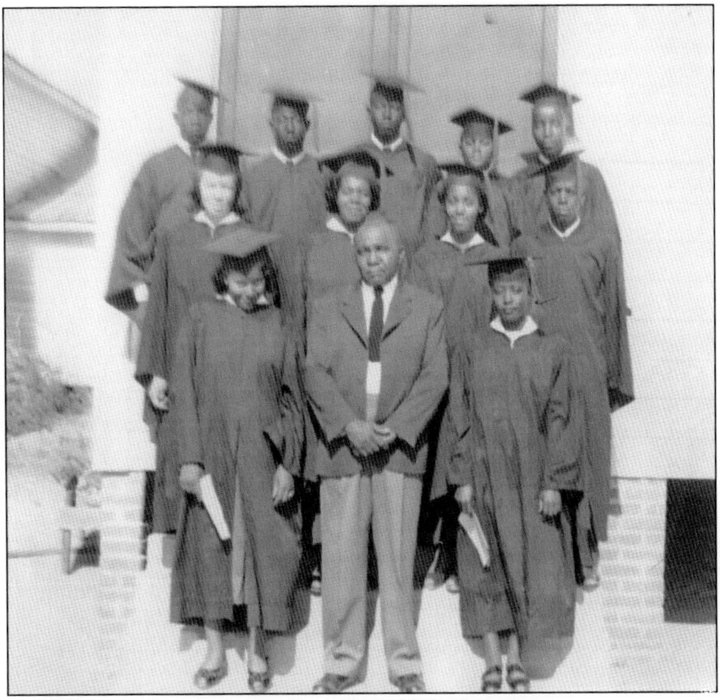

This is a graduating class of the Faucett School, which was located in Brent. (Courtesy of Gwendolyn Valentine.)

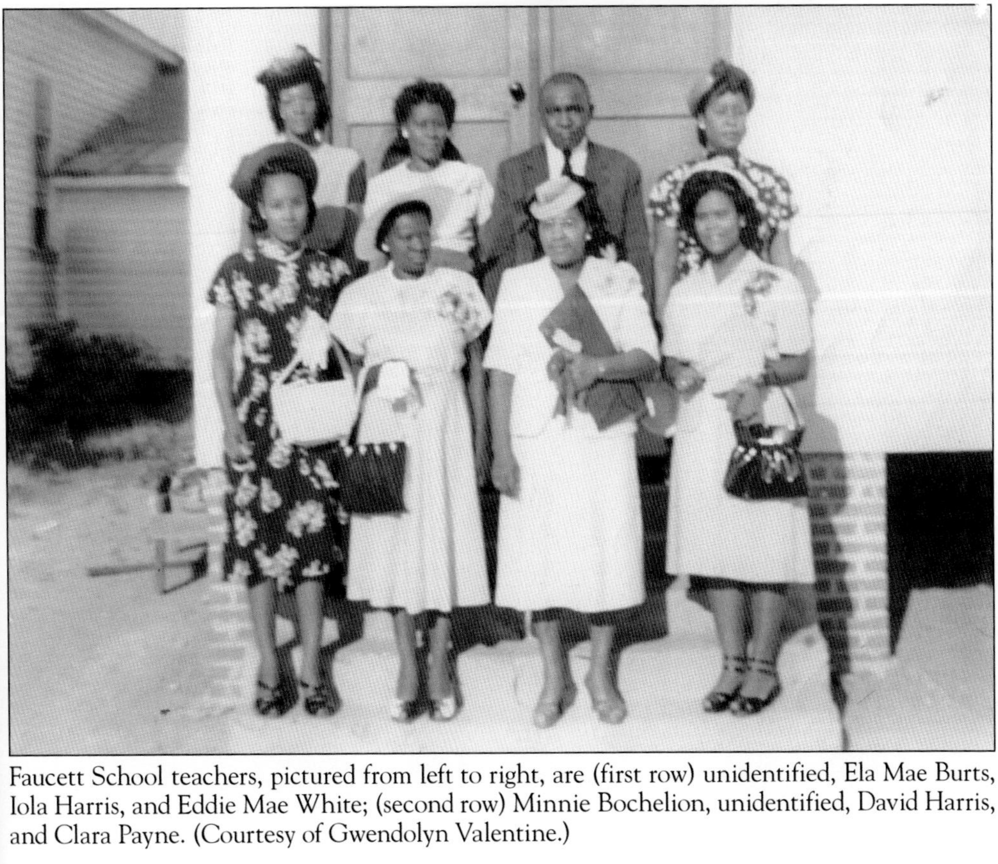

Faucett School teachers, pictured from left to right, are (first row) unidentified, Ela Mae Burts, Iola Harris, and Eddie Mae White; (second row) Minnie Bochelion, unidentified, David Harris, and Clara Payne. (Courtesy of Gwendolyn Valentine.)

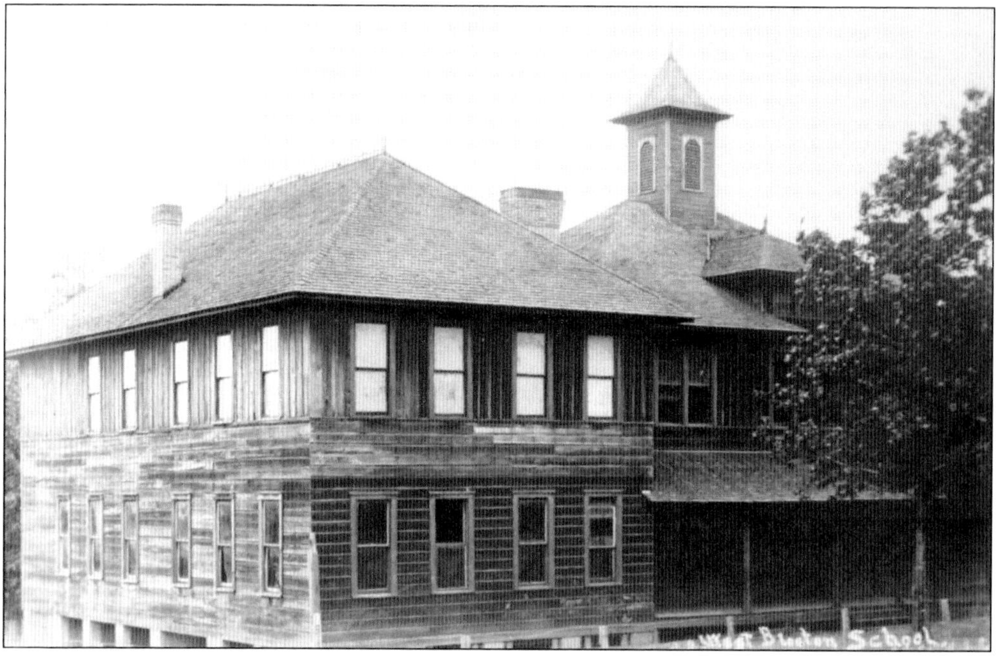

In the fall of 1903, the West Blocton High School opened its doors with eight grades. The old green school was located on Magnolia Street, just one block off Main Street, with an auditorium located underneath the steeple. (Photograph by John T. Weeks, courtesy of Beverly Weeks Beasley.)

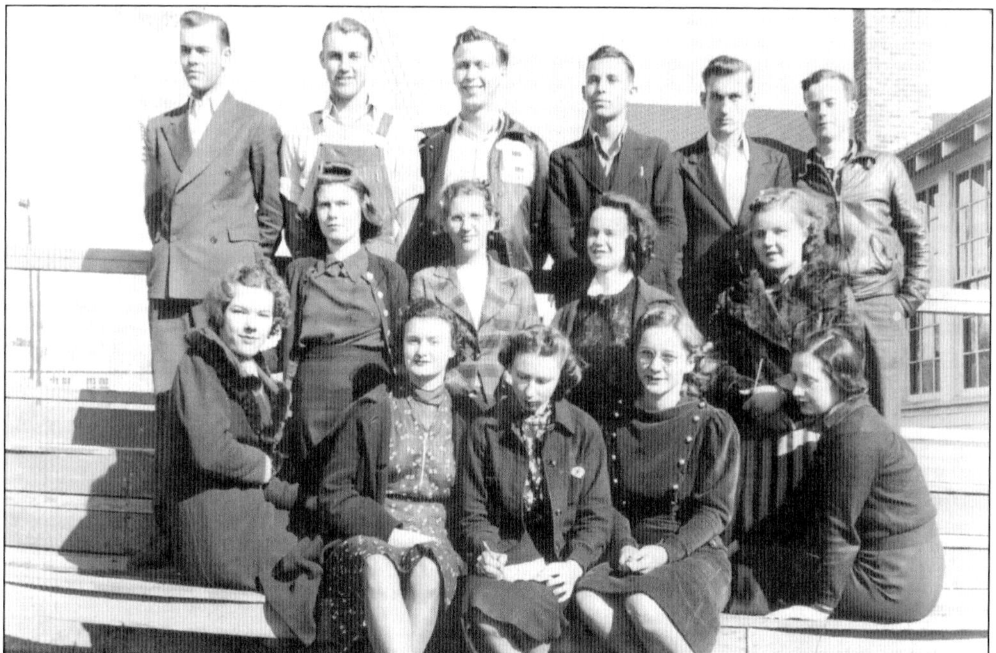

This photograph of the West Blocton High School Club was taken around 1939. Students from left to right are (first row) Virginia Lois Reed, Bobbie Thrasher Williams, and Christine Duncan; (second row) Margaret Parker, Margaret Kren/Koen, Frances Harris, Doris Goodwin, and two unidentified girls; (third row) Buddy George and five unidentified boys. (Courtesy of Paula Fancher.)

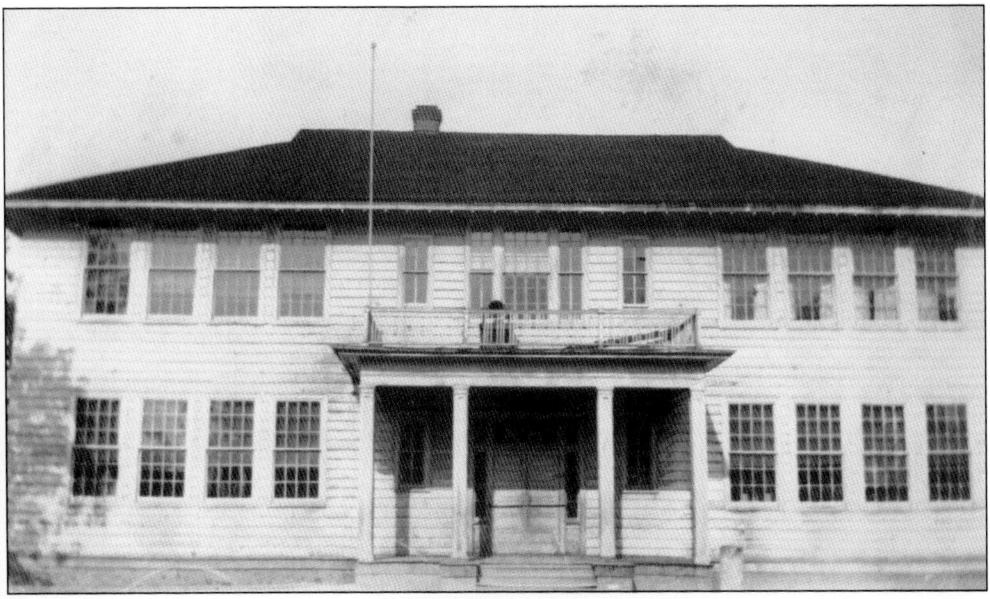

The Piper-Coleanor School was used for elementary and junior high classes until the early 1930s, when the senior high was added. This school was destroyed by fire in May 1940. (Courtesy of Mary Louise Jones Crider.)

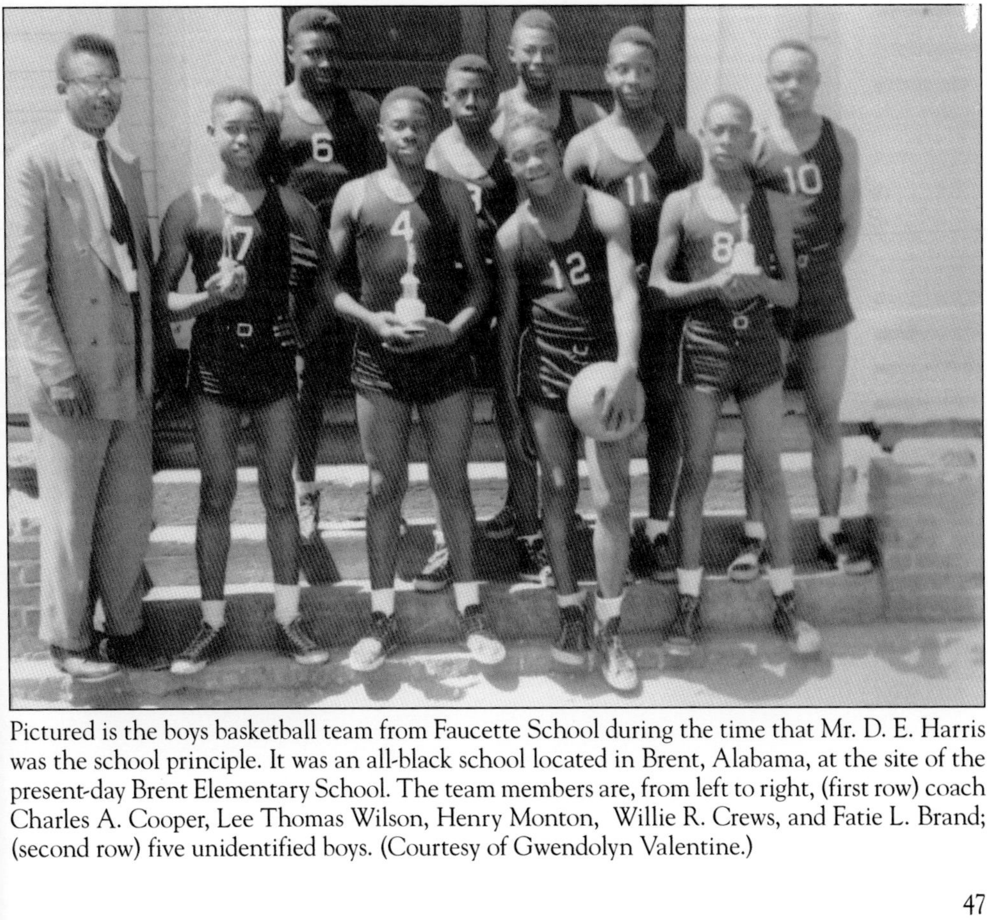

Pictured is the boys basketball team from Faucette School during the time that Mr. D. E. Harris was the school principle. It was an all-black school located in Brent, Alabama, at the site of the present-day Brent Elementary School. The team members are, from left to right, (first row) coach Charles A. Cooper, Lee Thomas Wilson, Henry Monton, Willie R. Crews, and Fatie L. Brand; (second row) five unidentified boys. (Courtesy of Gwendolyn Valentine.)

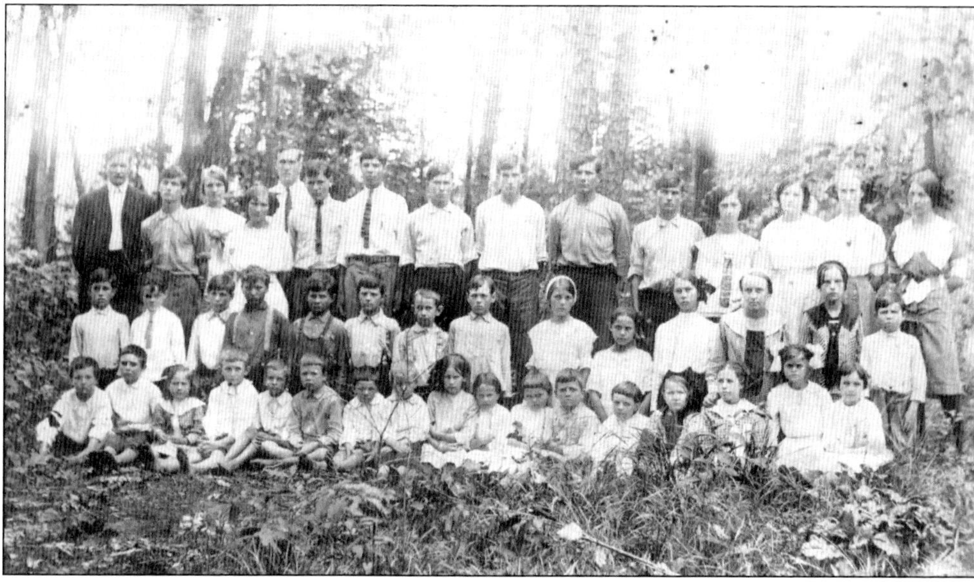

The Spencer School was located near the Spencer Church off Bear Creek Road and was named for Dr. J. W. Spencer, a local resident and physician in the last half of the 19th century. This photograph is the class picture of 1913. From left to right are (first row) Marlon Hayes, Herbert Yeager, Nola Cook, Fulton Meigs, Carl Bailey, Vick Murphy, Gilbert Yeager, Clifford Boyd, Ora Bailey, Nora Bailey, Jettie Ward, Brady Belcher, Lois Caddell, Edna Meigs, Levera Cook, Lola Belcher, and Ethel Yeager; (second row) Brady Murphy, Walton Yeager, Grady Snipes, Robert Boyd, Albert Belcher, Homer Caddell, Percy Bailey, Percy Hayes, Lena Belcher, Annie Maude Hayes, Charity Boyd, Theresa Meigs, Hattie Ward, and Clint Murphy; (third row) Prof. J. R. Alexander, Lonnie Snipes, Irene Tidwell, Maggie Snipes, Vincent Hunt, Clifton Logan, Nelson Murphy, Andrew Boyd, unidentified, Alvin Avery Shelby Belcher, Sam Snipes, Clyde Wyatt, Ola Caddell, Florence Boyd, and Stella Snipes. (Courtesy of Belcher Hobson.)

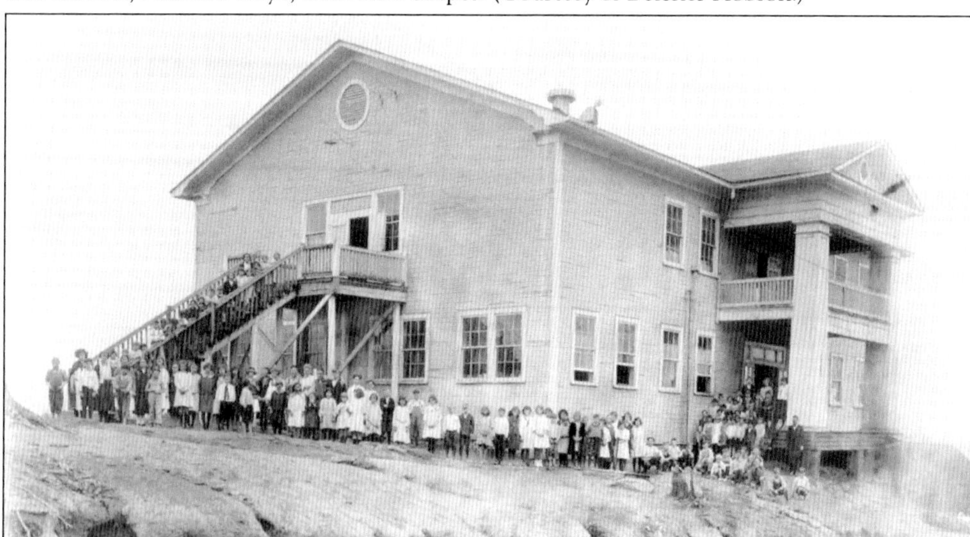

The Marvel School taught first through ninth grades. The school had four rooms on the first floor and two rooms and an auditorium on the second. It ran the full length of the building and took up about 60 percent of the upper level. (Courtesy of Marshall Goggins.)

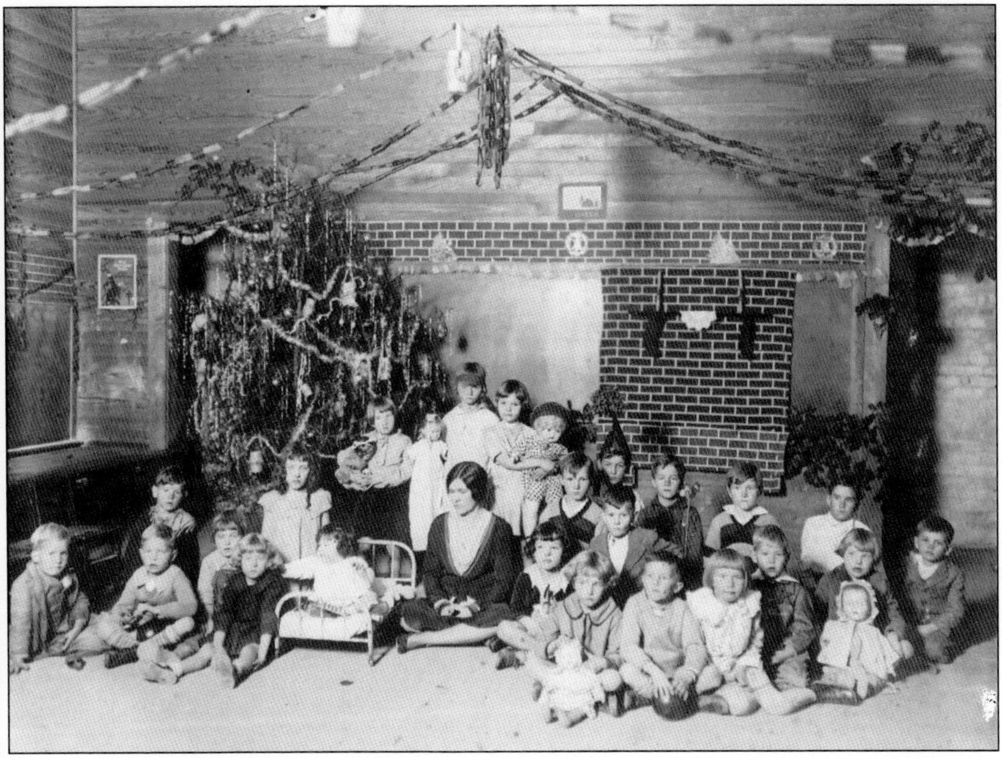

This was a Christmas gathering of elementary school students in Brent. The teacher in the center is Grace Ward, and the child to the right of her is Henri Ruth Owens. The other children are unidentified. (Courtesy of Henri Ruth Owens.)

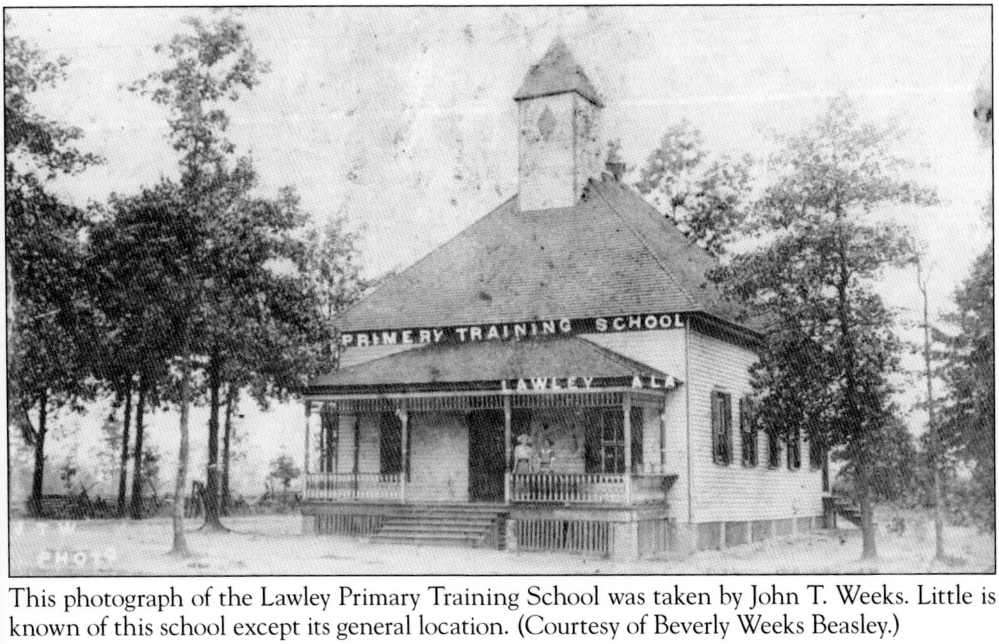

This photograph of the Lawley Primary Training School was taken by John T. Weeks. Little is known of this school except its general location. (Courtesy of Beverly Weeks Beasley.)

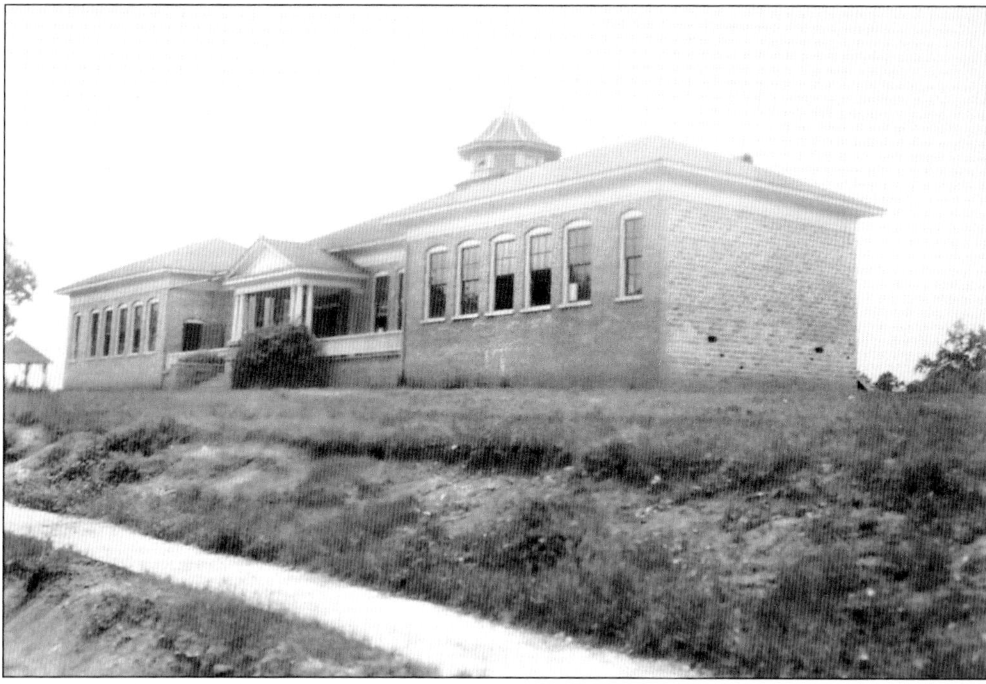

The Alexander Consolidated School—also known as the Centreville Elementary School—was named after Prof. J. R. Alexander of Anniston, who was the first principal of the school. The school building was destroyed by fire in February 1958. (Courtesy of Birmingham Public Library.)

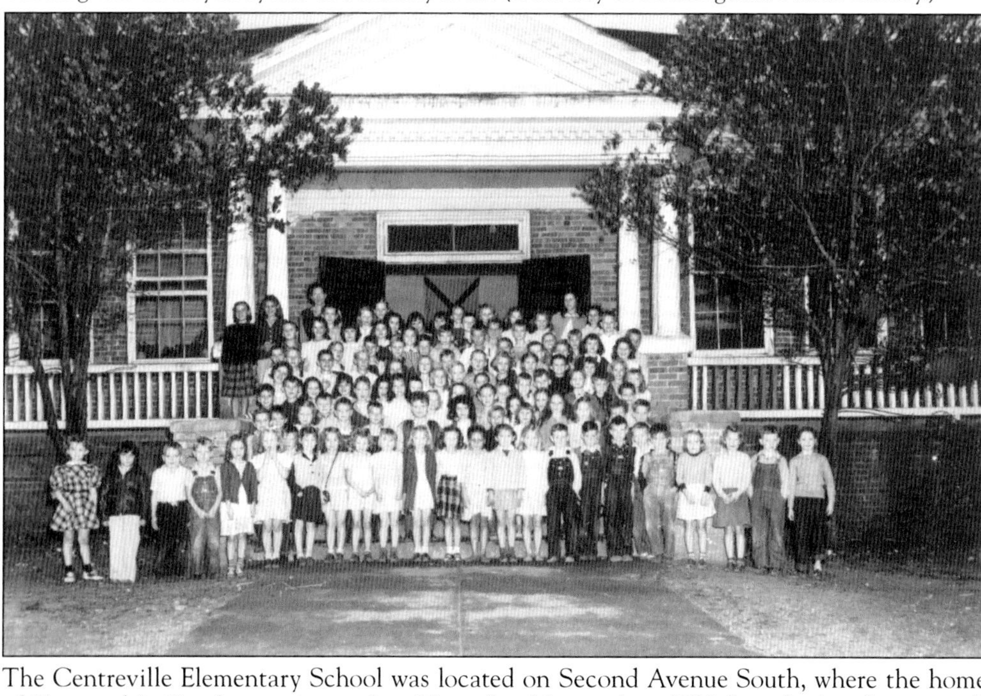

The Centreville Elementary School was located on Second Avenue South, where the home of Tom and Jo Bamberg exists today. The school burned in 1958, but the lunchroom still stands and is currently being used as the Community Service Program building. (Courtesy of Hal Cottingham.)

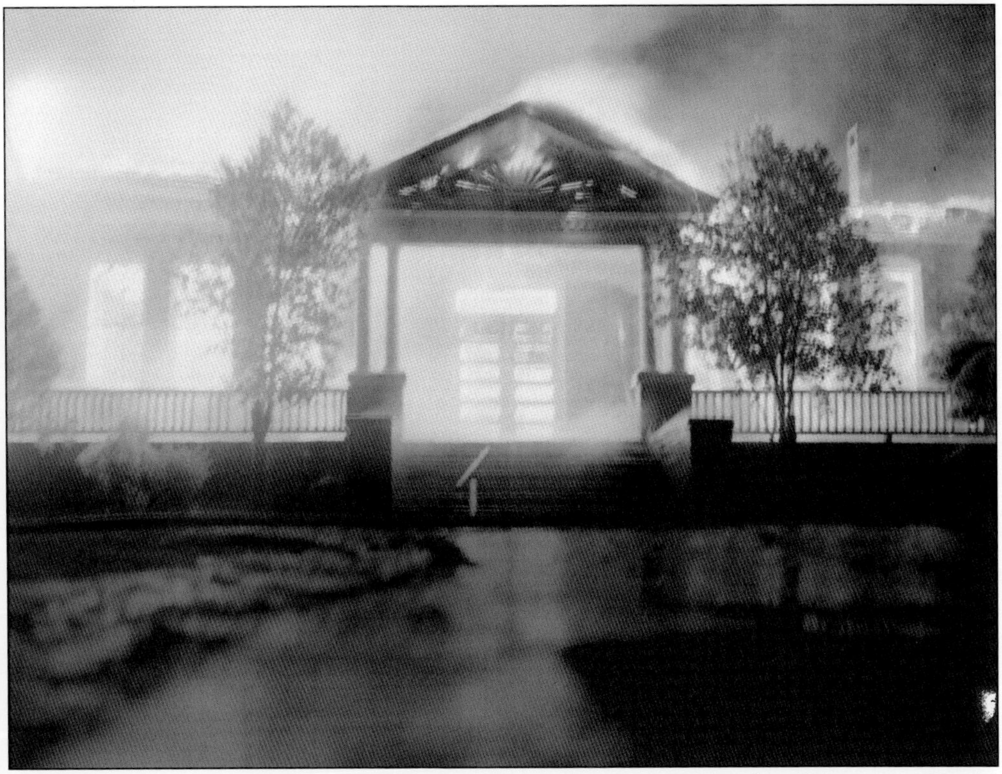

After the burning of the Alexander Consolidated Elementary School in February 1958, the students were relocated to local churches to continue their education. This photograph was taken by the editor of the *Centreville Press*, Jim Oakley Jr. (Courtesy of Jim Oakley Jr.)

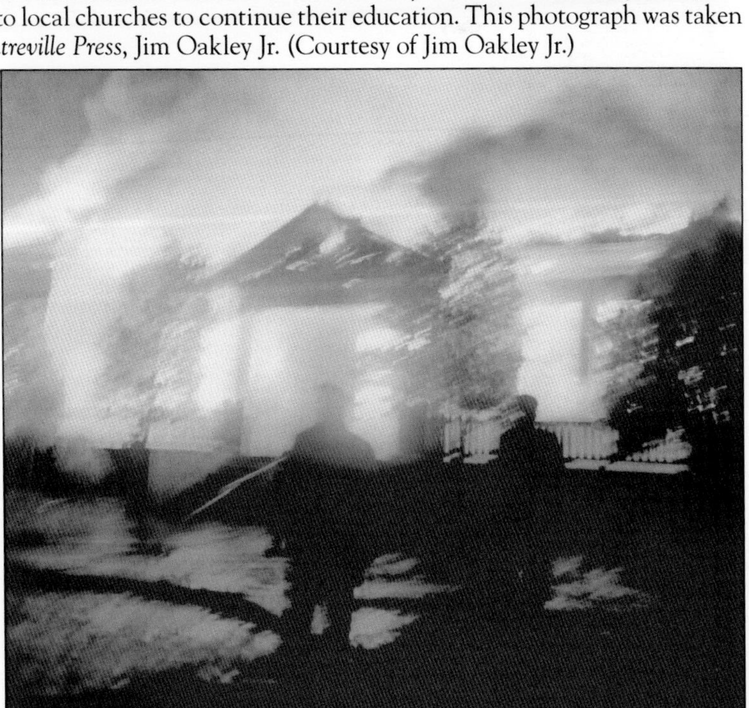

The Alexander Consolidated School sat on a hill above the town square. This four-classroom structure was built in 1908. Local newspaper owner Jim Oakley caught this image during the school's burning in February 1958. (Courtesy of Jim Oakley Jr.)

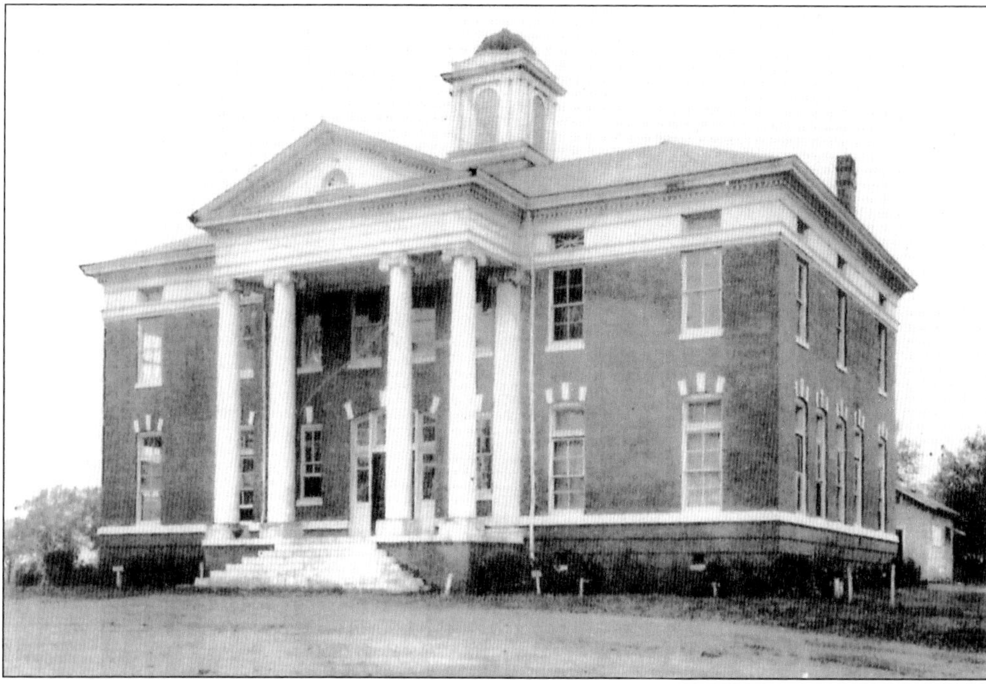

The Bibb County High School (BCHS) is shown as it stood in 1909 prior to additions that were made in later years. The first class to graduate from BCHS was in 1912. This building is now being used as the Bibb County Junior High School. (Courtesy of Roger Brothers.)

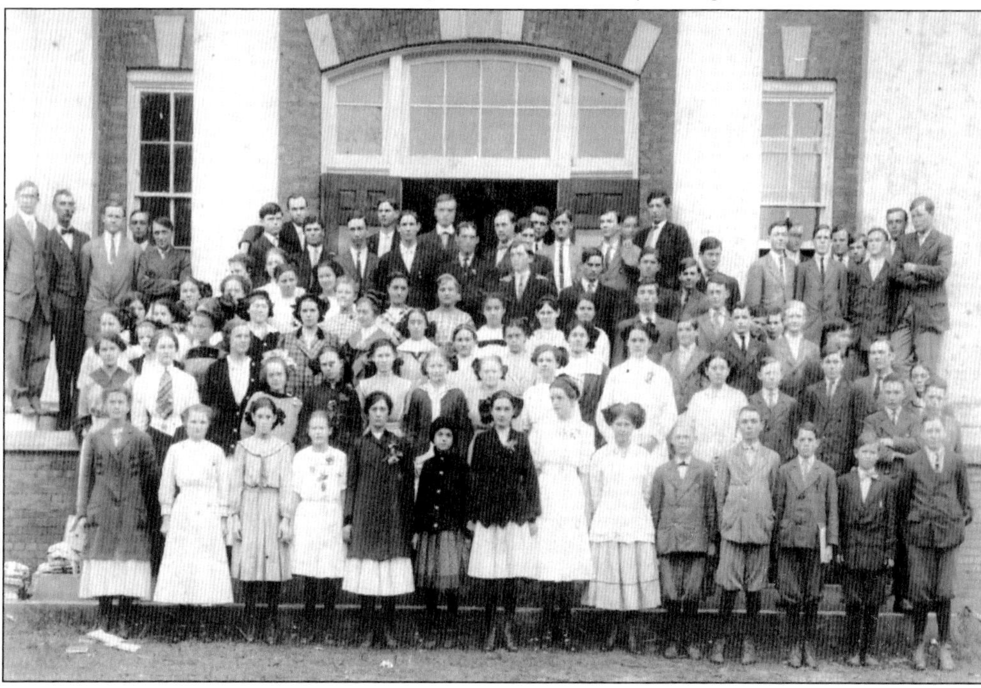

This is the original Bibb County High School in the early 1900s. There were four large classrooms and an auditorium that could seat 500 people. The names of these students are unknown. (Courtesy of Cecil Crews.)

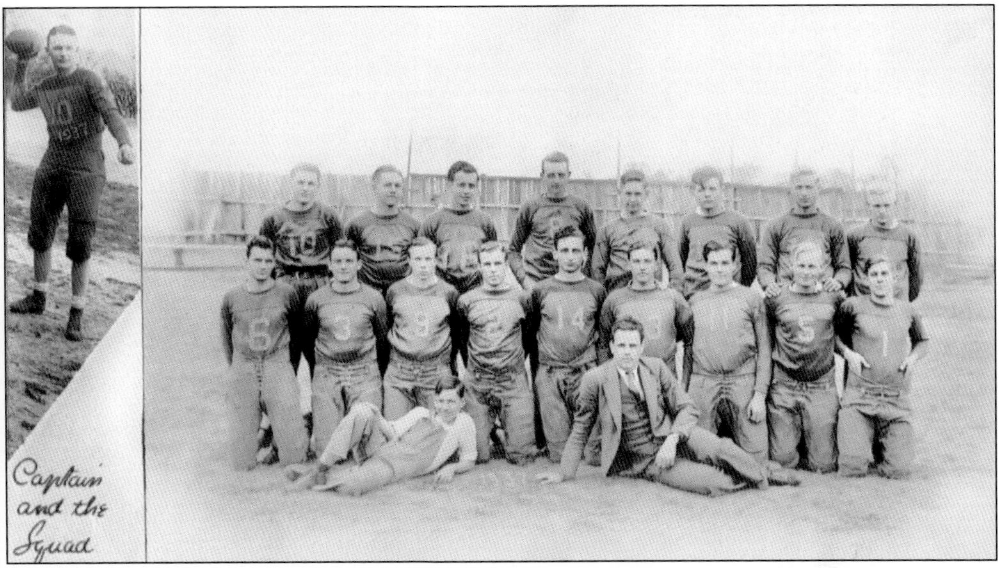

The 1938 Bibb County High School football squad is pictured here. From left to right are (sitting) Harry Meigs and coach ? Dobbin; (kneeling) Elbre Mitchell, Bert Snead, Glenn McGee, Stanley Boyd, Cary Jones, Vernon Medders, L. B. Bearden, Leonard Nichols, and Avery Kinnard; (standing) captain Jimmy Harbin, Louie Meigs, Buddy Cottingham, Gordon Avery, George Stacy, Belcher Hobson, Taylor Parker, and Cotton Stewart. (Courtesy of Belcher Hobson.)

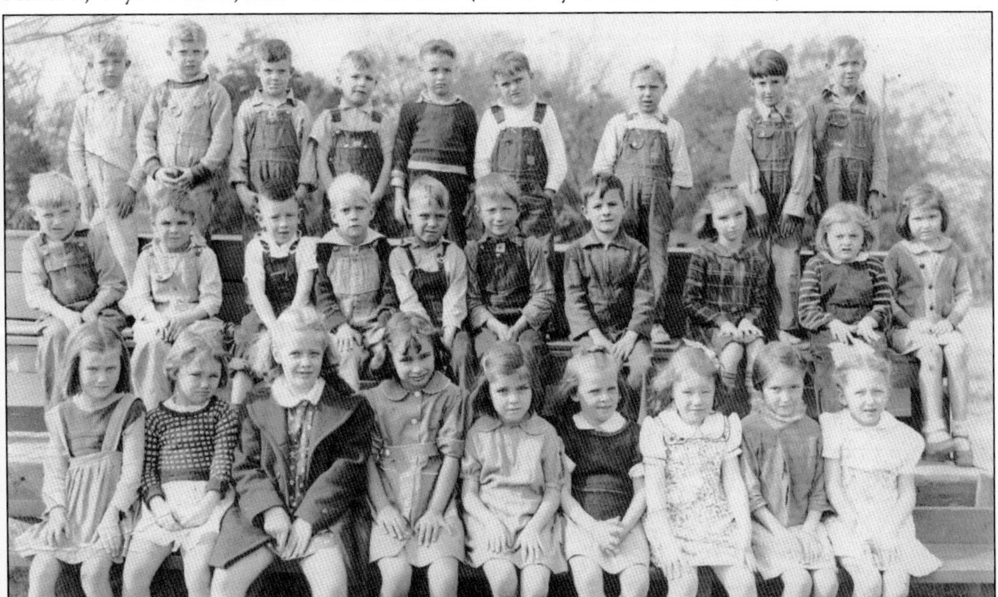

Pictured is the Alexander Consolidated School 1941 first-grade class. Students from left to right are (first row) Beverly Ann Champion, Lois Red, Ruby Fosher, Myrtle Sewell, Mary Sue Langston, Bettye Ann Deason, Mary Jane Stallings, Pauline Riley, and Sylvia McCalla; (second row) R. F. Smith, Buddy Reynolds, Stevie Rogan, Joe Ingram, Clyde Lawley, M. J. Geeslin, Harold Murphy, Bettye Ann Babb, Joyce Filgs, and Alean ?; (third row) Leo Phillips, Raymond Freeman Jr., Parson Wires, Reed Smitherman, Joe Elliott Jr., Charles Fowler, J. C. Lawrence, Young Clemmons, and Lorrie Parker Dailey. (Courtesy of Betty Burt.)

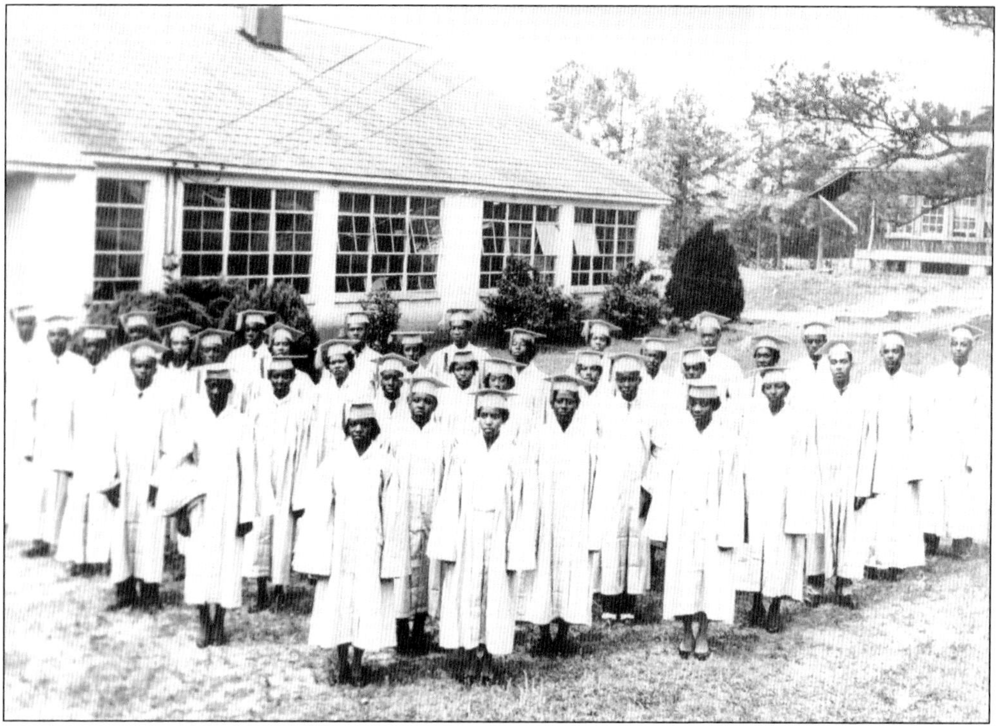

Picture here is a graduating class of Davidson School. (Courtesy of Gwendolyn Valentine.)

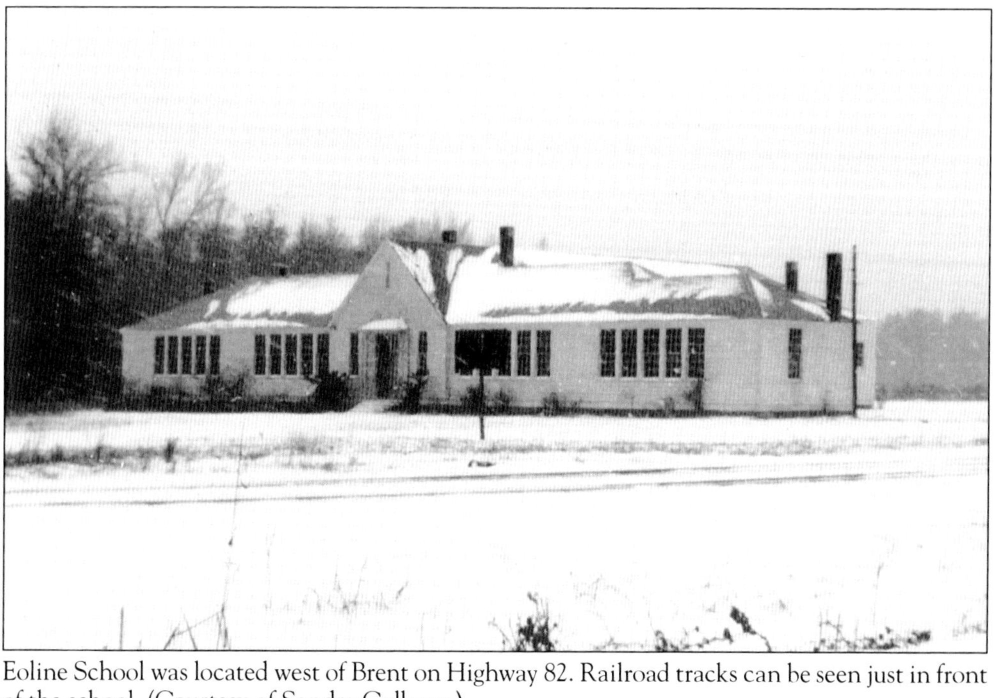

Eoline School was located west of Brent on Highway 82. Railroad tracks can be seen just in front of the school. (Courtesy of Sandra Colburn.)

Four

BUSINESSES AND OCCUPATIONS

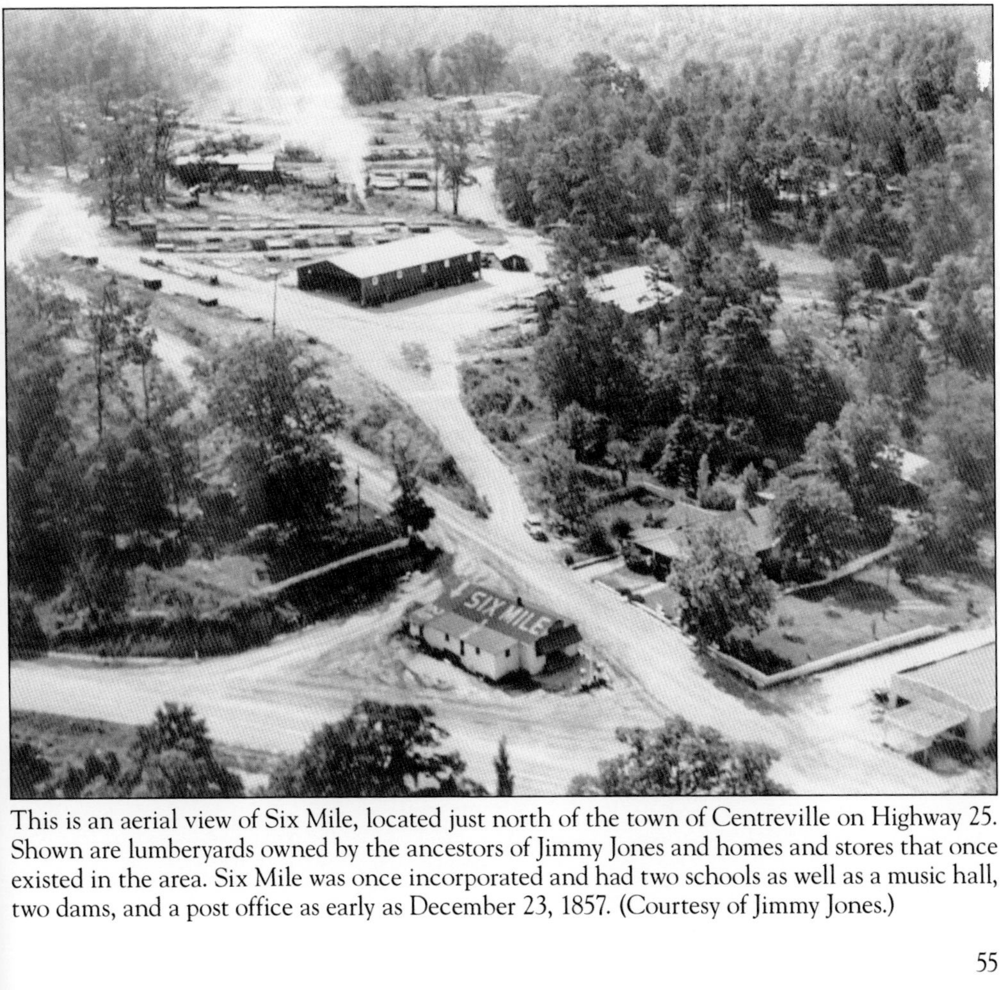

This is an aerial view of Six Mile, located just north of the town of Centreville on Highway 25. Shown are lumberyards owned by the ancestors of Jimmy Jones and homes and stores that once existed in the area. Six Mile was once incorporated and had two schools as well as a music hall, two dams, and a post office as early as December 23, 1857. (Courtesy of Jimmy Jones.)

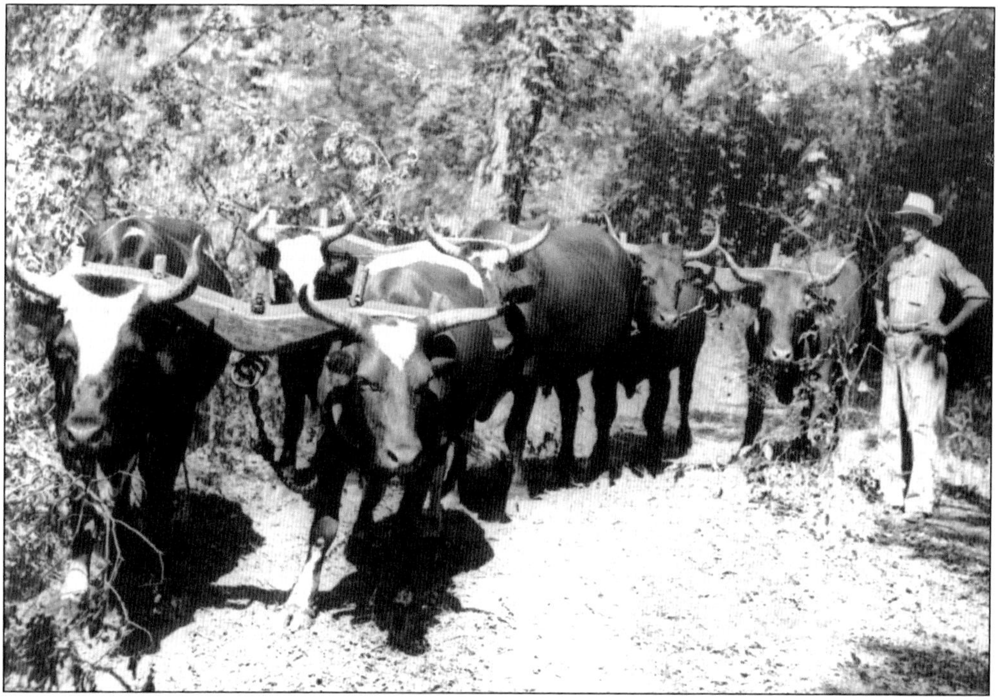

Richmond Pearson (1897–1986) is seen here as he skids logs on the banks of the Little Cahaba River in 1947. The steers were used to get logs in wet places where trucks could not go. Dickie Pearson, the son of Richmond Pearson, said that his step-brother, Billy Ragland, was asked to take the steers to get a drink of water and during their drink, still yoked together, they decided to go for a swim. The now-worried teen ran back and told his father what had happened. Then his father walked back down to the water and started talking to the steers, and when they heard his voice, they came swimming back to the shore and back to work. The steers (from left to right) are (front) Buck and Tig; (middle) Pobe and Doc; and (back) Let and Lemon. This photograph was taken by Jim Oakley Sr. (Courtesy of Dickie Pearson.)

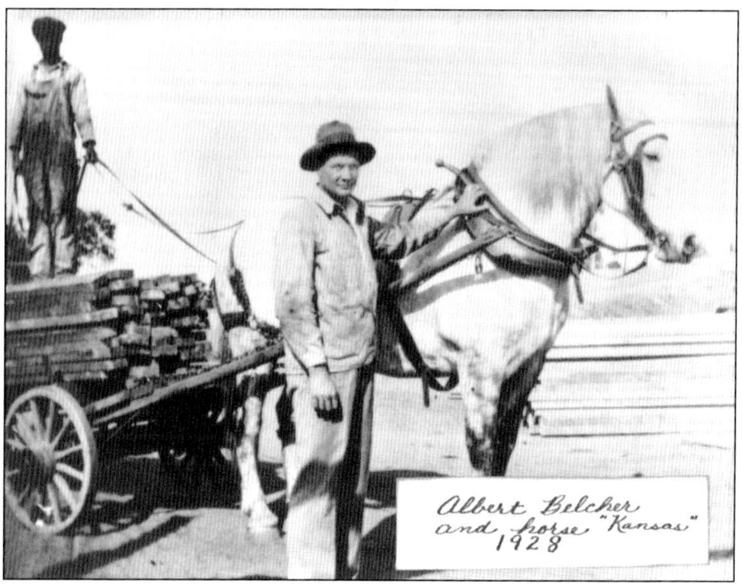

From left to right, unidentified, Albert Belcher, and Belcher's horse, Kansas, are hauling sawn lumber in 1928. (Courtesy of Belcher Lumber Company.)

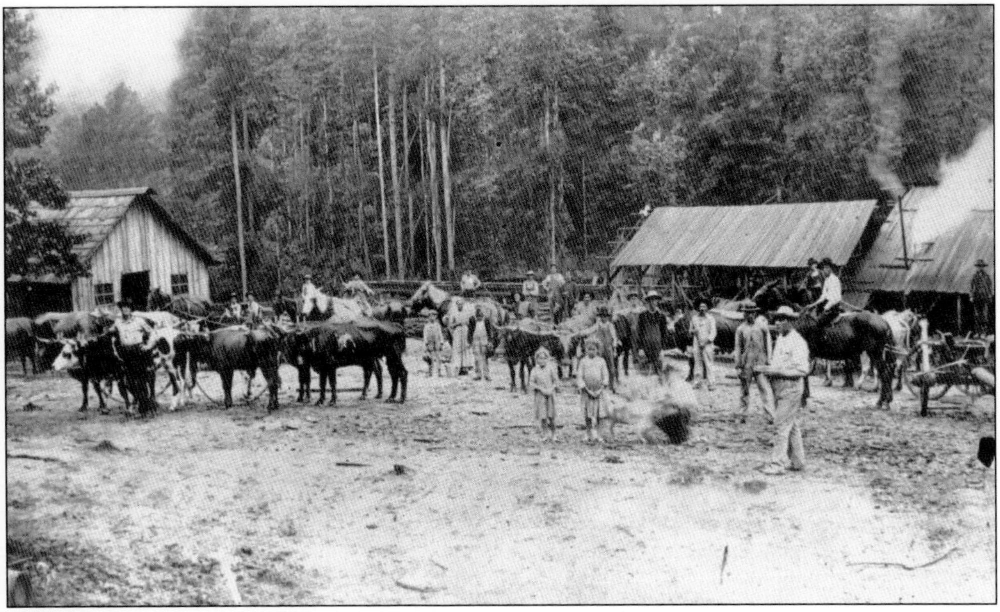

The first Belcher Lumber Mill was built in 1906 in Brent by Addy, Eddy, and Andrew Belcher. (Courtesy of Belcher Lumber Company.)

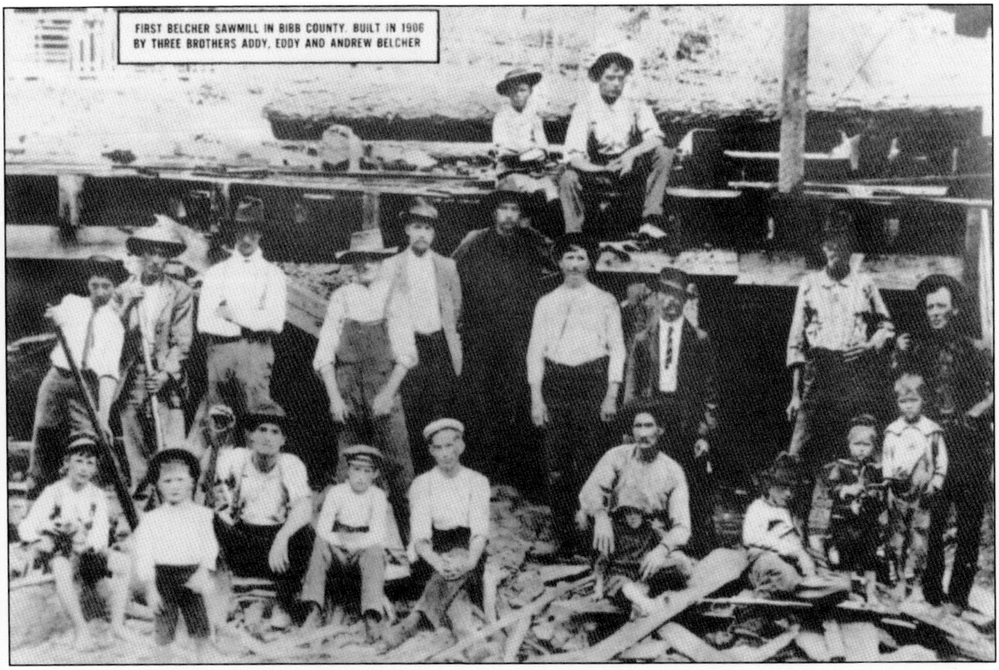

Pictured are workers employed by the Belcher Lumber Company. Lumber was one of the primary industries in the early days of Bibb County. (Courtesy of Belcher Lumber Company.)

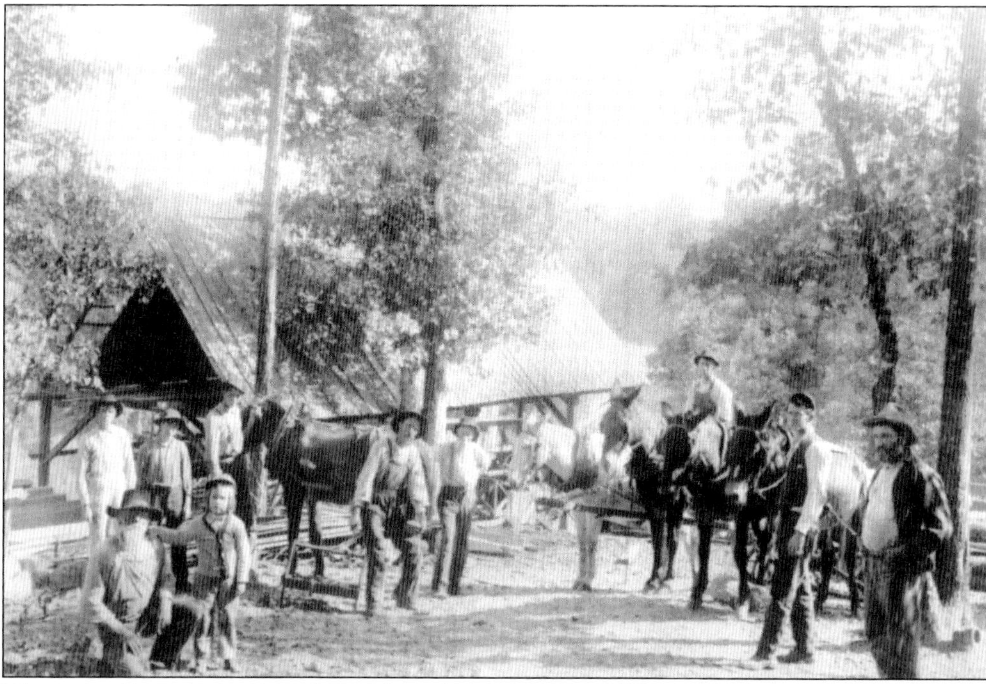

This sawmill was located on the Little Cahaba River at Bulldog Bend. John Frost, who is seen kneeling on the far left with his granddaughter Doris Fancher, built the mill. Others in this photograph are unidentified. (Courtesy of Paula Fancher.)

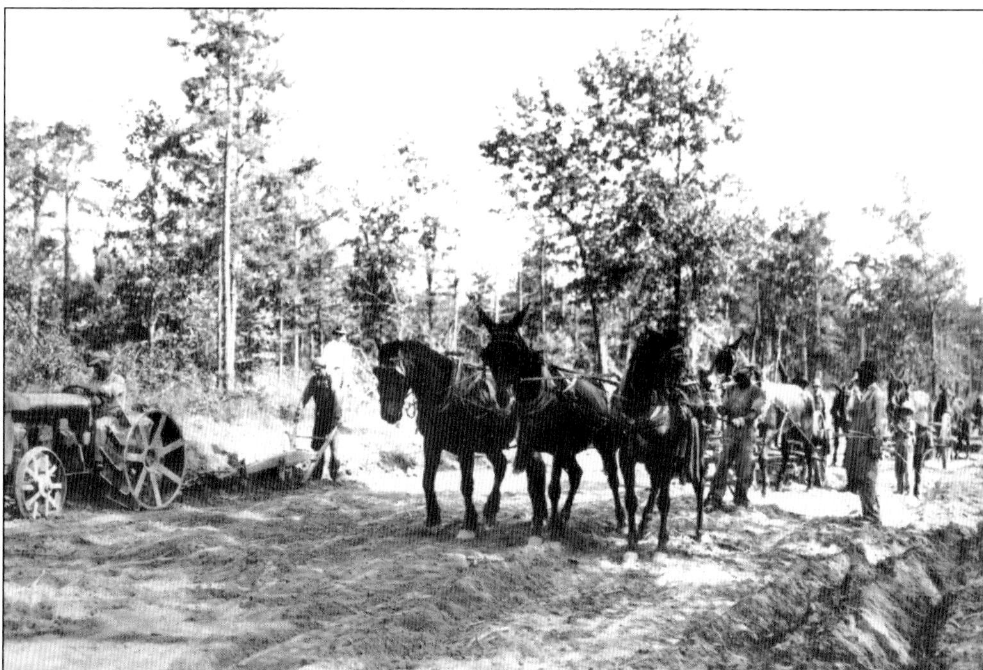

Building roads was sometimes a long and tedious project of the U.S. Forestry Service. This photograph was taken as horse-drawn equipment, along with a Fordson Tractor, cleared property in 1920. (Courtesy of Belcher Lumber Company.)

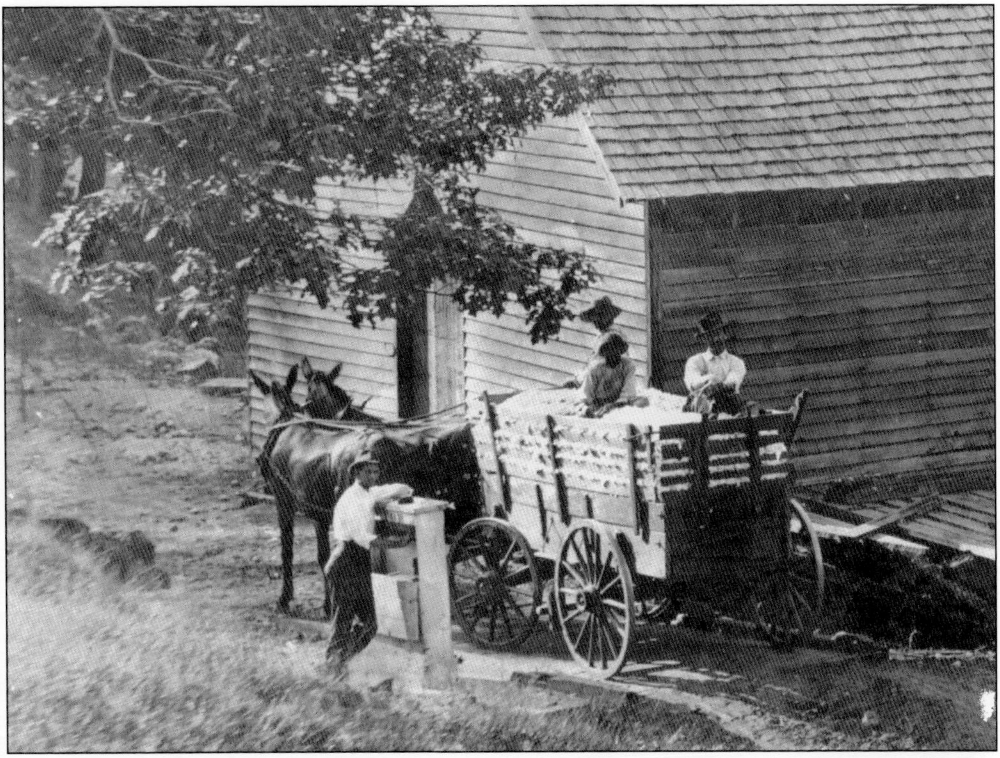

The cotton gin, located on Six Mile Creek at the Trott Dam, was owned and operated by Pop John Battle and his wife, Arvazena Arnold Farrington Battle, during late 1800s and early 1900s. (Courtesy of Mary Louise Jones Crider.)

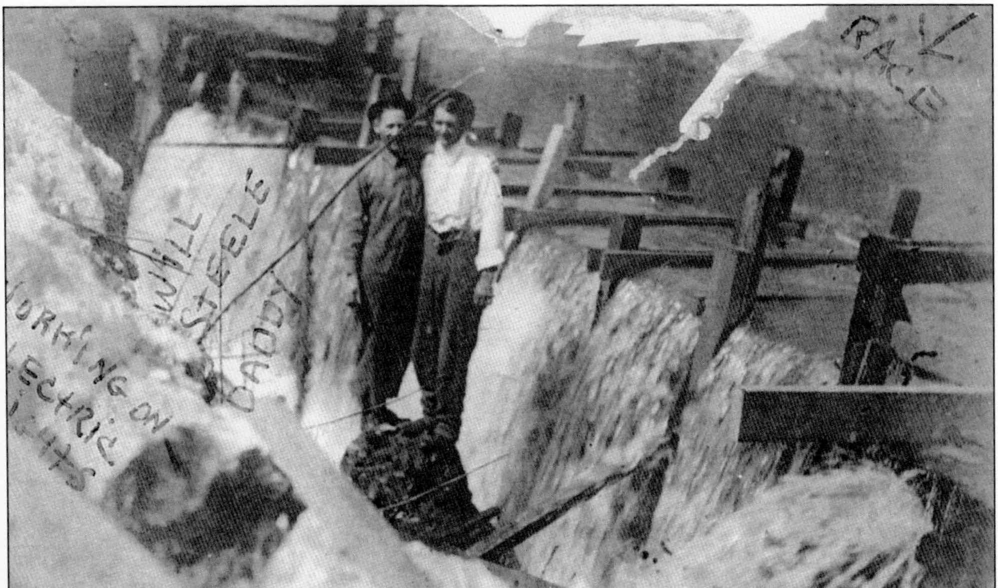

Will Steele (left) and Julian Fancher bravely stand on a rock at the sawmill and dam on the Little Cahaba River at Bulldog Bend while working on the electric lights. (Courtesy of Paula Fancher.)

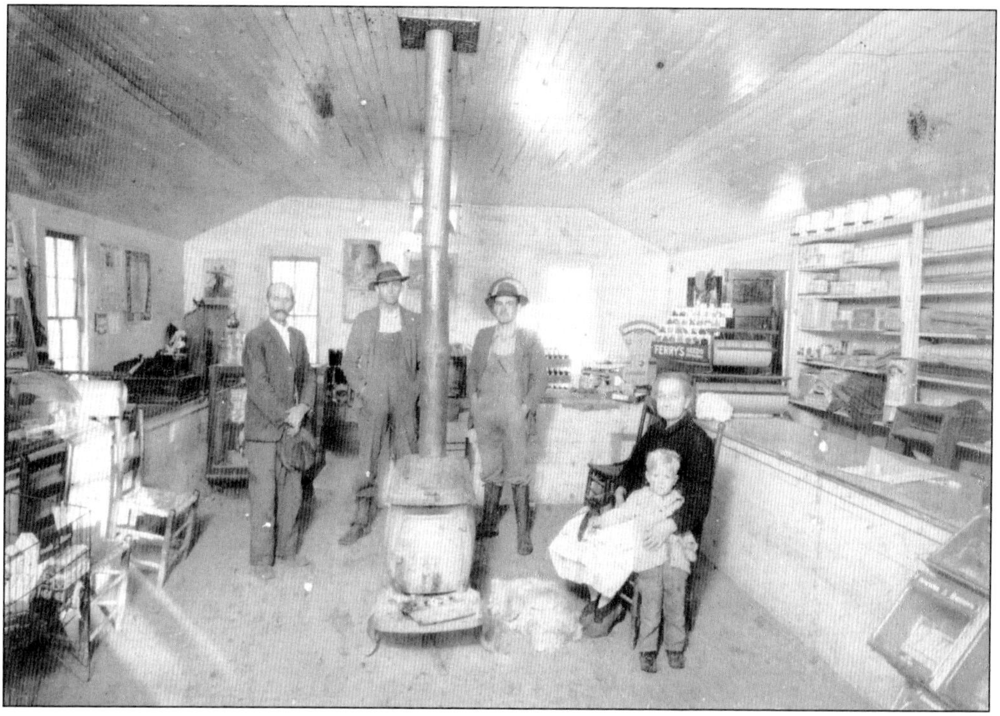

This is a photograph of the inside of Pop John Battle's store, located at Six Mile Bridge. Battle also had a flour mill, gristmill, and sawmill. (Courtesy of Mary Louise Jones Crider.)

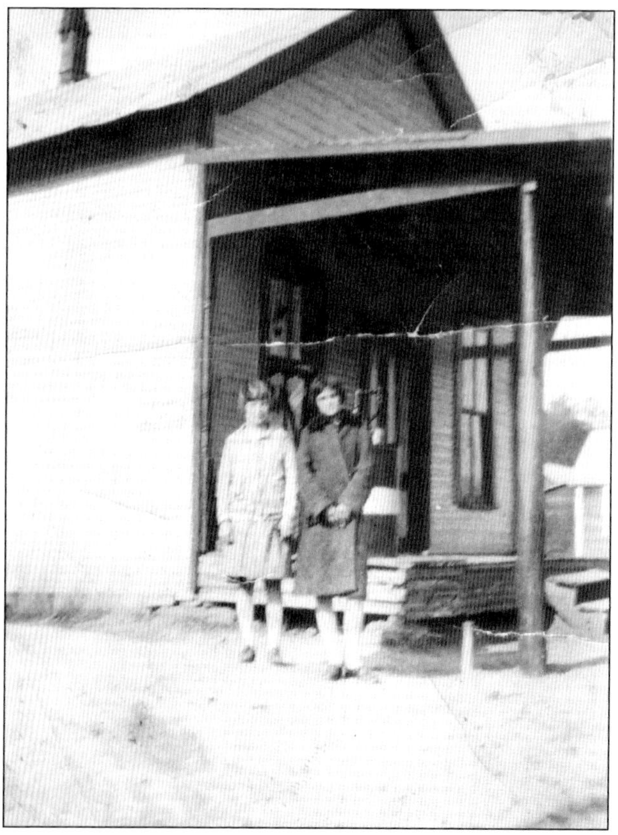

The country store is pictured here between 1927 and 1928. It once stood in Harrisburg, south of Brent, and was owned and operated by the Scott Young family. The store is now located in historic Tannehill State Park. The ladies are Odelle Fowler (left) and Mary Carr Worrells. (Courtesy of Grace Swartz.)

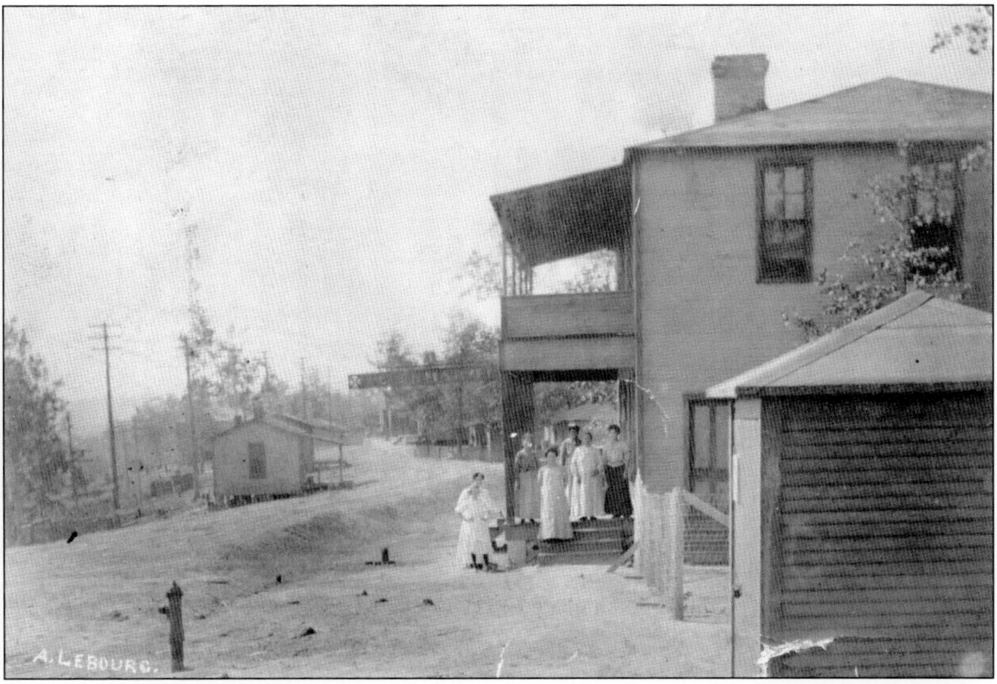

This photograph of the Hotel Marvel in Marvel was taken during the height of the coal mining era. (Courtesy of Mary Everse.)

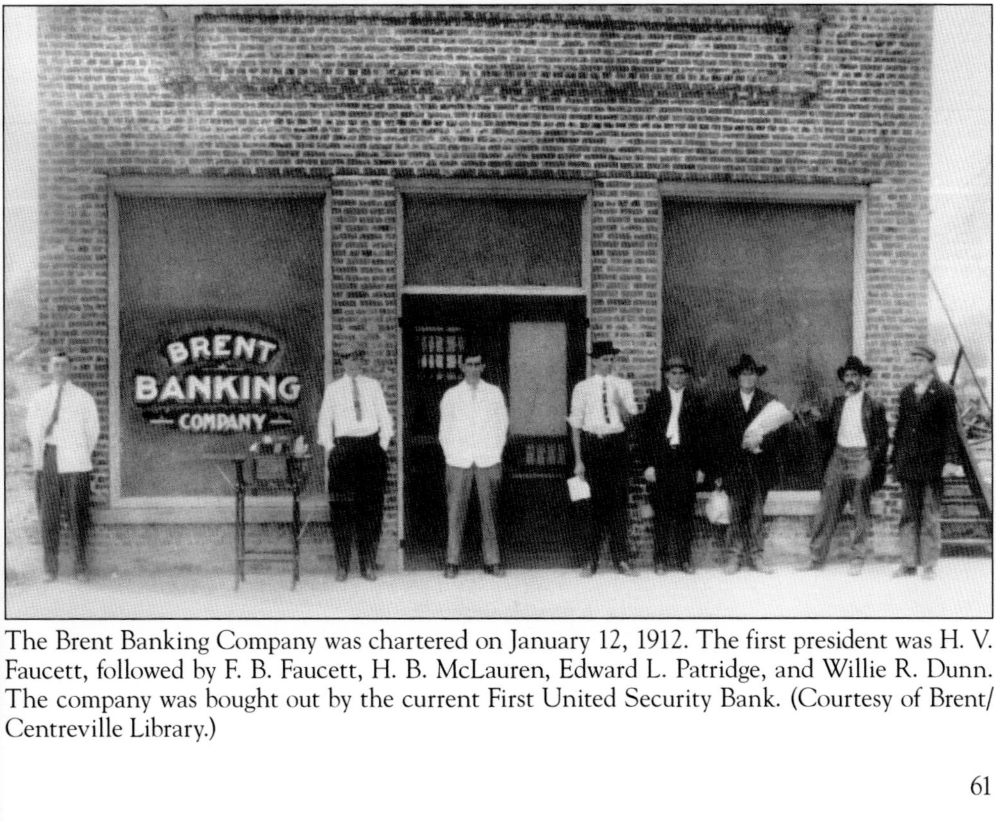

The Brent Banking Company was chartered on January 12, 1912. The first president was H. V. Faucett, followed by F. B. Faucett, H. B. McLauren, Edward L. Patridge, and Willie R. Dunn. The company was bought out by the current First United Security Bank. (Courtesy of Brent/Centreville Library.)

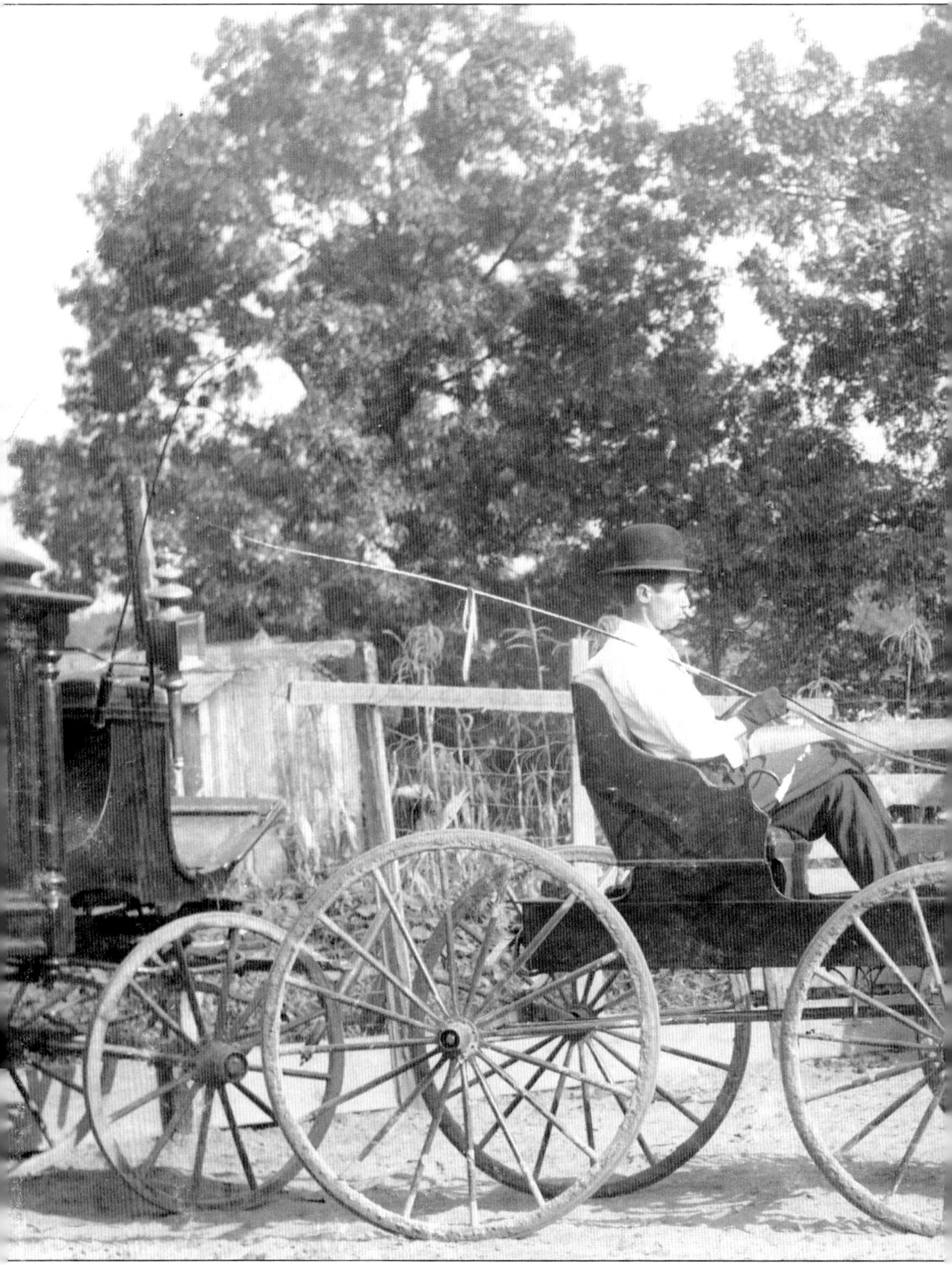

This photograph of Morgan Truman Smith was taken prior to 1915 in Blocton. Smith was the owner of a general store, where he sold a variety of things, including caskets and coffins that he

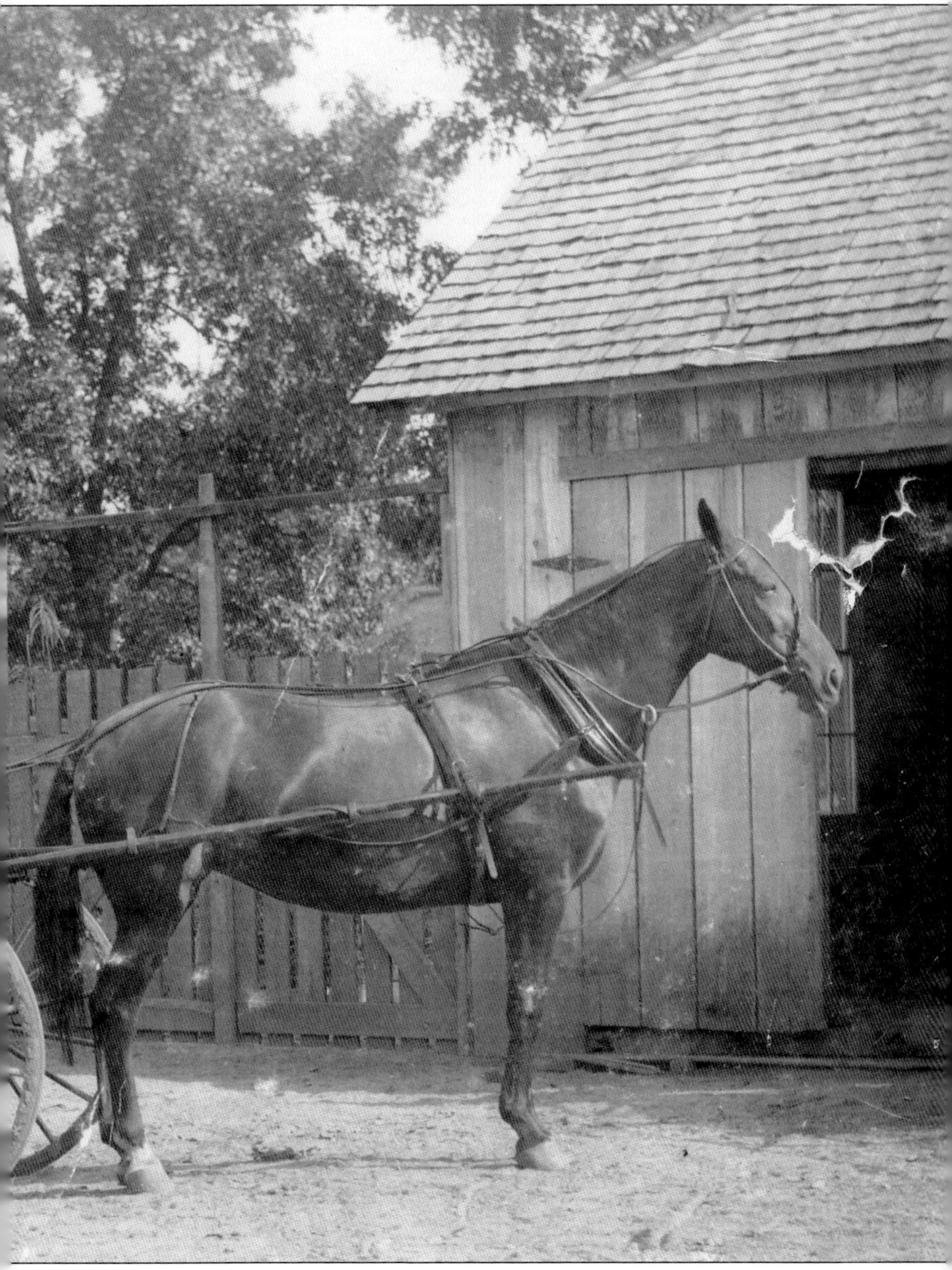

used at his other job as an undertaker. (Courtesy of Caroline Horton.)

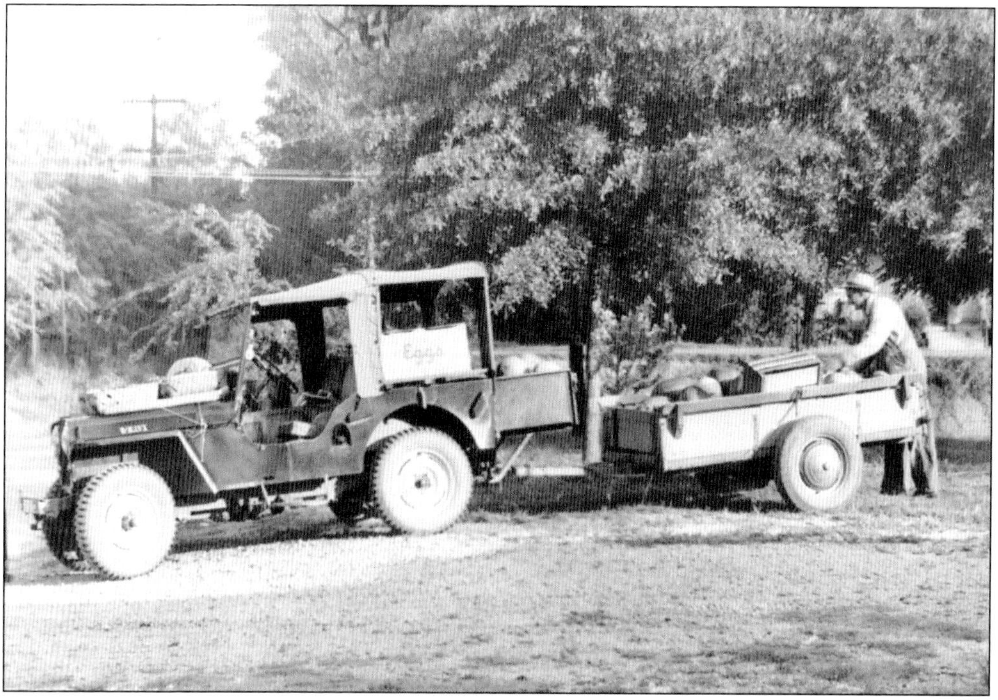

Pictured is truck farmer James Pilgreen in Brent. (Courtesy of Roselyn Vernon Pilgreen.)

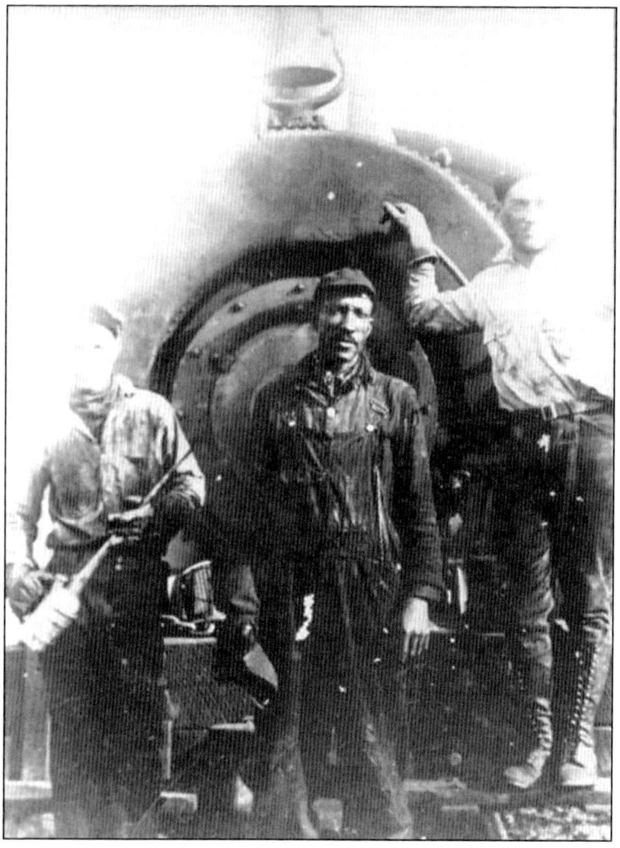

A Marvel dinky is shown with his crew. This was used to pull coal from Mine No. 3 to Mine No. 1's top house. The crew members from left to right are Bill Liddle, unidentified, and Jeff Liddle. (Courtesy of Marshall Goggins.)

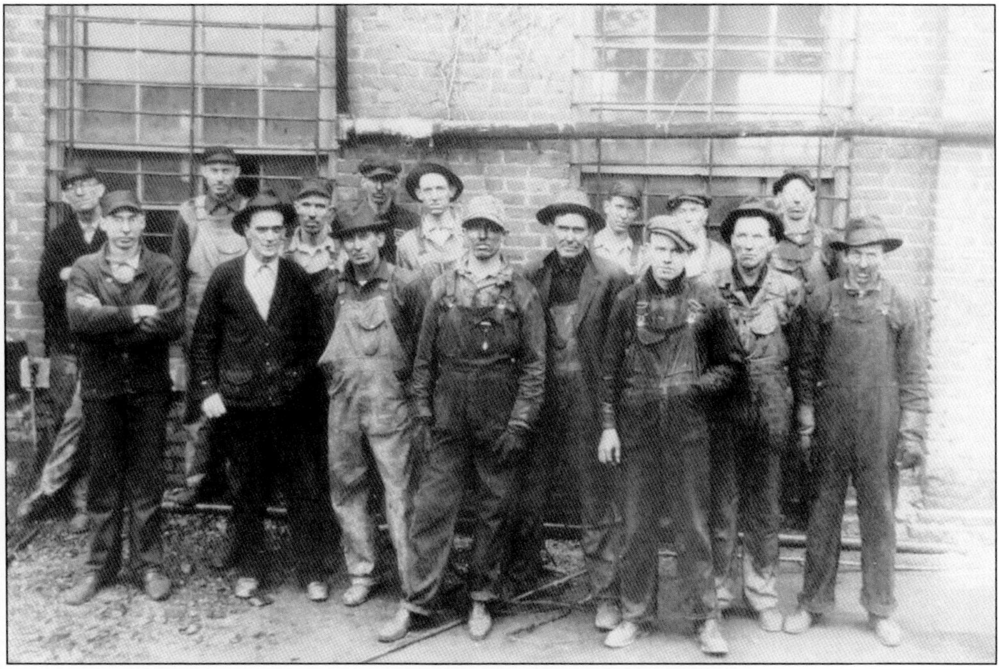

The Marvel Blacksmith shop crew includes, from left to right, (first row) Luke Lucas, Charlie Robinson, unidentified, O. C. Busby, Effie Harkins, Dewey McKenney, Lyde Seals, and unidentified; (second row) Ellis Finley, ? Lawrence, Cecil Busby, unidentified, Slim Smitherman, two unidentified men, and Joe Lucas. (Courtesy of Marshall Goggins.)

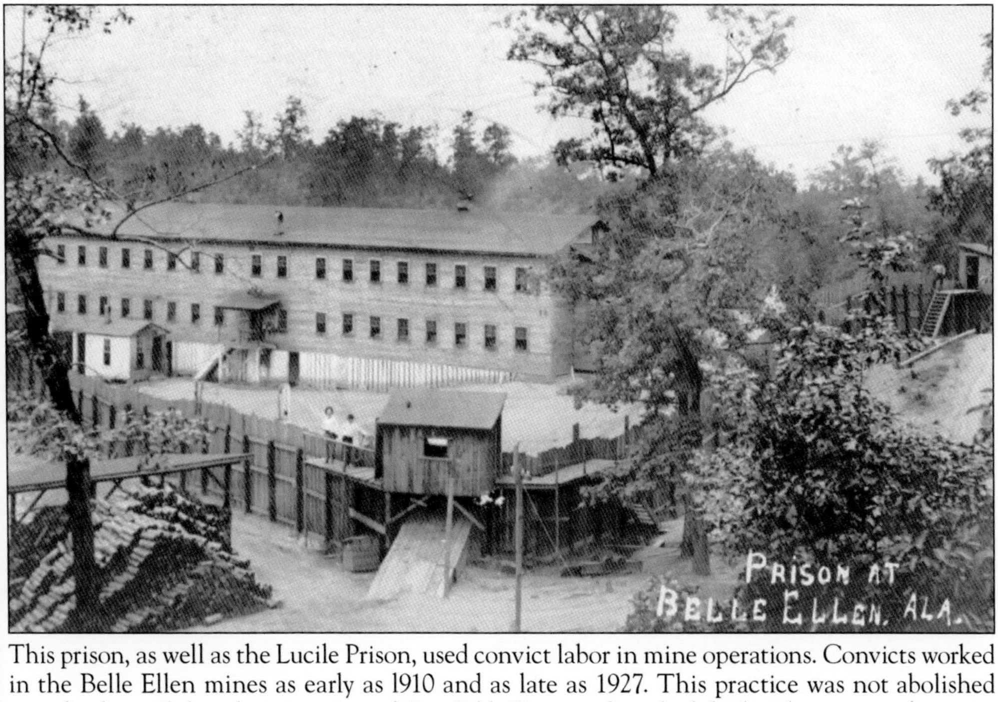

This prison, as well as the Lucile Prison, used convict labor in mine operations. Convicts worked in the Belle Ellen mines as early as 1910 and as late as 1927. This practice was not abolished completely until the administration of Gov. Bibb Graves, who asked the legislature to end convict labor. The system was brought to an end in June 1928. (Courtesy of Beverly Weeks Beasley.)

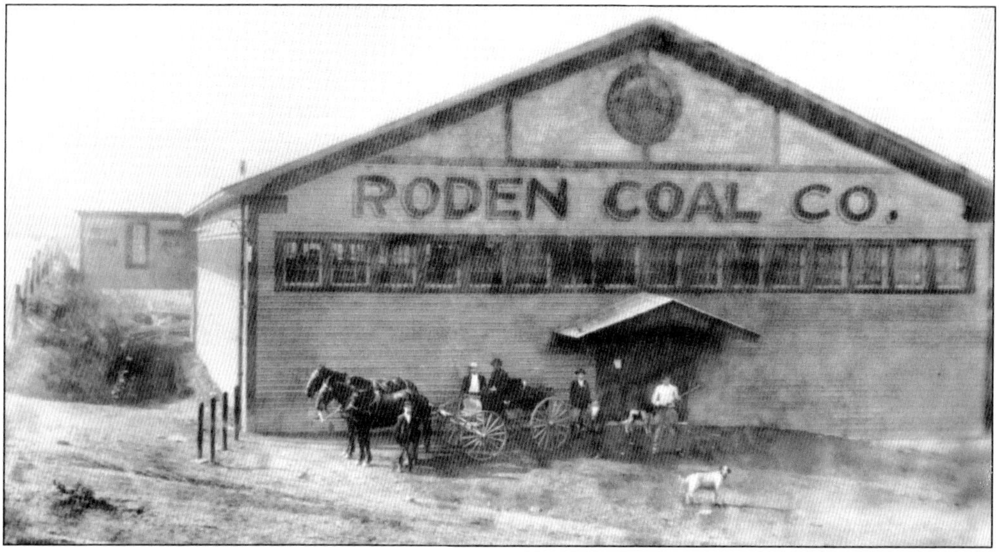

The Roden Coal Company was located in Marvel and operated until May 1951. The mine was owned by Ben Roden, who was a mining engineer. (Courtesy of Marshall Goggins.)

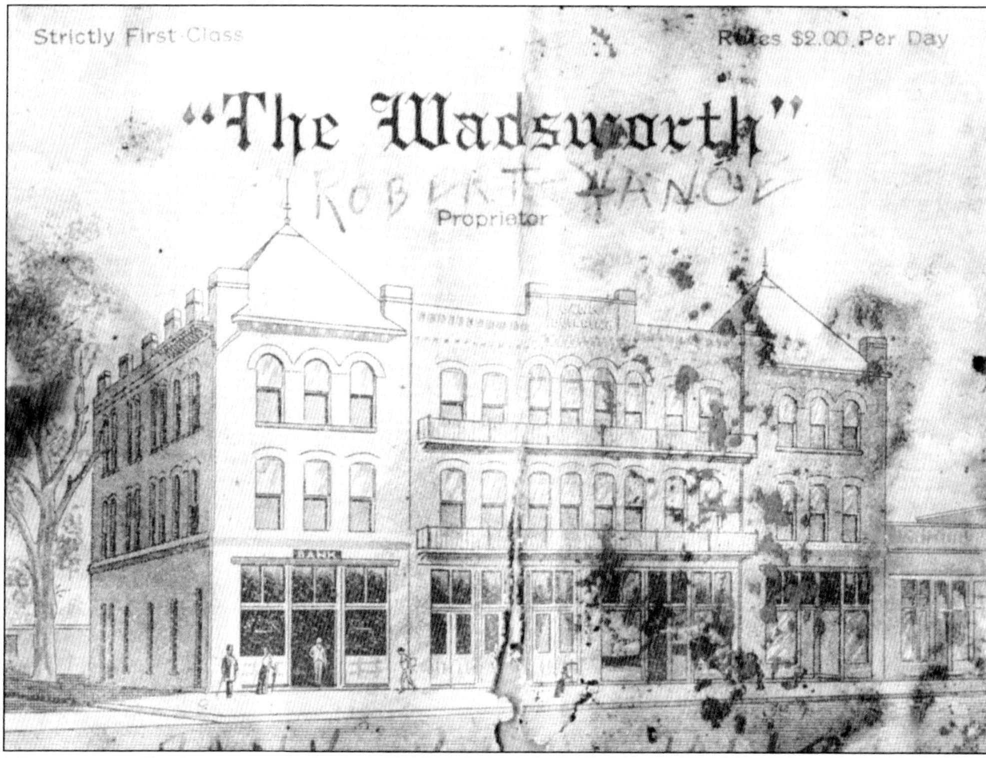

This image, which appears to be a type of business card or announcement, had sustained some water damage when it was discovered by county officials who opened the time capsule located in the cornerstone of the Bibb County Courthouse in 2002. The cornerstone and time capsule were placed in 1902 when the current courthouse was constructed. This item and many others removed from the time capsule can be seen today in several displays located in the main hall of the beautifully restored Bibb County Courthouse. (Courtesy of Bibb County.)

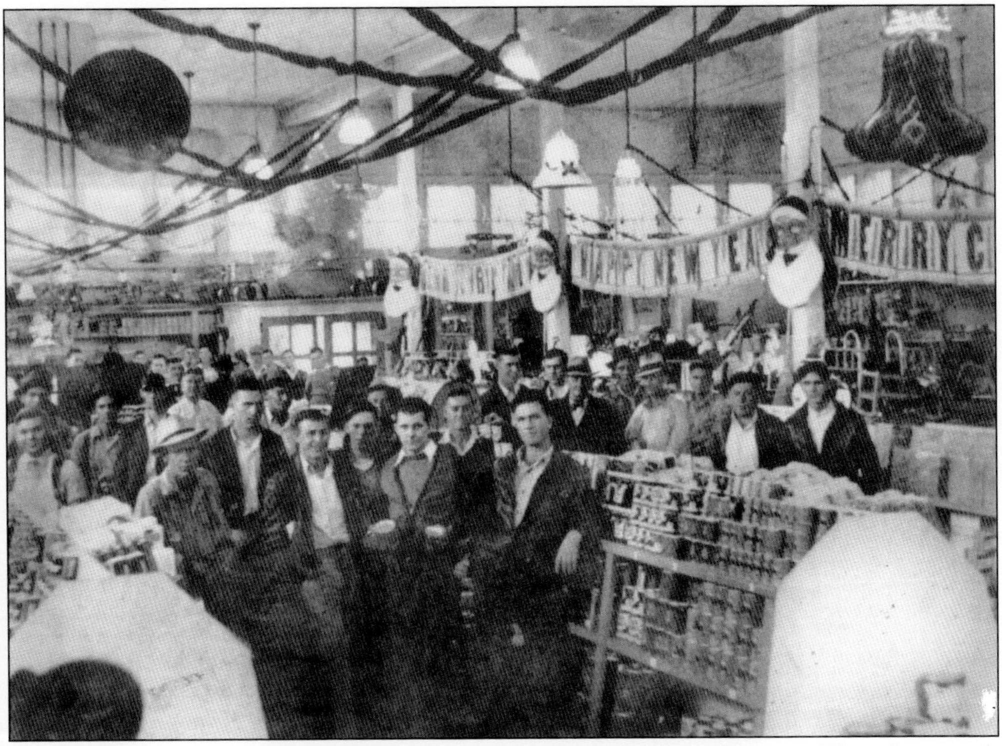

The Roden Coal Company in Marvel was in operation for about 50 years. This photograph shows one of the company's Christmas parties before hard times hit the coal industry. (Courtesy of Marshall Goggins.)

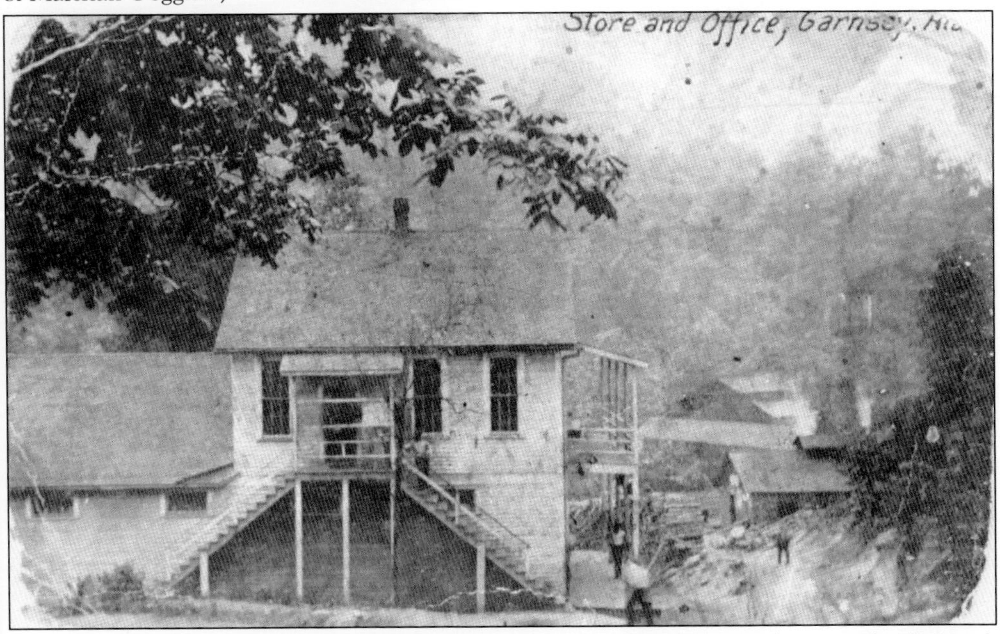

Pictured is the store and office building at the Garnsey Coal Mine, located just south of Marvel. The mine was named after Cyrus Garnsey, the mine owner, and it closed in 1925. (Photograph by John T. Weeks, courtesy of Beverly Weeks Beasley.)

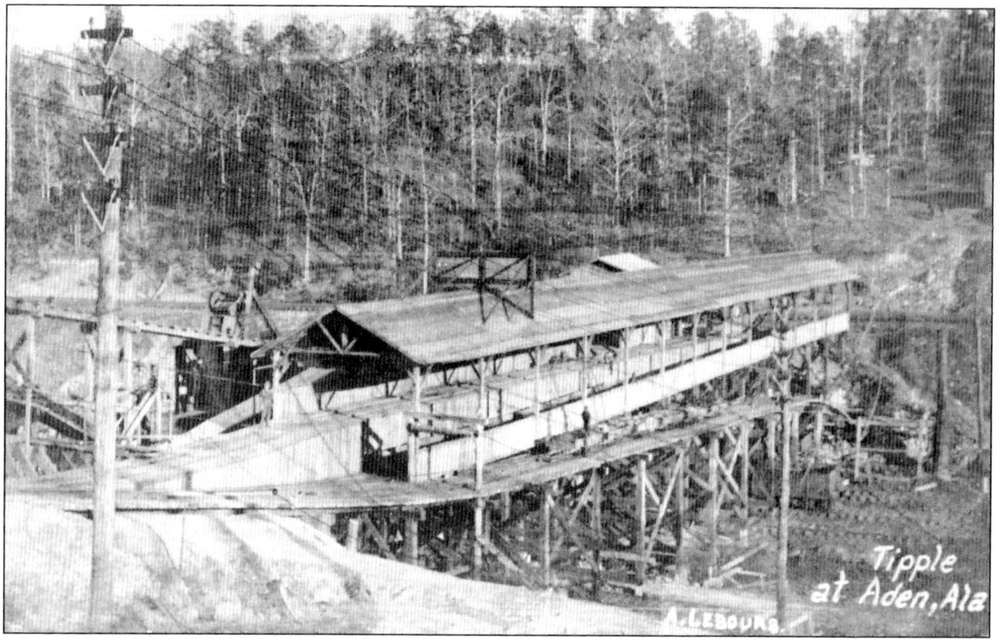

Here is the Tipple Coal Mining operation, located at Aden. (Courtesy of Beverly Weeks Beasley.)

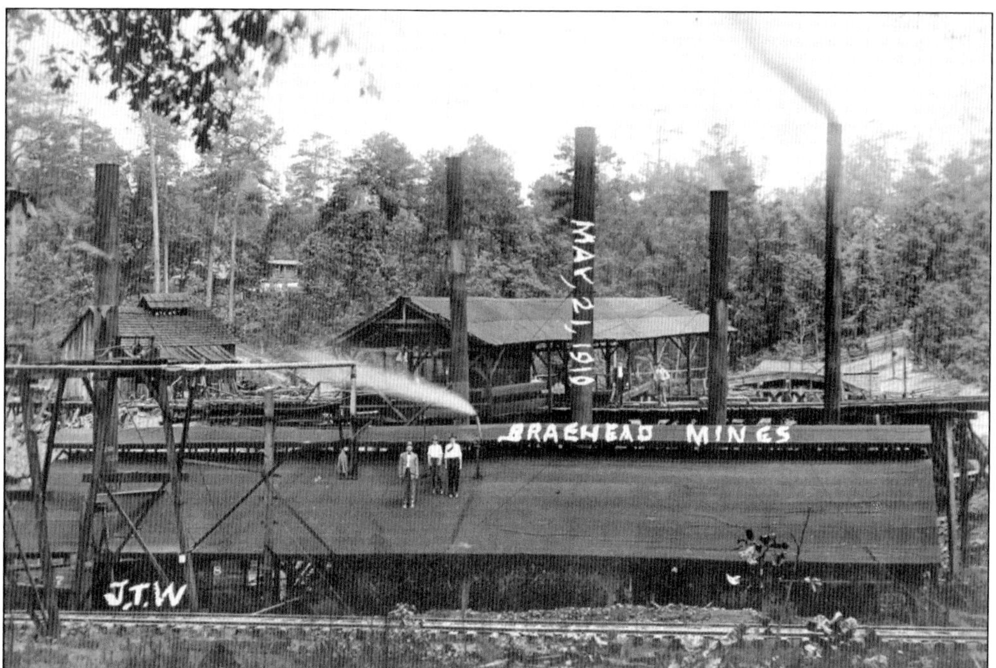

The Braehead Mine operation was photographed here by John T. Weeks on May 21, 1910. (Courtesy of Beverly Weeks Beasley.)

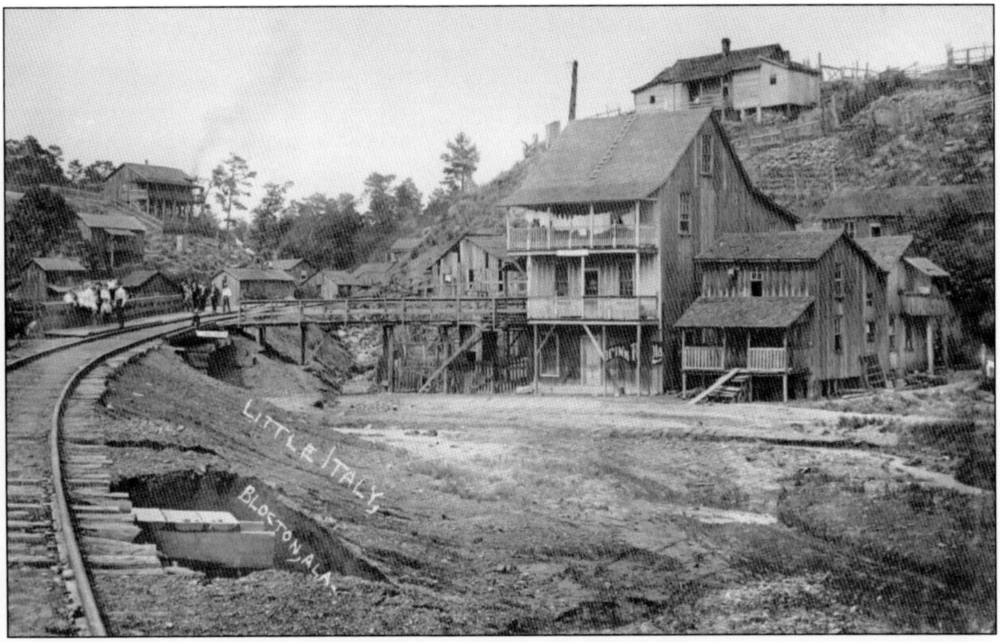

The mining community located in North Bibb was known as "Little Italy" for its many Italian immigrants. The community is no longer there, but a small Italian cemetery still sexists in West Blocton. (Photographed by John T. Weeks, courtesy of Beverly Weeks Beasley.)

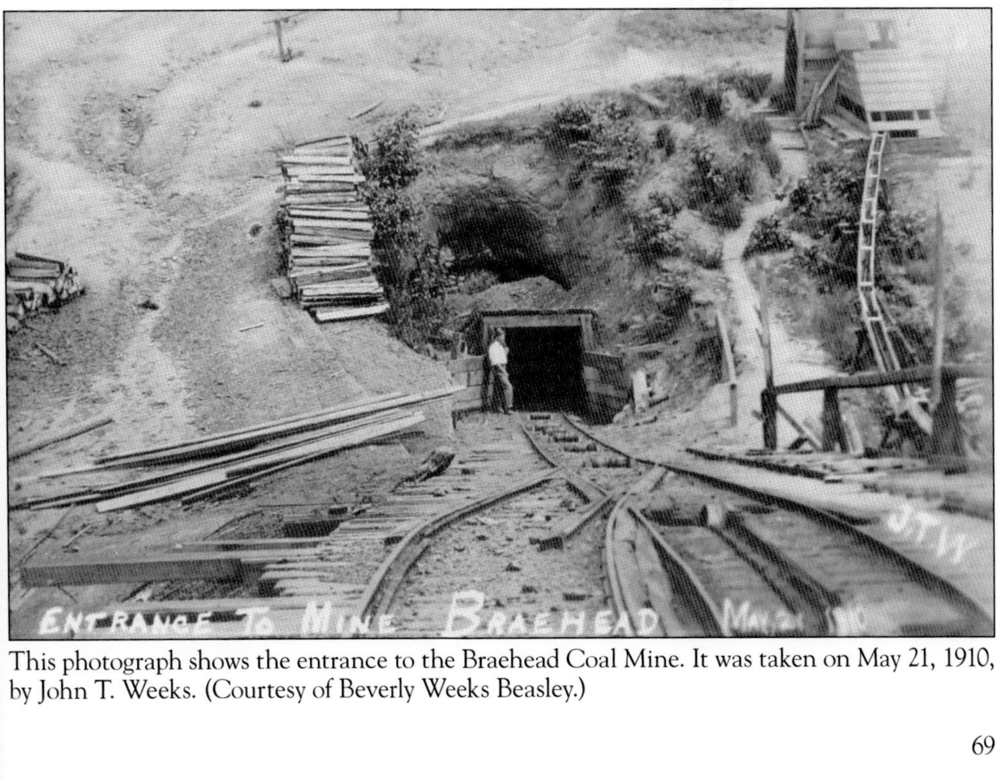

This photograph shows the entrance to the Braehead Coal Mine. It was taken on May 21, 1910, by John T. Weeks. (Courtesy of Beverly Weeks Beasley.)

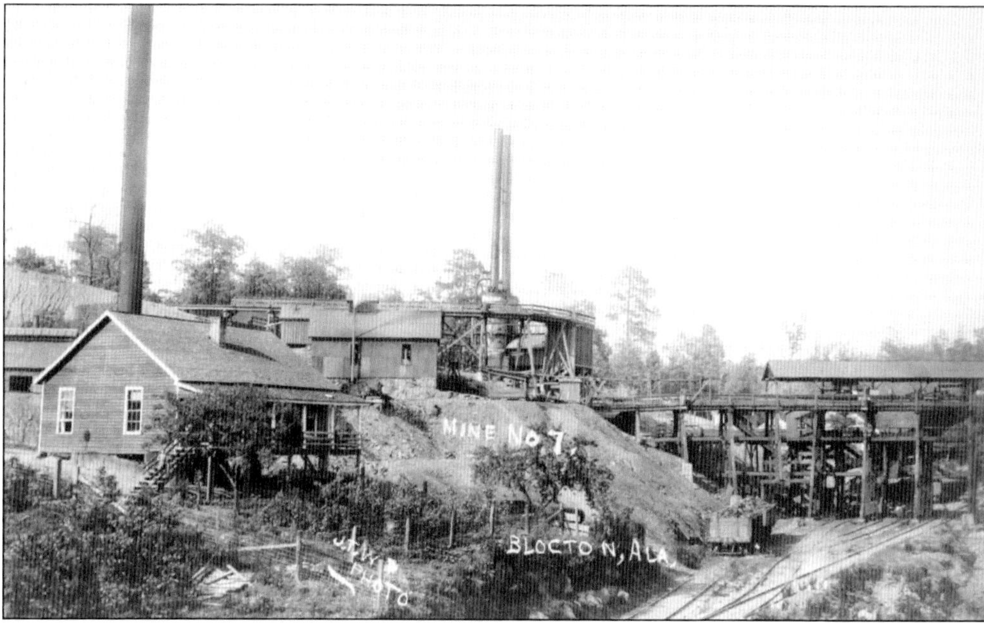

This image shows Coal Mine No. 7 in West Blocton. (Photograph by John T. Weeks, courtesy of Beverly Weeks Beasley.)

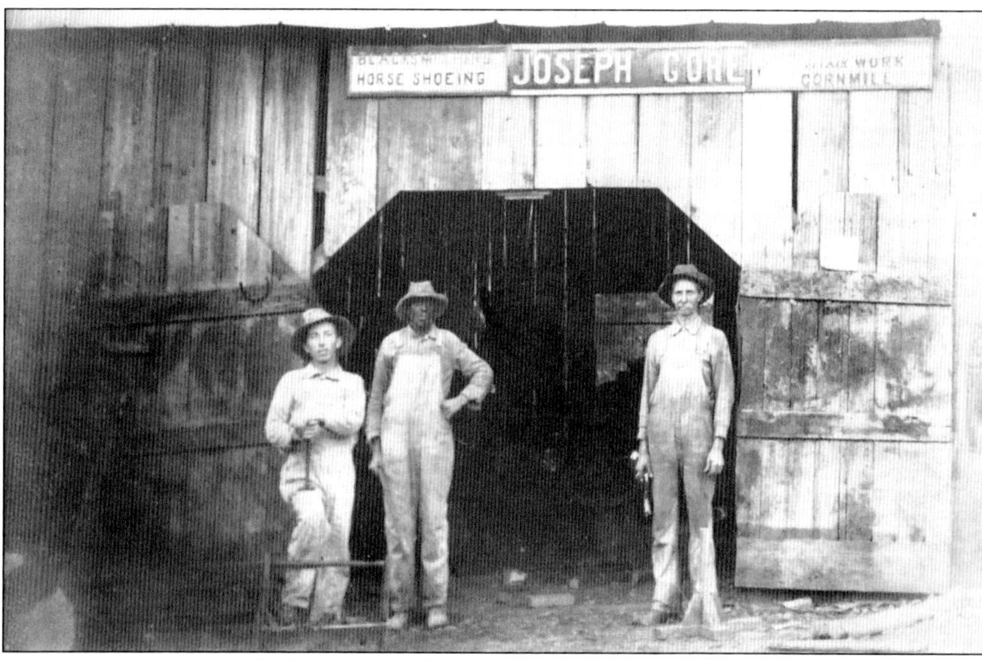

One early industry in Bibb County was blacksmithing. This establishment was called the Gore Blacksmith Shop. It was named for its owner, Joseph Gore. The shop was located on Market Street in Centreville, across from Judge L. S. Moore's home, near First Avenue South. (Courtesy of Betty Burt.)

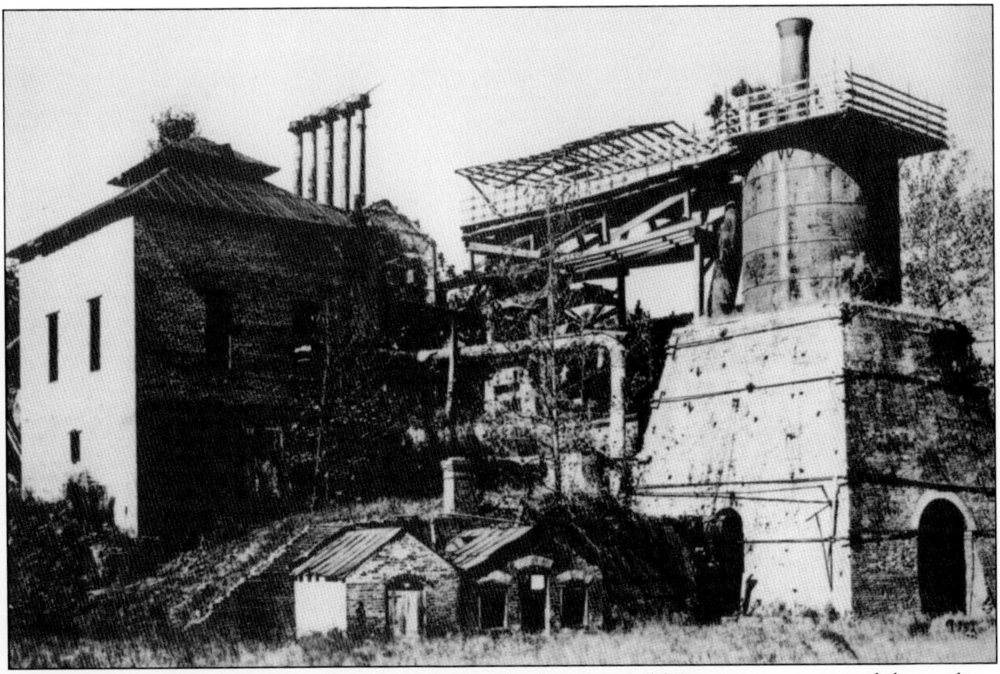

Located just north of Centreville on Highway 25, the Brierfield Furnace was one of the earliest ironworks in Alabama. It was built in 1862 and was almost totally destroyed during the Civil War. The ruins of the furnace have been preserved and can be seen today at Brierfield Ironworks State Park. (Courtesy of Marty Everse.)

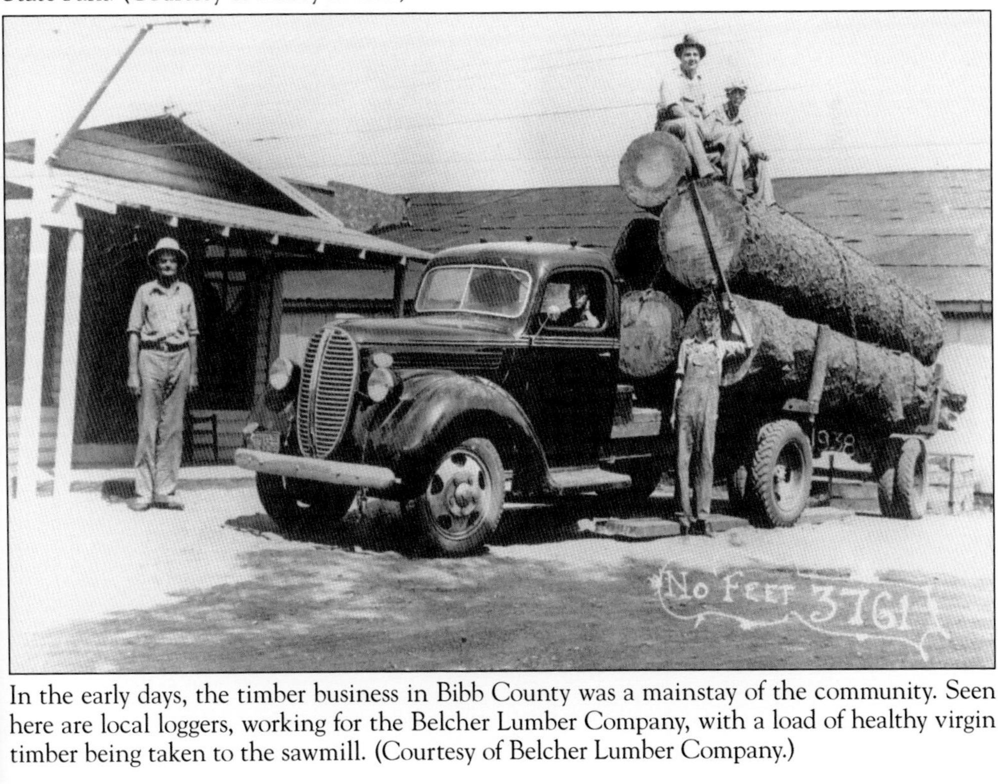

In the early days, the timber business in Bibb County was a mainstay of the community. Seen here are local loggers, working for the Belcher Lumber Company, with a load of healthy virgin timber being taken to the sawmill. (Courtesy of Belcher Lumber Company.)

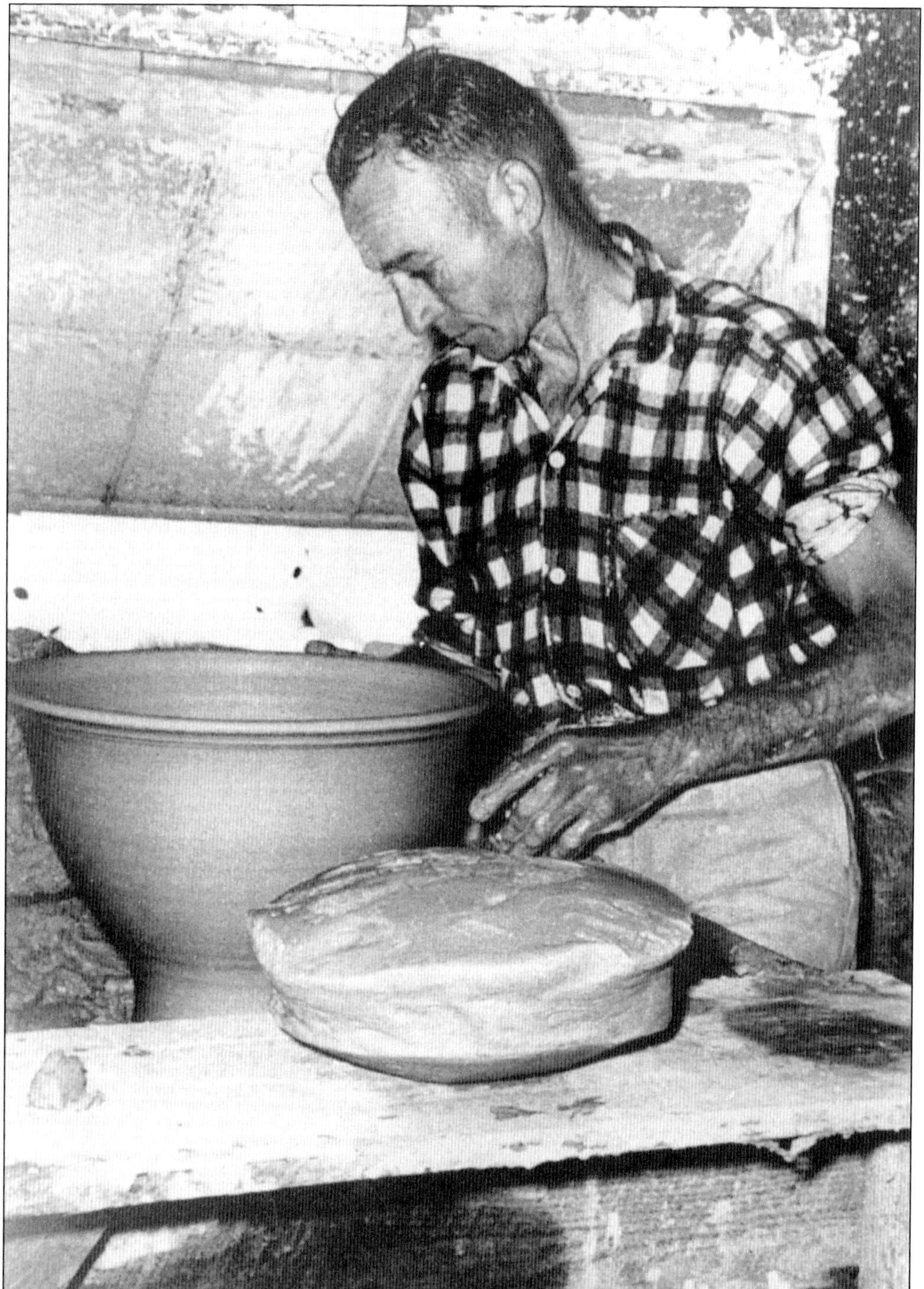

Hendon Miller is seen at work at the potter's wheel in his business, Miller's Pottery, which is located south of Brent. He is carrying on the tradition started by his ancestors Abraham and Frances Miller. Hendon Miller died in 1983, but his family still operates the business. (Courtesy of Steve Miller.)

Five

County Seat and Court Square

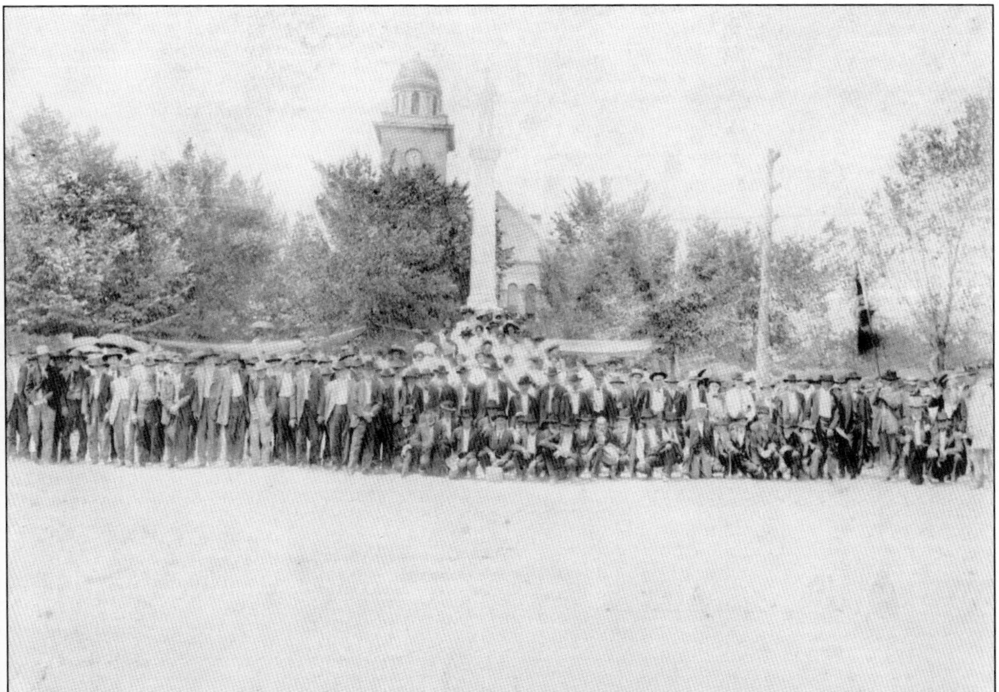

Four to five thousand residents and visitors saw the dedication and unveiling of the Confederate Monument, which sits on the courthouse lawn in uptown Centreville. Sen. Herbert Reynolds presided over the celebration. Centreville resident Perry Thomas, Congressman Oscar Underwood, and state auditor W. W. Brandon gave speeches. (Courtesy of Brent/Centreville Library.)

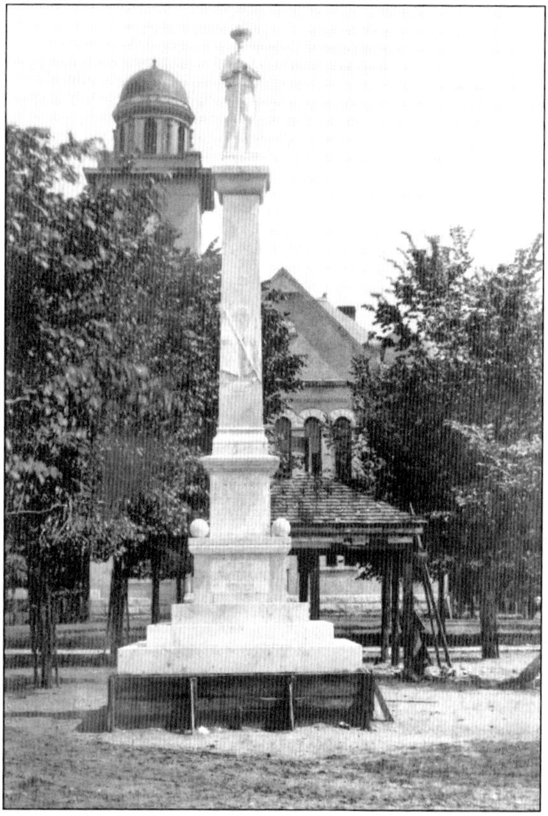

The Confederate Monument was spearheaded by the Leonard Callaway Pratt Chapter of the United Daughters of the Confederacy and was dedicated and unveiled on July 22, 1910. It is still located on the Centreville Historic Town Square lawn but has since been moved closer to the courthouse. This location is currently a parking lot. The structure in back with a covering over it is the city well. (Courtesy of Brent/Centreville Library.)

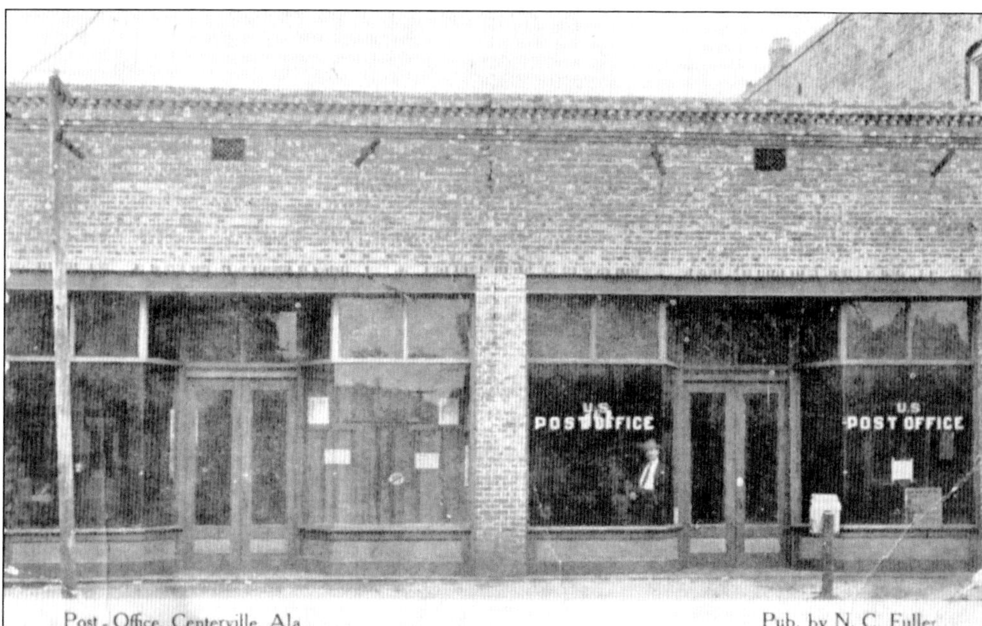

The Centreville Post Office is pictured around 1919. The postmaster at this time was N. C. Fuller, who owned the building. The post office was moved to the Bank Building in 1920. (Courtesy of Betty Burt.)

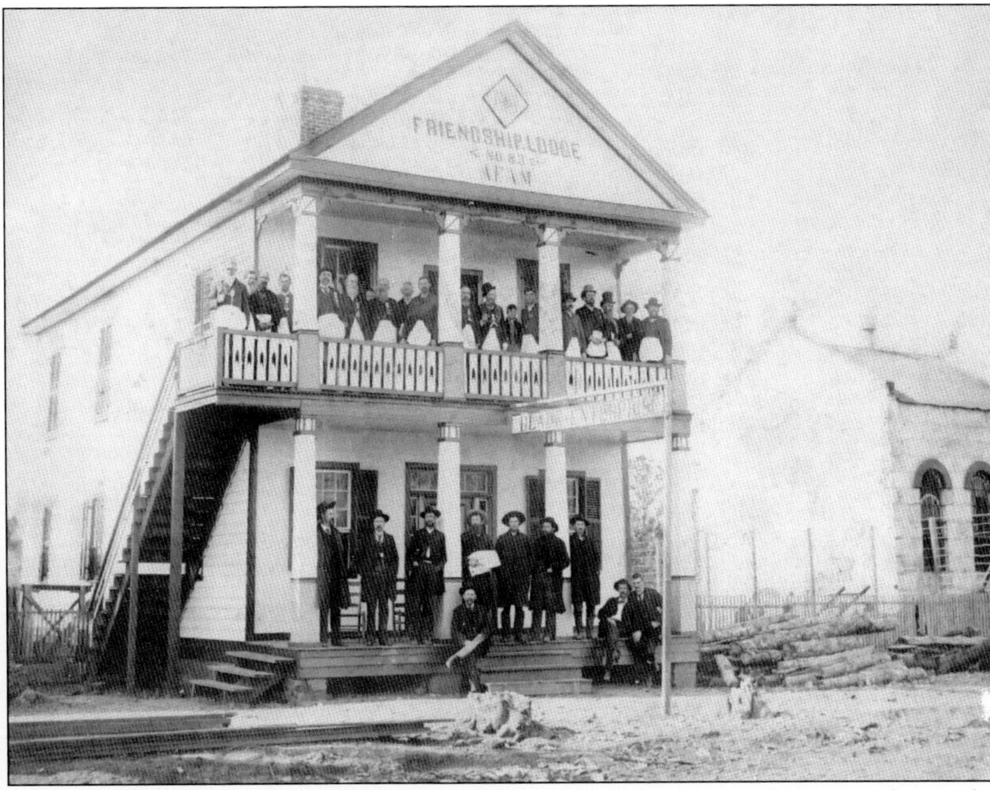

Friendship Lodge No. 83 was home to the Bibb County Freemasons, a fraternity of men who were joined by common links around the world by their desire to serve their fellow man and their belief in a Supreme Being. Located to the right in this photograph is the old jail, which sits on the site of the existing jail. The bottom floor was the home of the *Bibb Blade*, a local newspaper. (Courtesy of Wayne and Jonlee Melton.)

Friendship Lodge No. 83 was located on Centreville Historic Town Square in the 1920s. The staircase that was located on the left side was removed and placed in the front at some time. Compared to the earlier picture, some of the left side of the lodge has been removed. Note the chimney. Today the building is the home of the *Centreville Press*, Bibb County's weekly newspaper. (Courtesy of Cliff and Vicky Clemmons.)

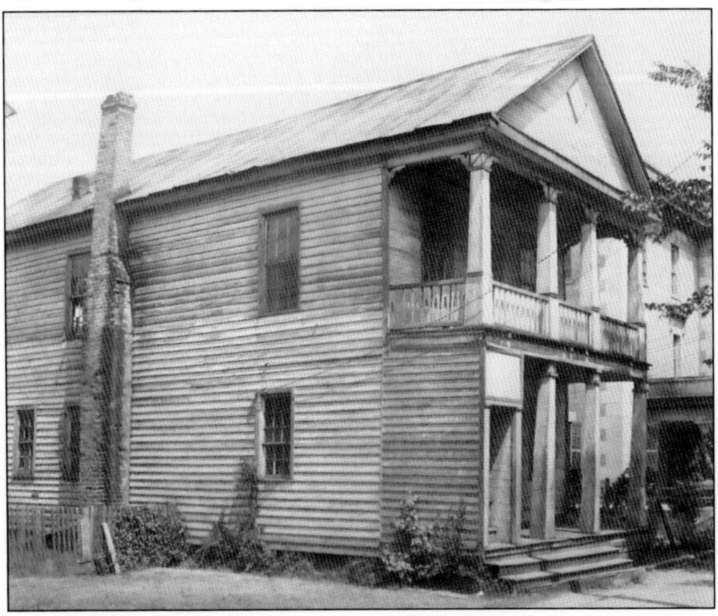

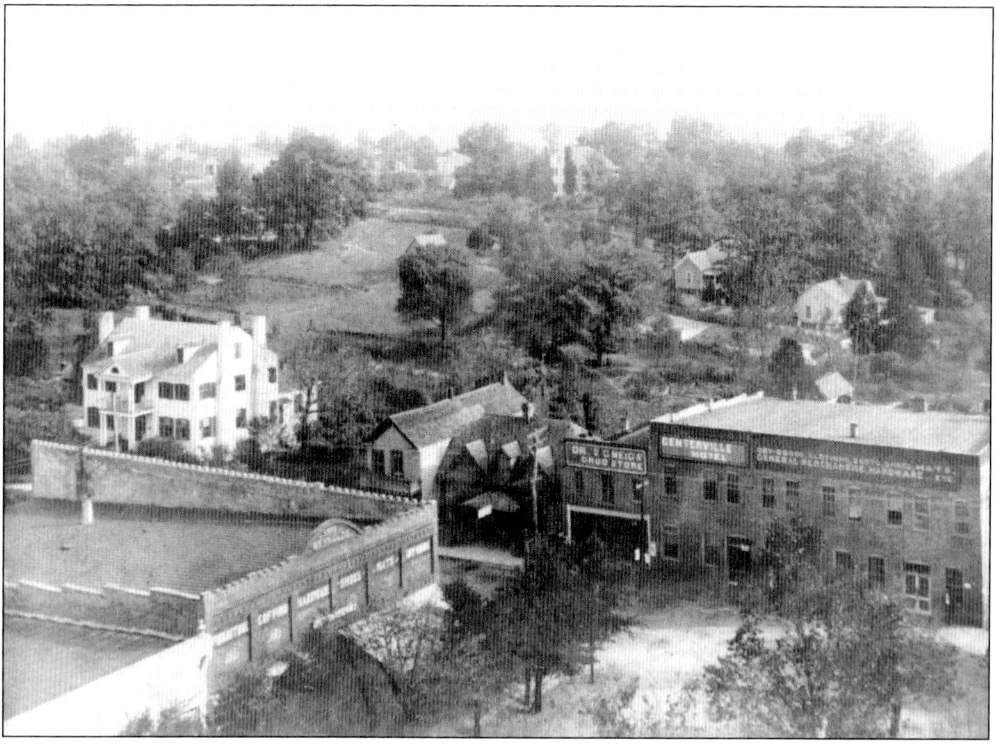

This is a 1913 view of the southeast corner of Centreville Historic Town Square. The buildings from left to right are the Reynolds General Store (foreground), which sold furniture, coffins, hardware, shoes, hats, and dry goods; the Kennedy House; the original Cleveland store (the former site of Green Calhoun's store); the office of attorney S. D. Logan; the office of Dr. T. E. Schoolar; Dr. S. C. Meigs Drug Store; the Centerville Hotel; and General Merchandise Hardware. The Reynolds General Store building burned in 1926. This photograph belonged to John Percy and Annie Kennedy. (Courtesy of Hal and Edna Earl Cottingham.)

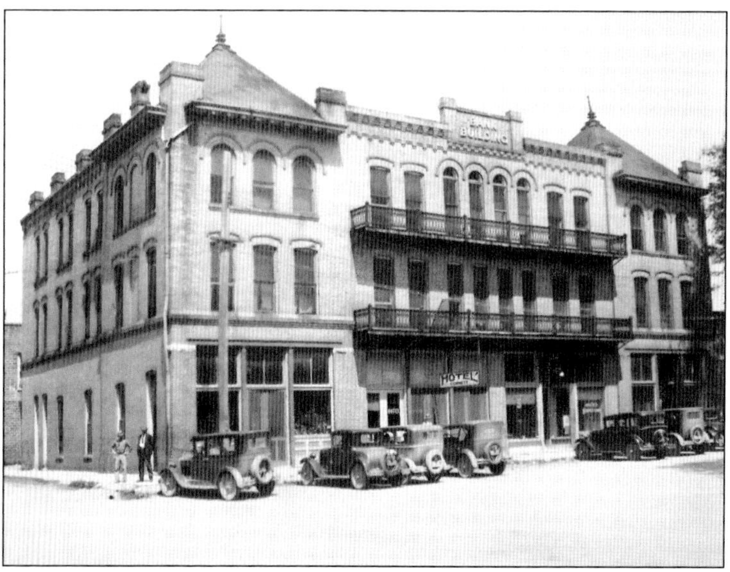

The Bibb County Bank and Trust Company Building is still located on Court Square in Centreville and was restored in 1992. It is listed on the National Register of Historic Places and is currently empty. Construction of the building began in 1898 and was finished in September 1899. It has served as a tavern, post office, and a bank to name a few. (Courtesy of Brent/Centreville Library.)

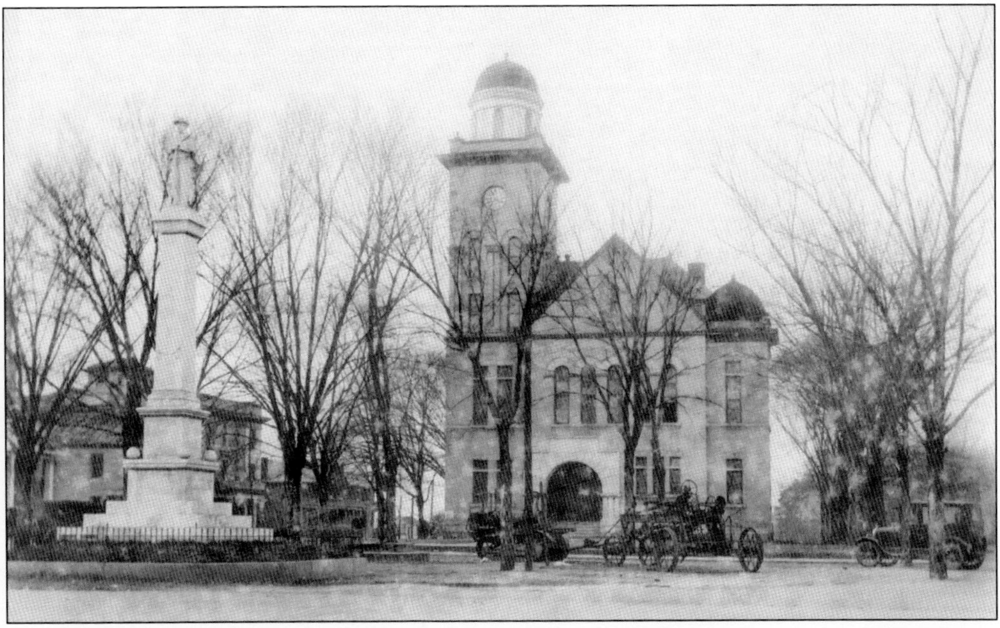

The Bibb County Courthouse is located on the Centreville Historic Town Square. This picture was taken sometime around 1925 before the Confederate Monument was relocated closer to the courthouse. This building is listed on the National Register of Historic Places and was constructed in 1902 by contractor F. M. Dobson of Jasper. This courthouse was the fifth in the county and the third to be built in Centreville. (Courtesy of Birmingham Public Library.)

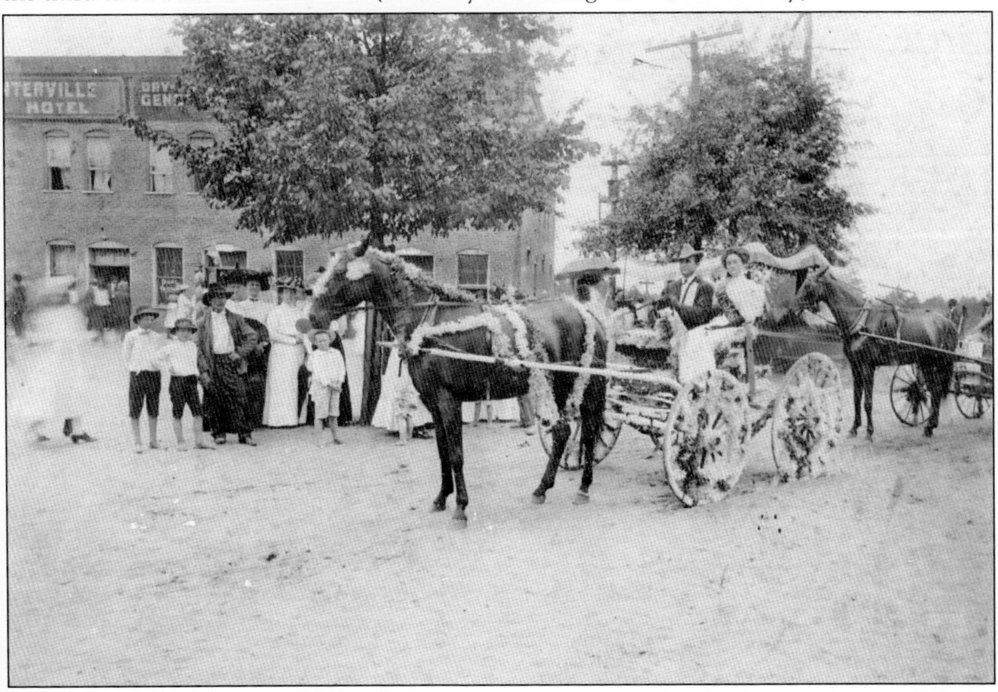

Beulah Avery and her unidentified escort are pictured on July 22, 1910, in the Confederate Parade either before or after the unveiling of the Confederate Monument. (Courtesy of Brent/Centreville Library.)

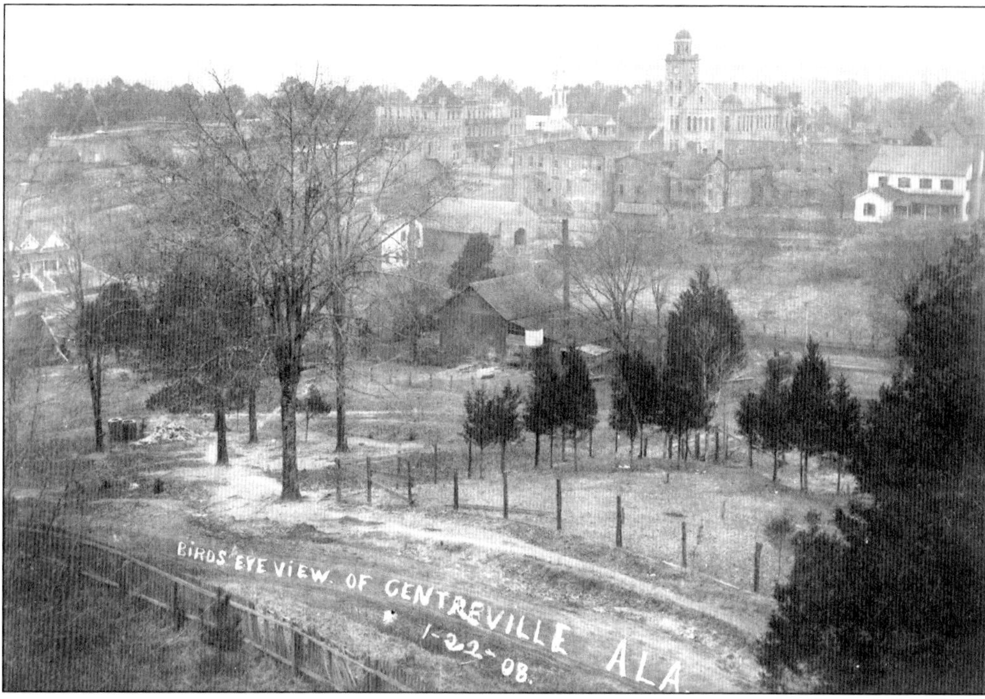

This picture was taken from the upper porch of the Davidson-Smitherman-Leggett House, which is located on a high hill southeast of the town square. This is the town of Centreville as it looked on January 22, 1908. The Davidson-Smitherman-Leggett House is still standing and is located on Fourth Avenue and Second Street South. (Courtesy of Hal and Edna Earl Cottingham.)

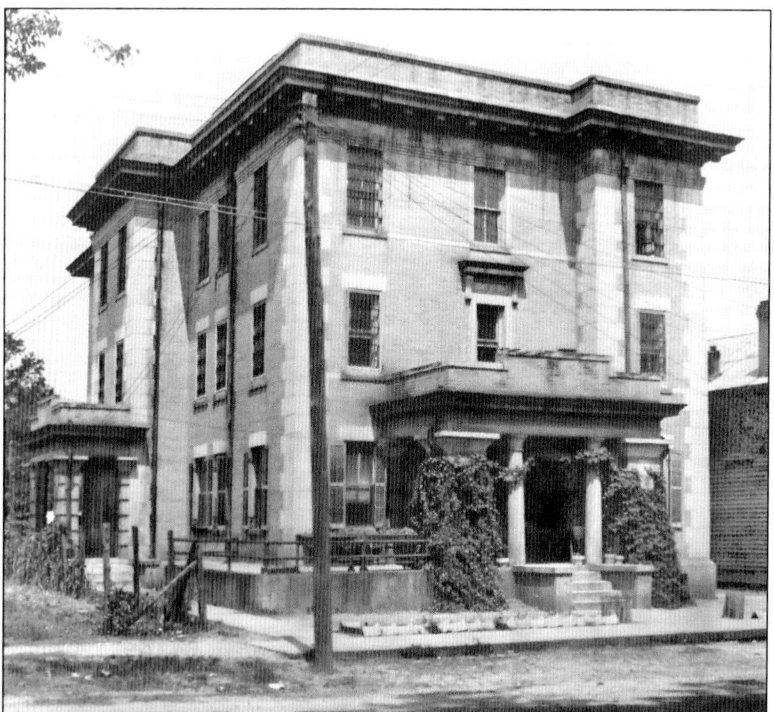

The Bibb County Jail was located on the Centreville Historic Town Square in the 1920s. This jail was built around 1909 and has since been replaced with a new jail in Brent. This building still exists and is currently being considered for restoration by the Better Hometown Group of Bibb County. (Courtesy of Jim Oakley.)

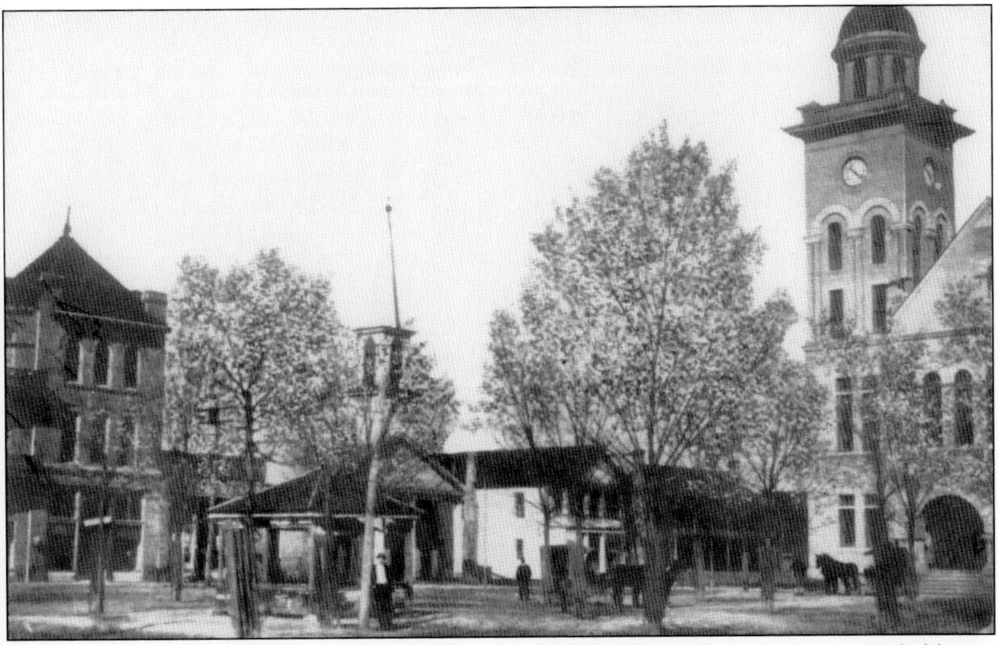

This courthouse replaced the old one built around 1858. The well covering was probably put there by jail prisoners in 1893 during a period of renewal and improvements. This picture was made sometime around 1908. The buildings from left to right are the Hotel-Bank Building, the Presbyterian Church of Centreville, the Masonic building, the residence of J. T. Casey, and the new courthouse. (Courtesy of Hal Cottingham.)

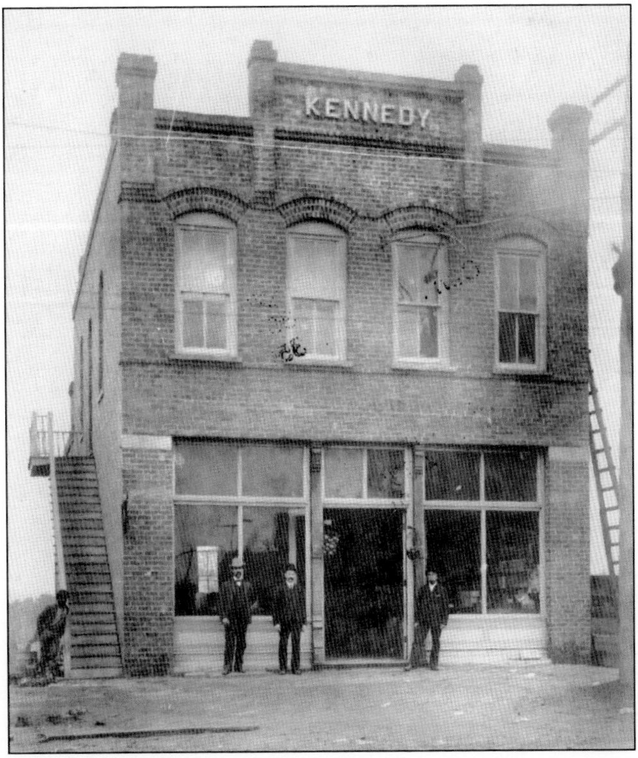

This photograph, taken prior to 1909, shows the Kennedy Building, which was constructed by Josiah Kennedy. The building was remodeled after a fire, and the upper level was removed. It is currently the location of Bizzy Beans and Ashleys Clothing. (Courtesy of Hal Cottingham.)

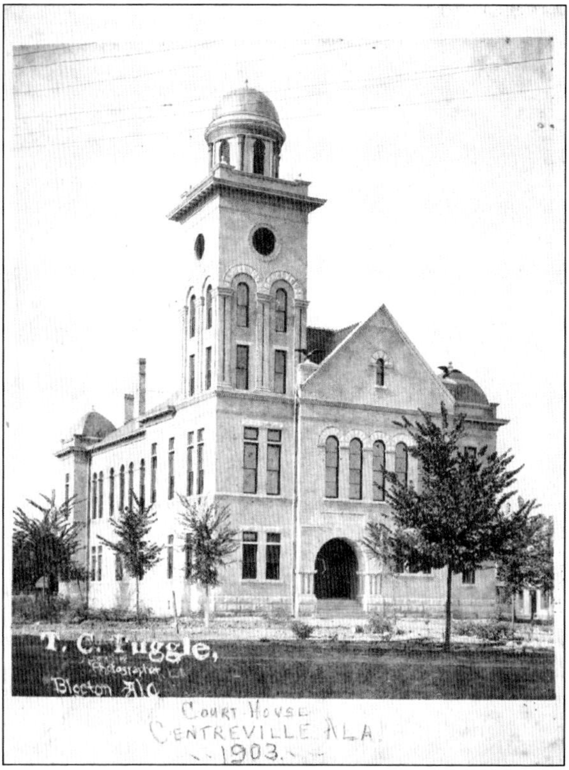

This 1903 photograph was taken by noted photographer T. C. Tuggle. It shows the existing Bibb County Courthouse, which was built in 1902. The courthouse is located in Centreville, which was incorporated in January 1832. (Courtesy of Hal Cottingham.)

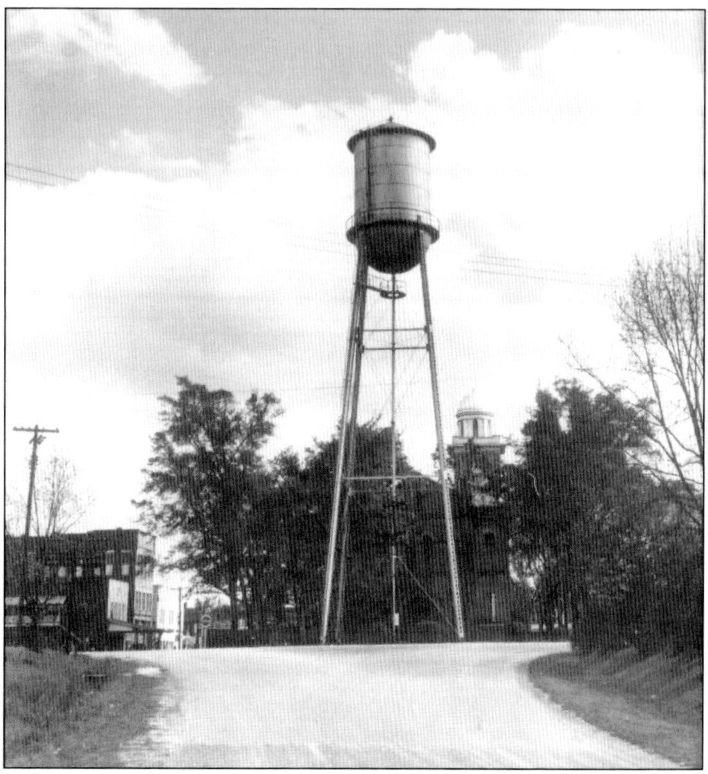

The water tank once stood on the back lawn of the Bibb County Courthouse. The water supply has been moved to Walnut Street. (Courtesy of Harold Cottingham.)

Six

Transportation and Bridges

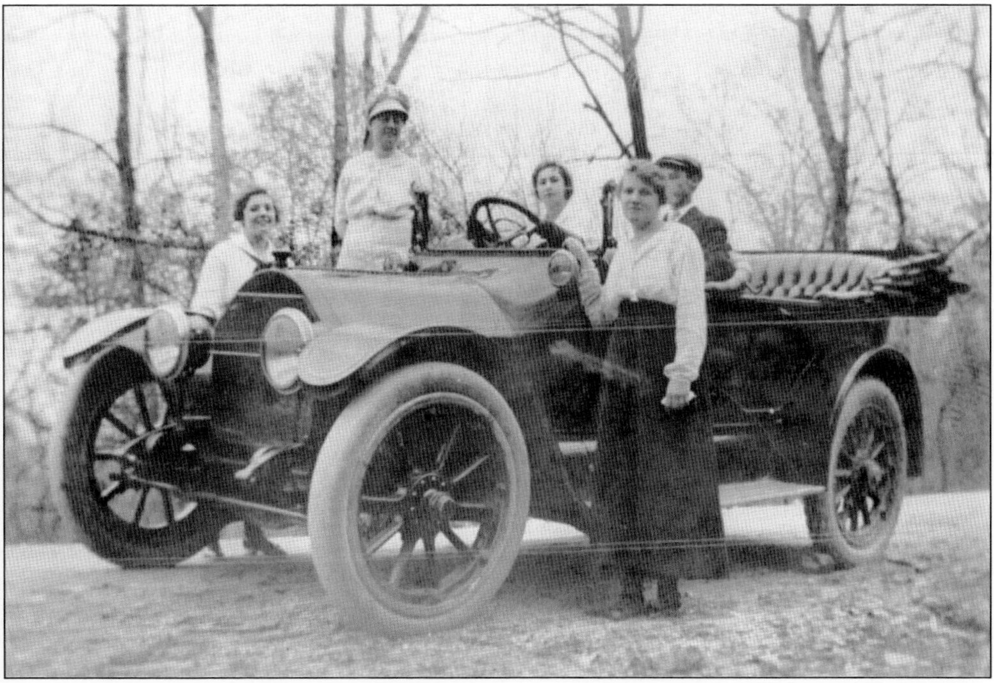

In the early days, a car ride was a luxury in Hargrove, which was located close to West Blocton. Seen in this photograph from left to right are Nancy Virginia Turner, unidentified, Lelia Payne Turner (driver), Johnny Stewart, and Martha Dodd. (Courtesy of Paula Fancher.)

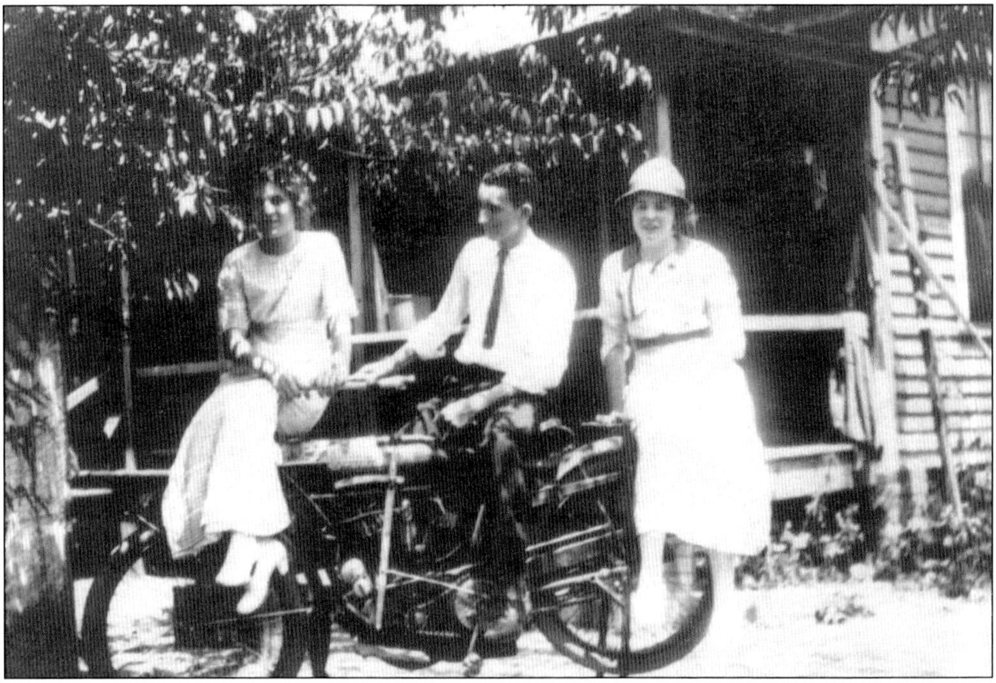

Few people in Hargrove had cars in the 1920s, and fewer still had motorcycles. Posing with this 1920s Indian motorcycle are, from left to right, Valla Davis, Dan Cannon, and Virginia Turner. The owner of the motorcycle is unknown. (Courtesy of Paula Fancher.)

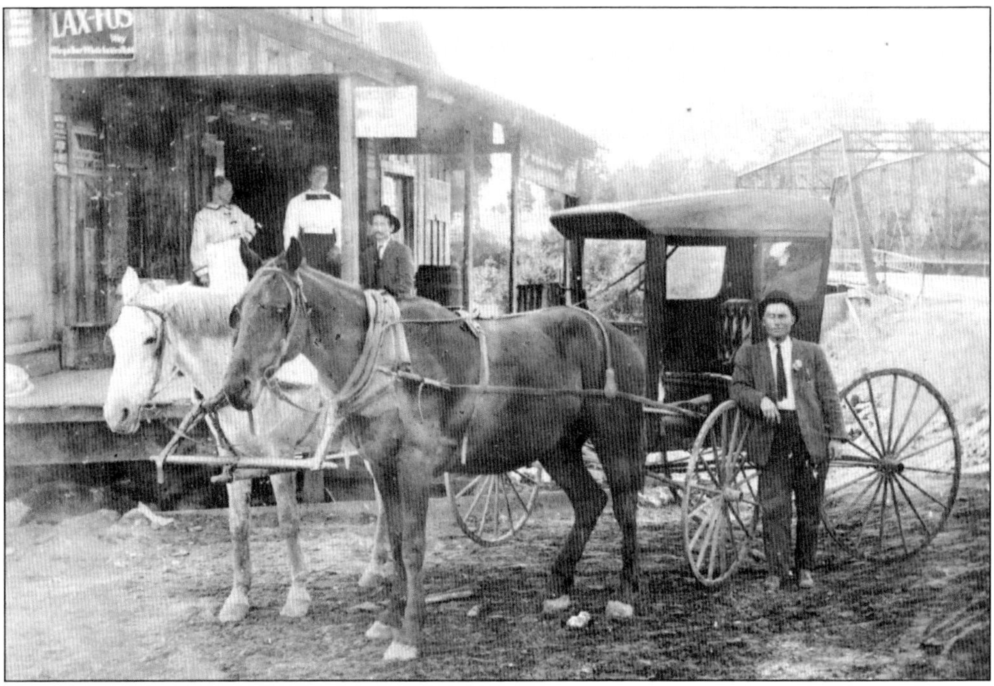

Pictured is Pop John Battle's store, which was in Six Mile near Six Mile Creek. Battle is standing near the post at the corner of the store. The man with the buggy is possibly the postman. (Courtesy of Jimmy Jones.)

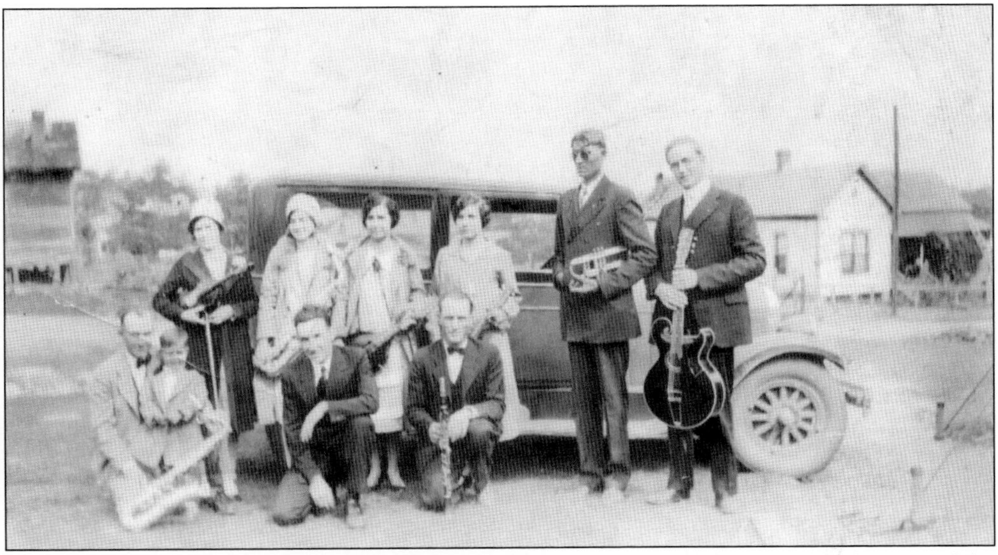

This is the orchestra that played with the Evangelists' party from Michigan. The identities of the musicians are unknown. (Courtesy of Marty Everse.)

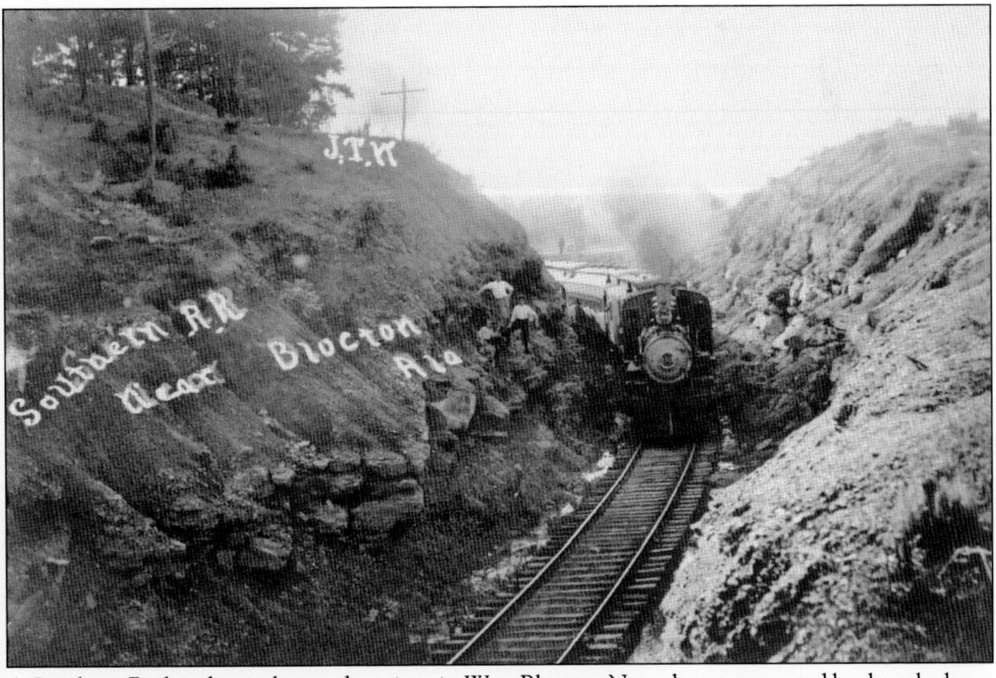

A Southern Railroad train leaves the mines in West Blocton. Note the cross created by the telephone pole just above the initials. (Photograph by John T. Weeks, courtesy of Beverly Beasley.)

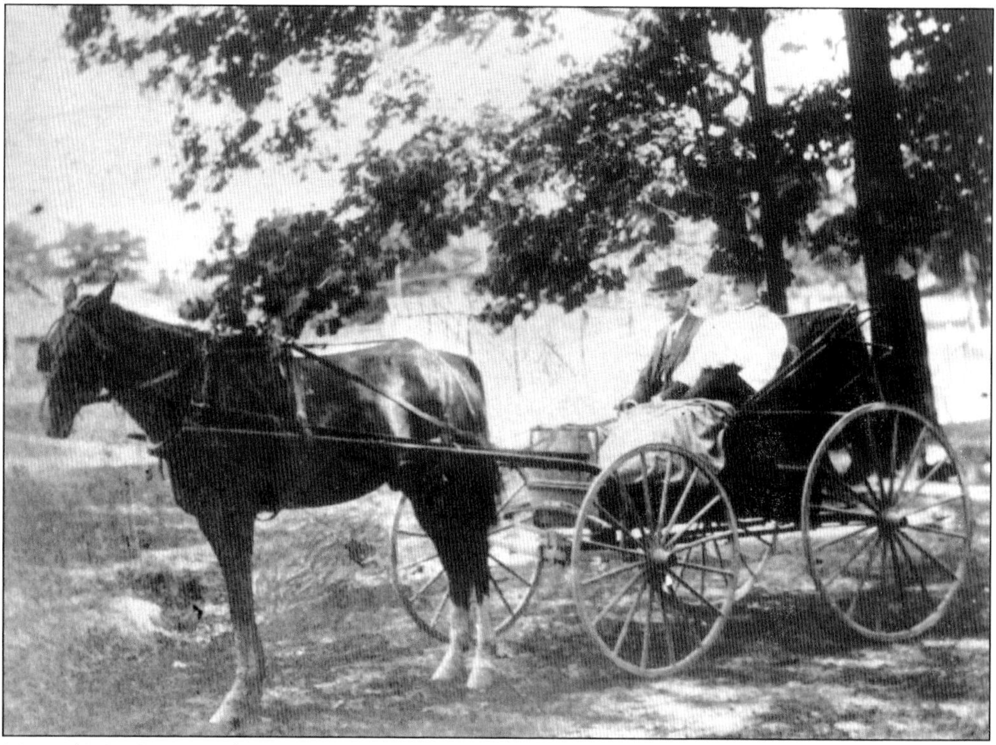

Mr. and Mrs. James Wilcox were seen out for a ride in their horse-and-buggy in one of the mining regions of Bibb County. This was a common mode of transportation used in this area for visiting nearby communities, work, and church. (Courtesy of Marshall Goggins.)

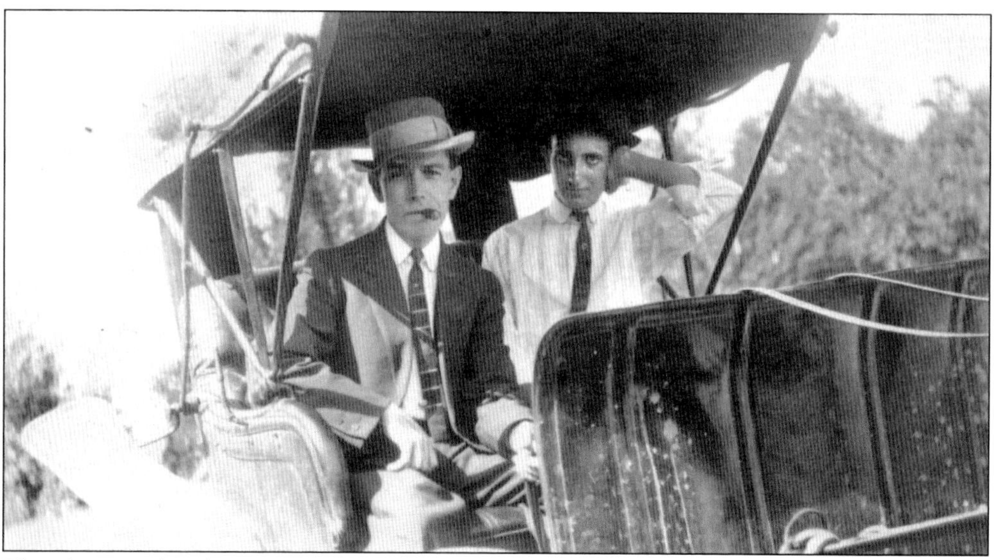

This photograph, taken in Hargrove, shows town physician Dr. William Bloomer (left) and Dan Cannon. (Courtesy of Paula Fancher.)

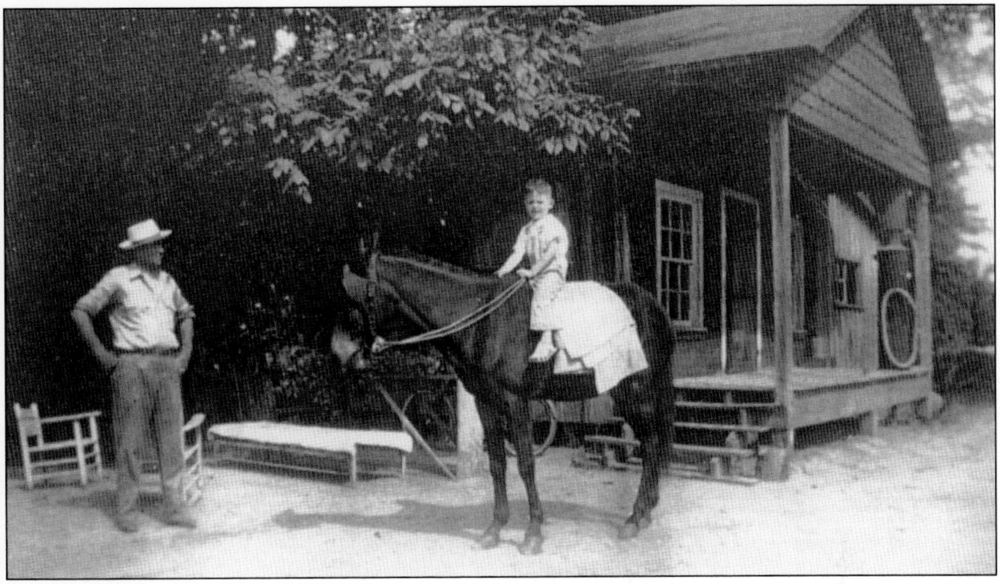

Taken at the old store at Bulldog Bend, this photograph shows three modes of transportation: foot, horse, and bicycle. Pictured are Julian Fancher (left) and Jimmy Suttle. (Courtesy of Paula Fancher.)

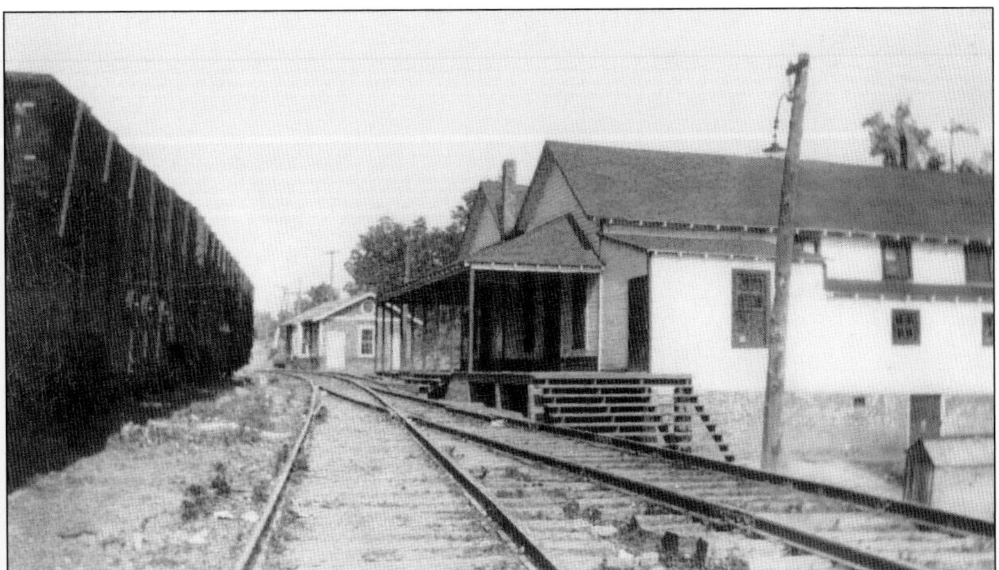

The Piper Depot is the first building on the left. From here, locals could catch the Louisville and Nashville (L&N) passenger train for work, school, or entertainment between Piper and Birmingham. (Courtesy of Mary Louise Jones Crider.)

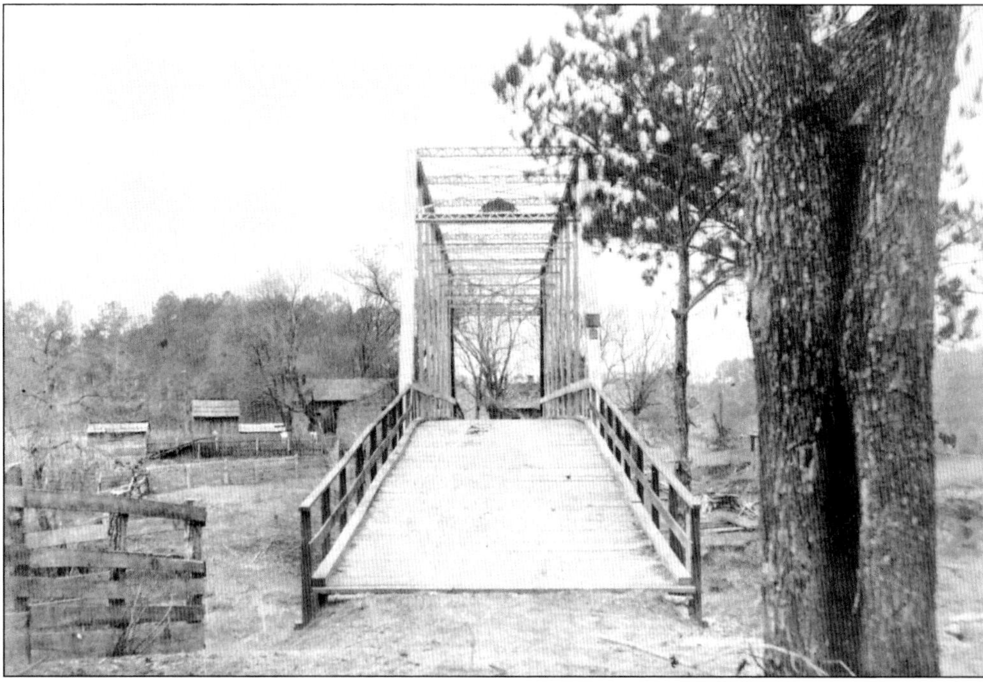

This photograph shows a newly constructed bridge over the Cahaba River, but the exact location is not known. According to writing on the back, the image probably belonged to John Kennedy. (Courtesy of Brent/Centreville Library.)

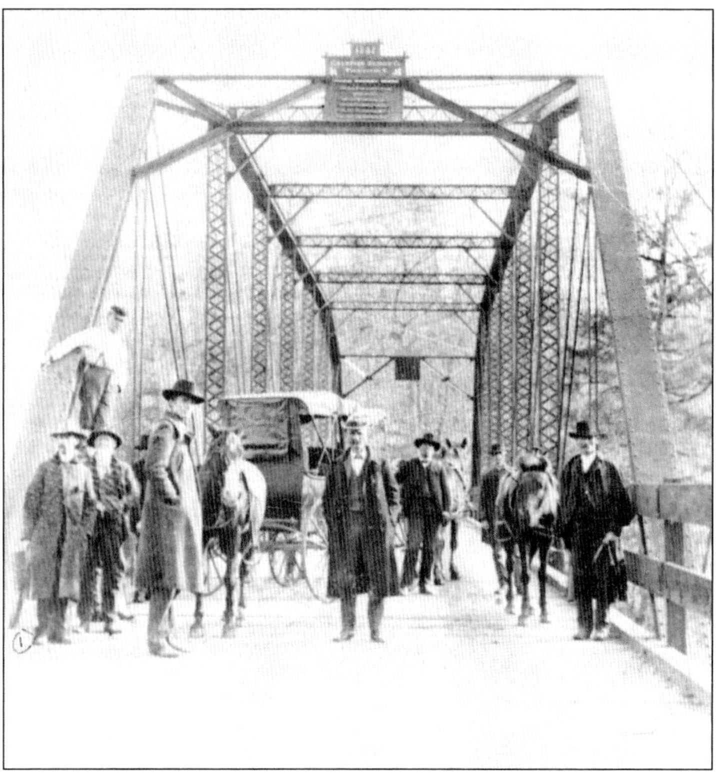

Pictured is the Pratt Ferry Bridge across the Cahaba River, located just south of its confluence with Cottingham Creek in River Bend. It was named the Pratt Ferry for the Pratt family that owned it. A plaque on the bridge shows that it was built in 1902. Standing on the bridge are commissioners W. C. Trott, W. H. Cleveland, C. T. Ragland, N. E. Stewart, and Judge W. L. Pratt. (Courtesy of Hal Cottingham.)

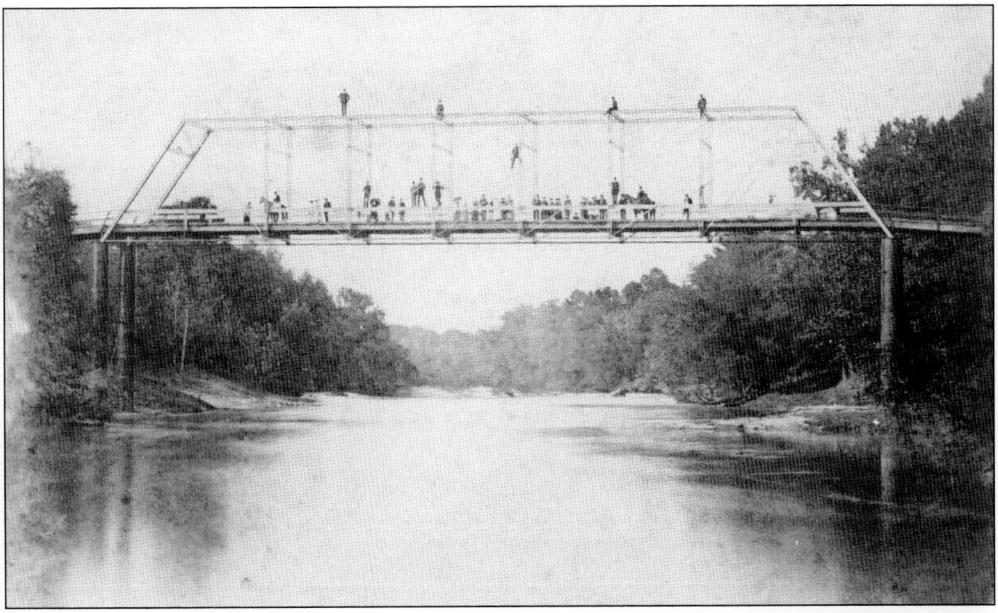

The iron bridge over the Cahaba River at Centreville was erected in 1885 by the King Bridge Company of Cleveland, Ohio. The central span was 175 feet, the eastern approach was 76 feet, and the western approach was 99 feet long. The height from the low-water mark to the top of the pier is 39 feet, with a total height of 65 feet. (Photograph by J. V. Quinn, courtesy of Brent/Centreville Library.)

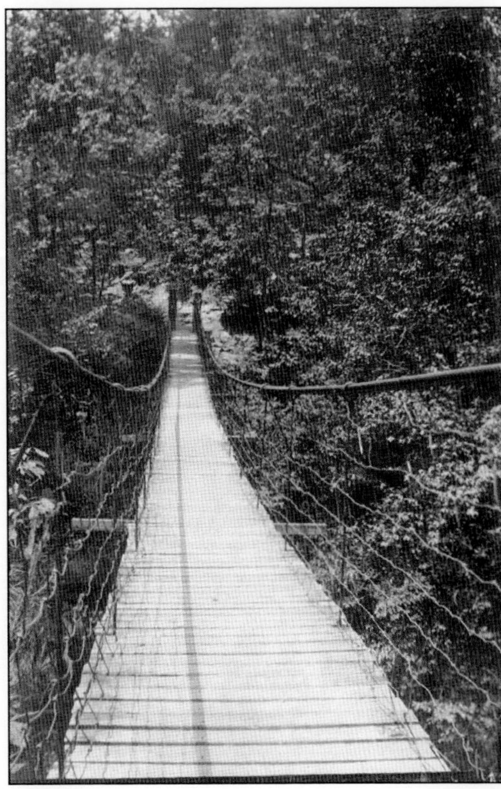

This swinging bridge stretched from Piper to Coleanor. It was built so the children from Coleanor could cross over to go to school. It was designed by Walter Henley and was constructed by Robert Raines. (Courtesy of Paula Fancher.)

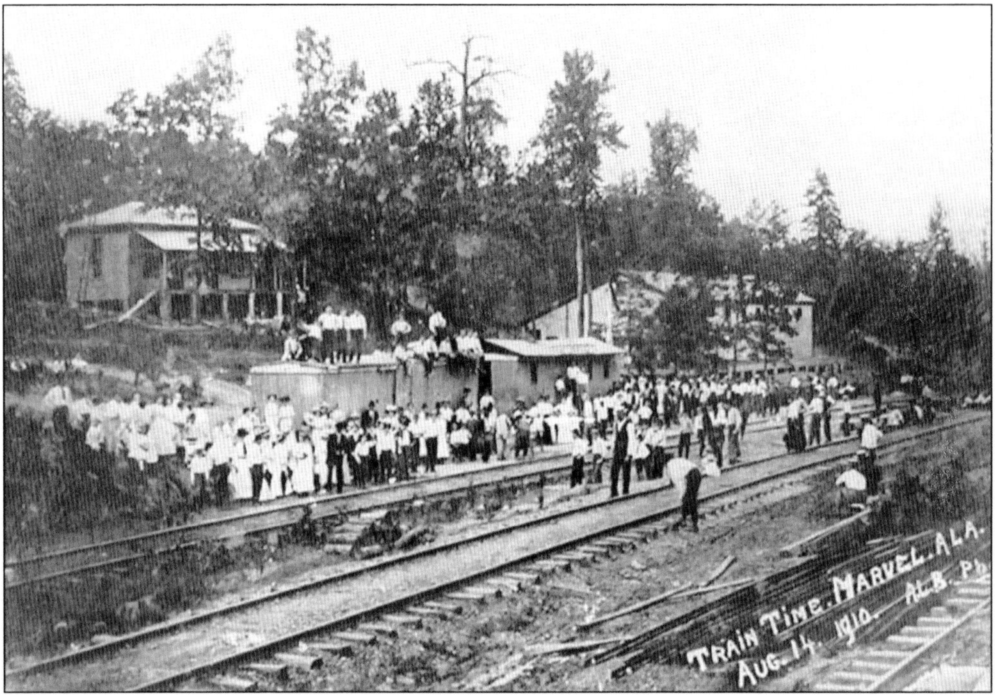

On August 14, 1910, the residents of Marvel gathered for the L&N "Joe Lee," perhaps to get their mail, which was delivered by the train twice a day. (Courtesy of Marshall Goggins.)

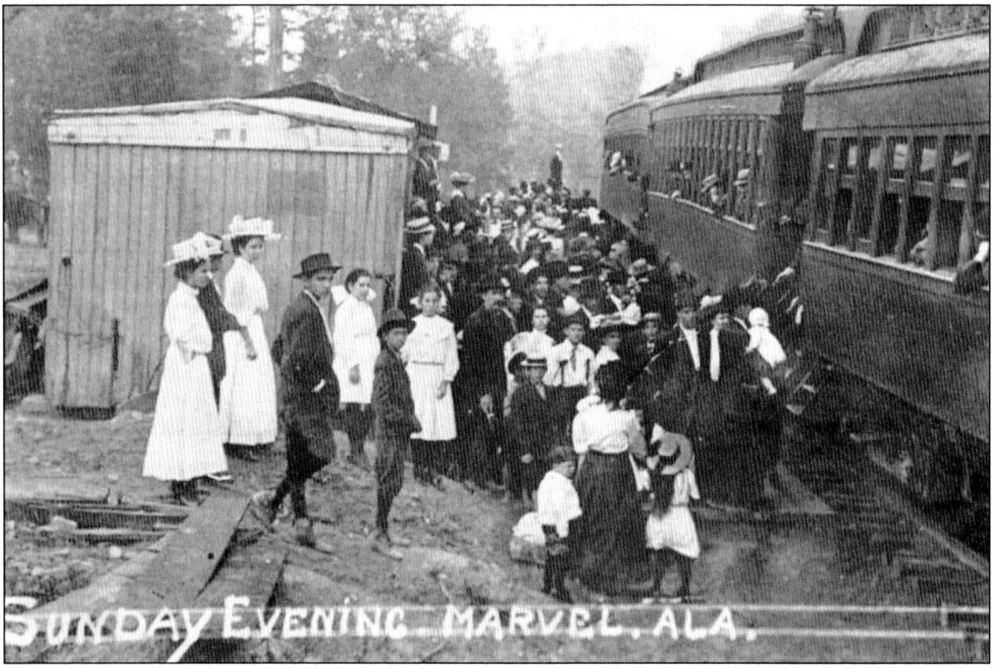

On a Sunday evening in Marvel sometime around 1910, the residents gather to watch the train come through the mining town. In *The Struggle and the Joy: An American Coal Town Piper, Alabama*, Cecil O. Sewell Sr. recalls people gathering in the morning and evening to watch the L&N "Joe Lee" pass by. (Courtesy of Marshall Goggins.)

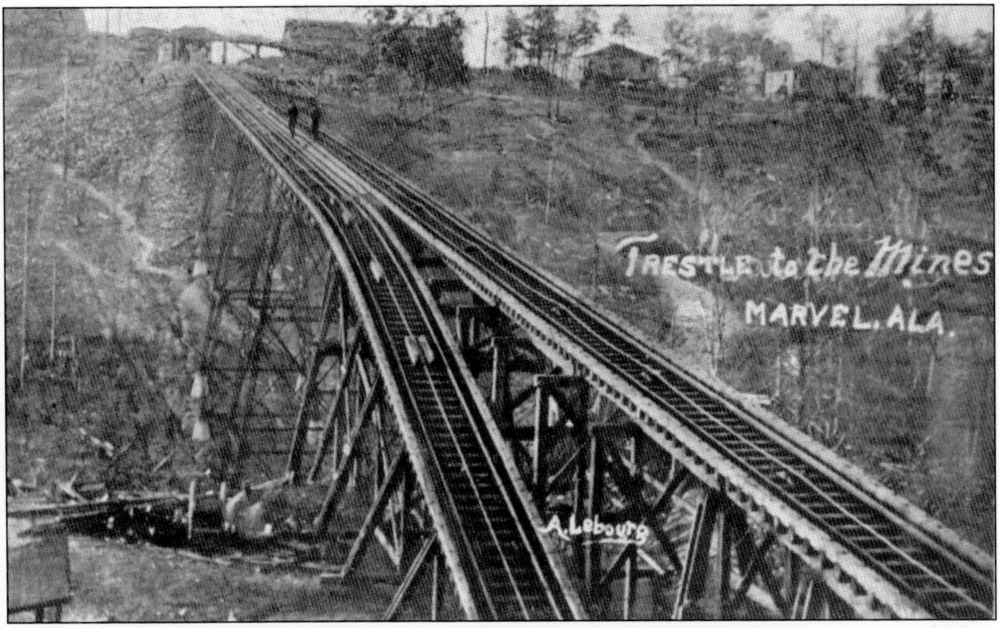

This railroad trestle linked the mines to Marvel during the height of the coal mining era. (Photograph by John T. Weeks, courtesy of Beverly Weeks Beasley.)

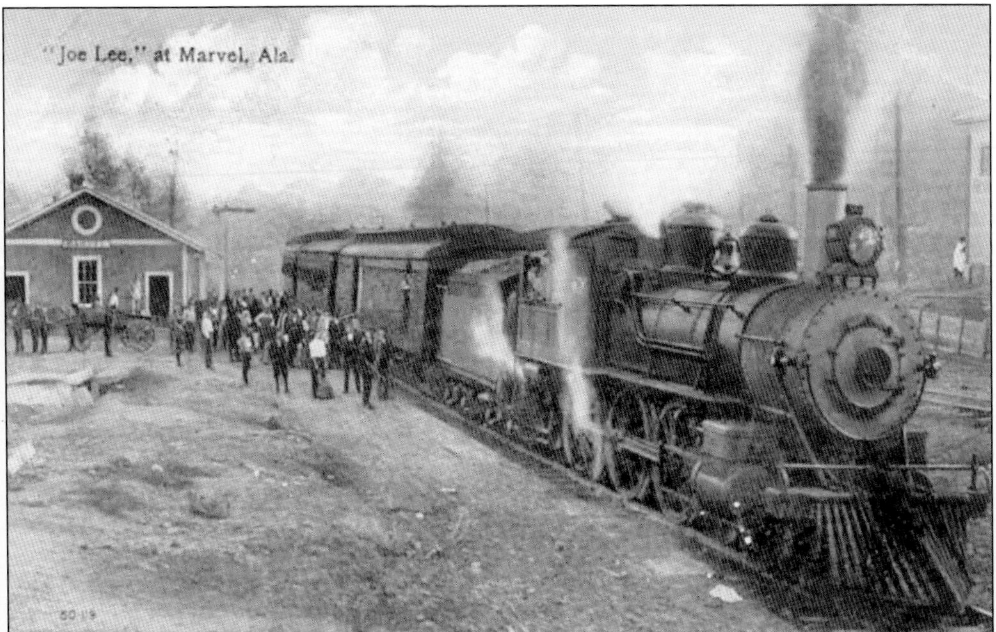

The L&N passenger train made two trips each day to Birmingham, one in the morning and one in the evening. The "Joe Lee" was named after its conductor. He was a man of few words, but he was fast to stop the train and dismiss disorderly passengers. The "Joe Lee" also commuted Piper-Coleander students to West Blocton High School. (Courtesy of Marshall Goggins.)

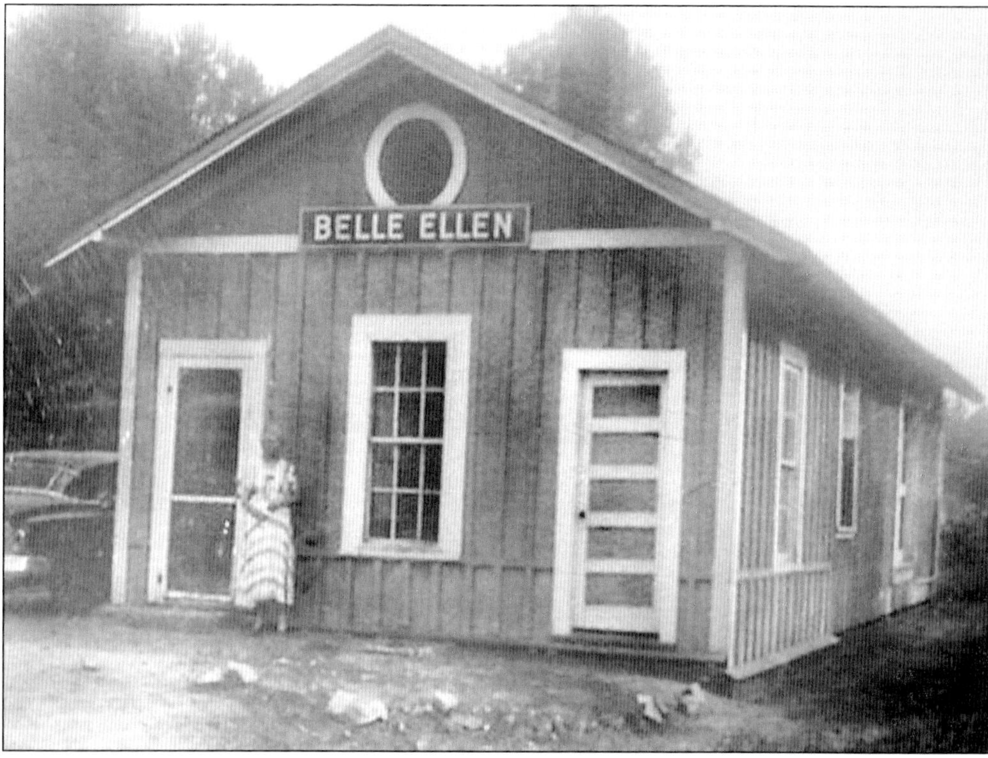

In the early 1950s, the last steam engine in the Southern Railway System was taken out of service, bringing an end to the need for coal for steam engines. In 1953, it was reported that there were only 16 families left in Belle Ellen, and shortly after, the town was all but forgotten. (Courtesy of Marshall Goggins.)

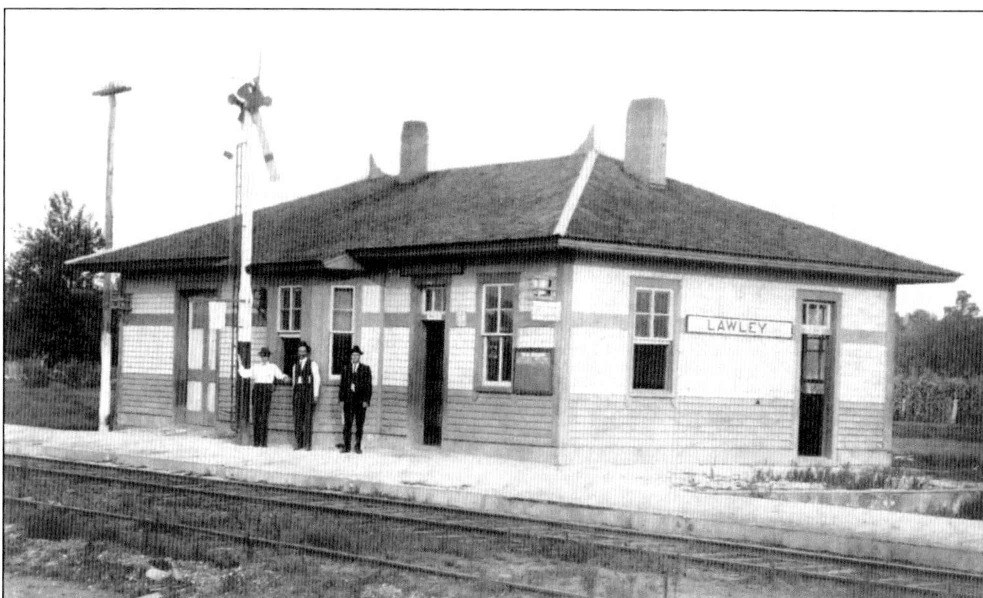

This is an early photograph of the train depot in Lawley. (Photograph by John T. Weeks, courtesy of Beverly Weeks Beasley.)

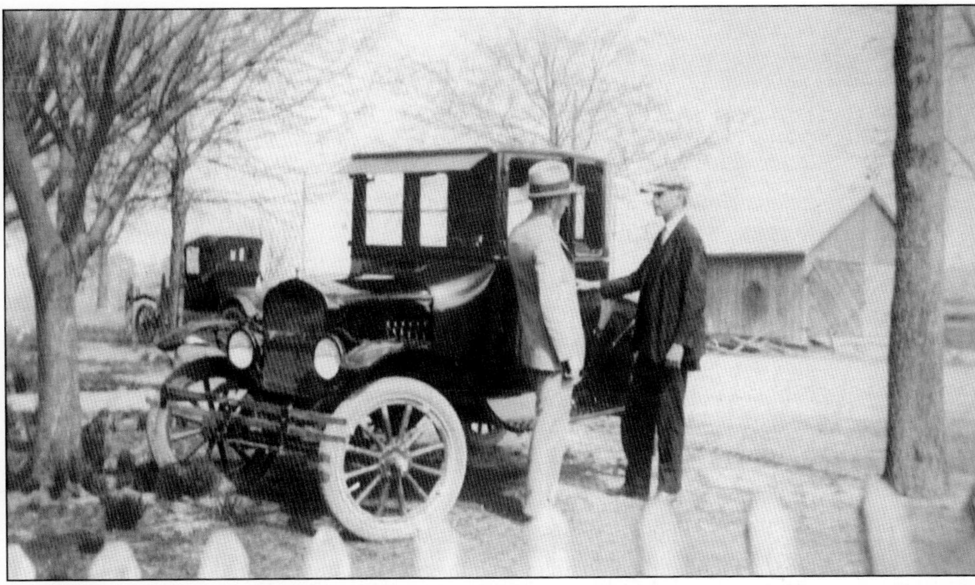

Two of the James brothers are pictured at an unknown location. Daniel Ward James was the older brother of John Howard James. John (right) was a businessman and farmer, while Daniel (left) was a cashier at the Brent Banking Company. (Courtesy of Ruth Dailey.)

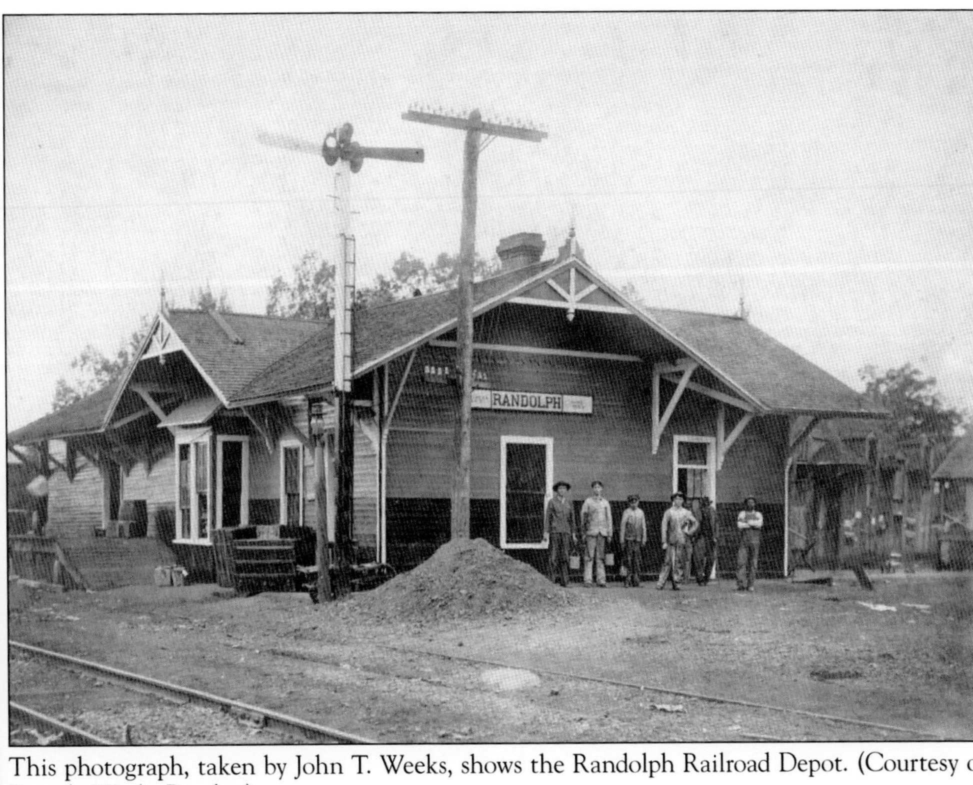

This photograph, taken by John T. Weeks, shows the Randolph Railroad Depot. (Courtesy of Beverly Weeks Beasley.)

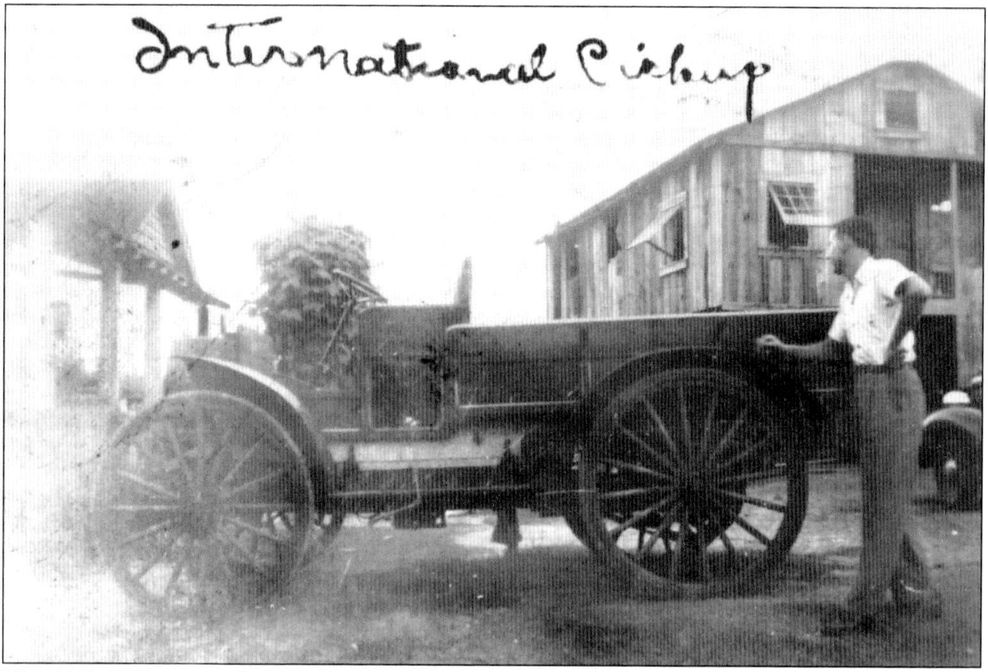

The 1910 International Harvester Auto Wagon was welcomed into the workforce both to help out on the farm and as a faster way to get where one wanted to go. The man in this picture is unidentified. (Courtesy of Ruth Dailey.)

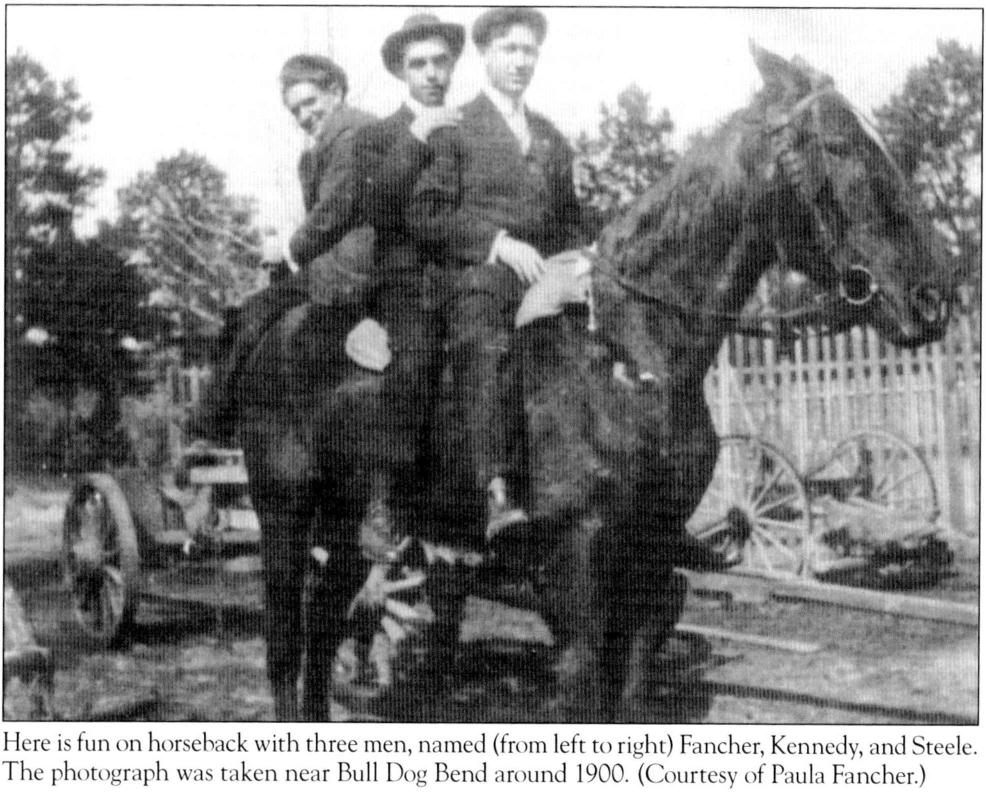

Here is fun on horseback with three men, named (from left to right) Fancher, Kennedy, and Steele. The photograph was taken near Bull Dog Bend around 1900. (Courtesy of Paula Fancher.)

Seven

Public Service and Military Service

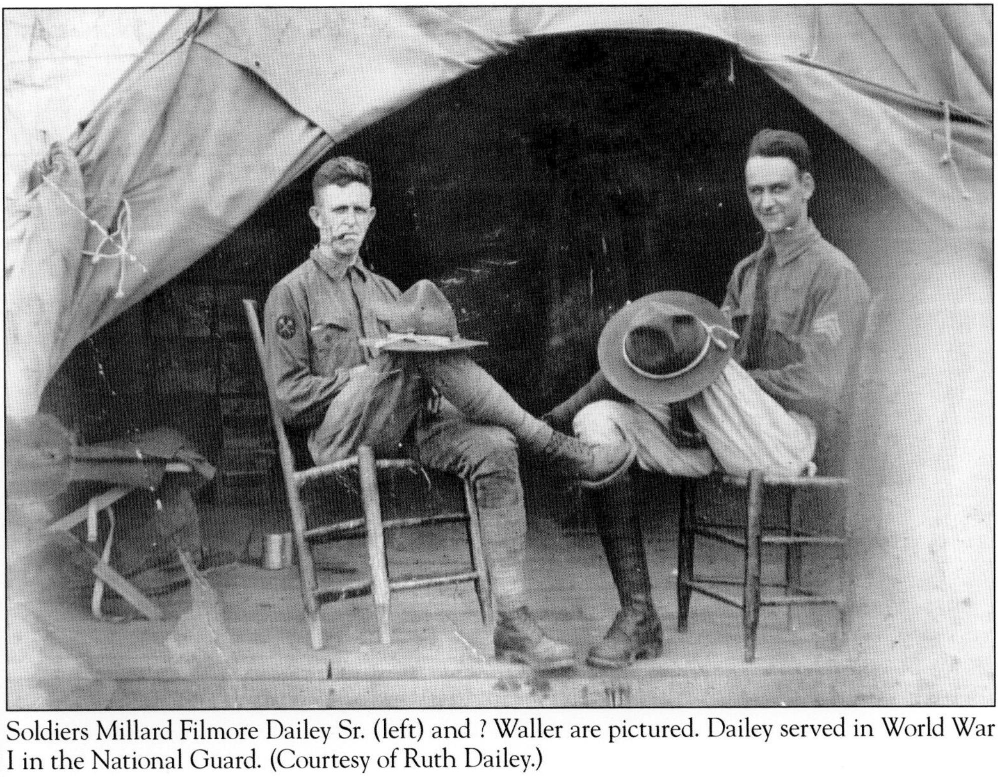

Soldiers Millard Filmore Dailey Sr. (left) and ? Waller are pictured. Dailey served in World War I in the National Guard. (Courtesy of Ruth Dailey.)

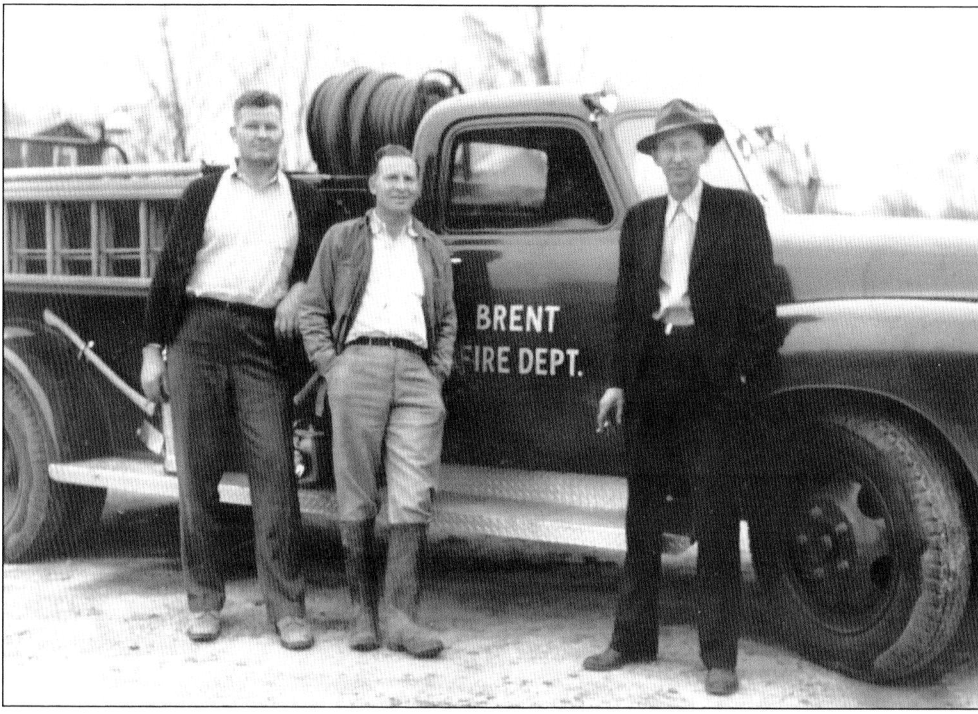

Pictured in 1948 is Brent's first fire truck. From left to right are Olon Belcher, Virgil Peak, and Murray Nichols. (Courtesy of Belcher Lumber Company.)

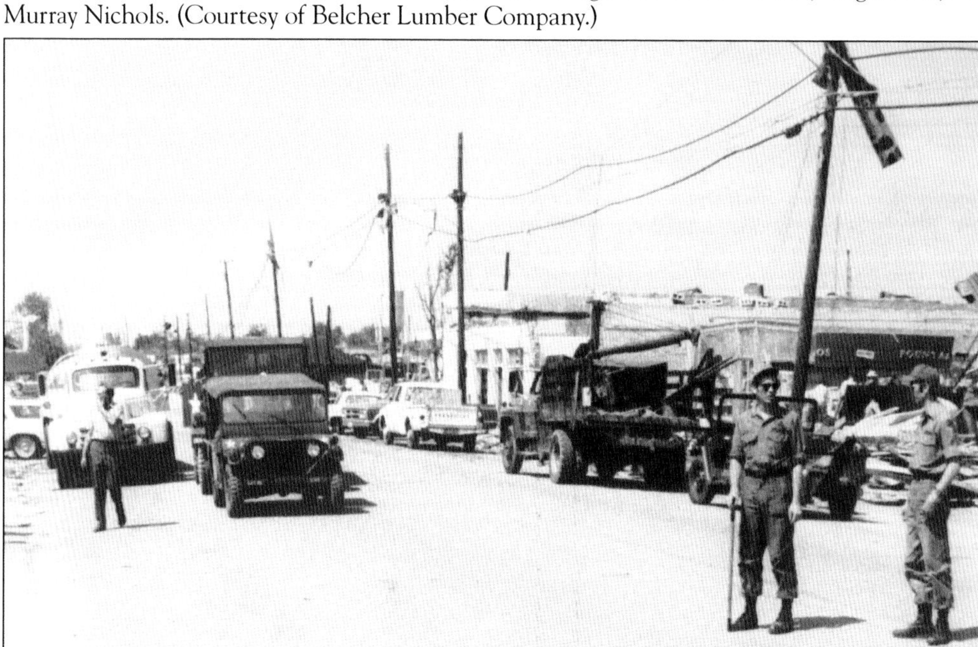

On May 27, 1973, Brent was hit by a tornado that devastated the entire community. The downtown was totally destroyed, but in a spirit of perseverance, residents soon started reconstruction. This picture is of the local National Guard on duty, helping to bring order to a chaotic time. (Courtesy of Ruth Dailey.)

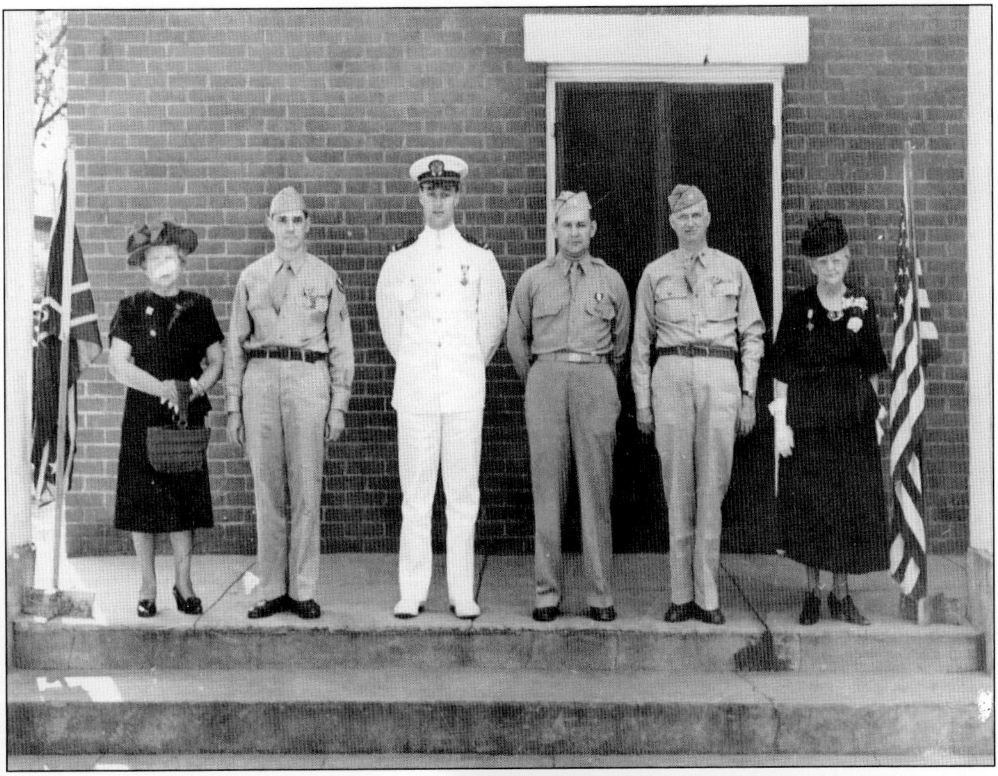

This photograph was taken in front of the Centreville First Presbyterian Church, located on the Court Square. From left to right are Mrs. ? Jamison, Josiah Kennedy, unidentified, George Harper Stacy Jr., John Percy Kennedy, and Annie Kennedy. John Percy and Annie Kennedy were members of the Centreville Presbyterian Church. (Courtesy of Bernise Stacy.)

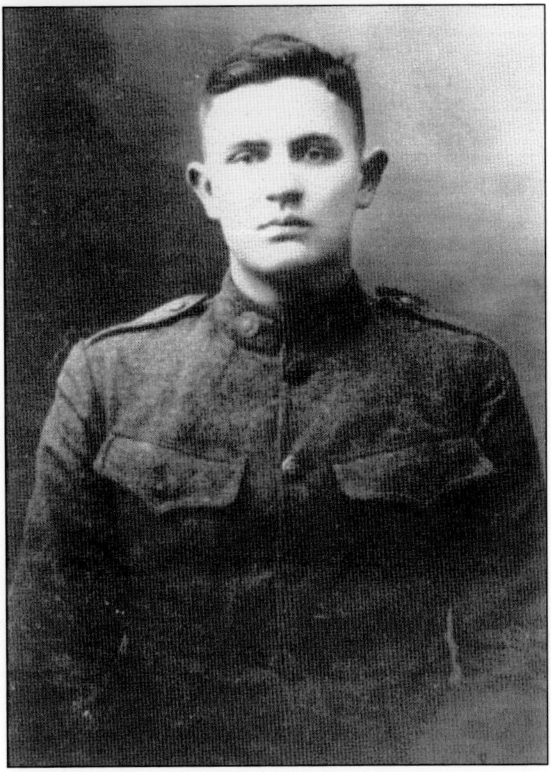

Robert Richard Farrington (1900–1967) was buried in Cedar Hill in Bessemer. He married Doris Fancher (1905–1994), the daughter of Julian L. and Jesse Frost Fancher. (Courtesy of Paula Fancher.)

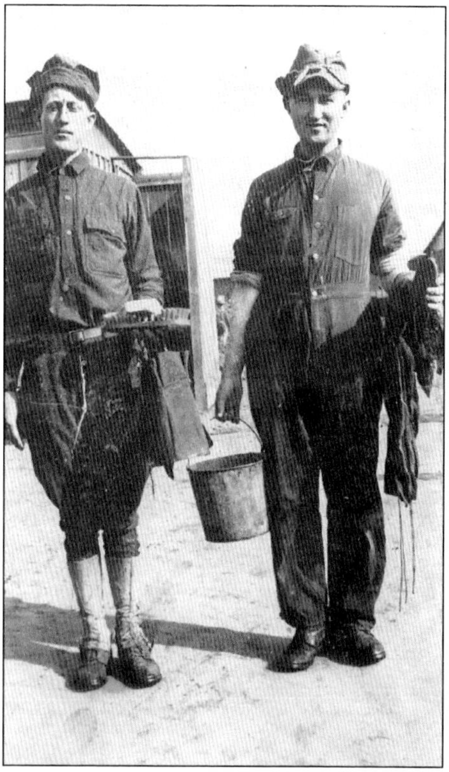

These soldiers, who served in World War I, are John Osborne Parker (left), born in Brierfield in 1890, and unidentified. Parker was the son of Reese Coleman and Caroline Childers Parker. (Courtesy of Paula Fancher.)

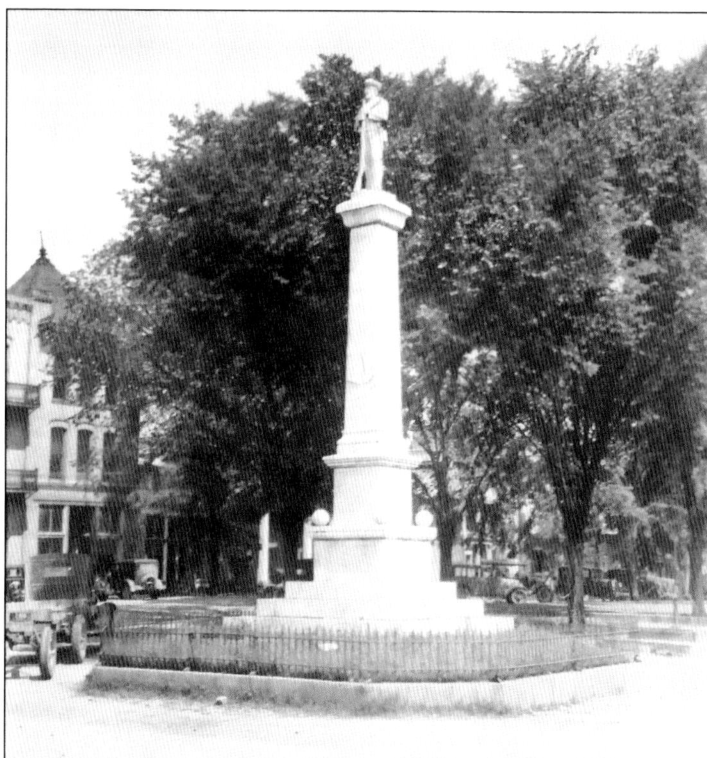

The Confederate Monument, located on the lawn of the Bibb County Courthouse, was dedicated and unveiled on July 22, 1910. It is still located on the courthouse lawn but has since been moved closer to the courthouse. (Courtesy of Brent/Centreville Library.)

George Phillips White (1915–1977) was the son of James Bailey and Berta Jones White. He graduated from the University of Alabama in 1939, and in that same year, he was admitted to the Alabama Bar. In 1952, White married Betty Ann Poag, and they had three children: George Phillips White III, Allison White, and Rachel White. George served from ensign to lieutenant in the Naval Air Force (1943–1946) with active duty aboard the Sangamon aircraft carrier in the South Pacific Theatre. He was also decorated with the Presidential Unit Citation Five Battle Stars. After his discharge, White returned to Centreville and practiced law until his death. (Courtesy of Betty Poag White.)

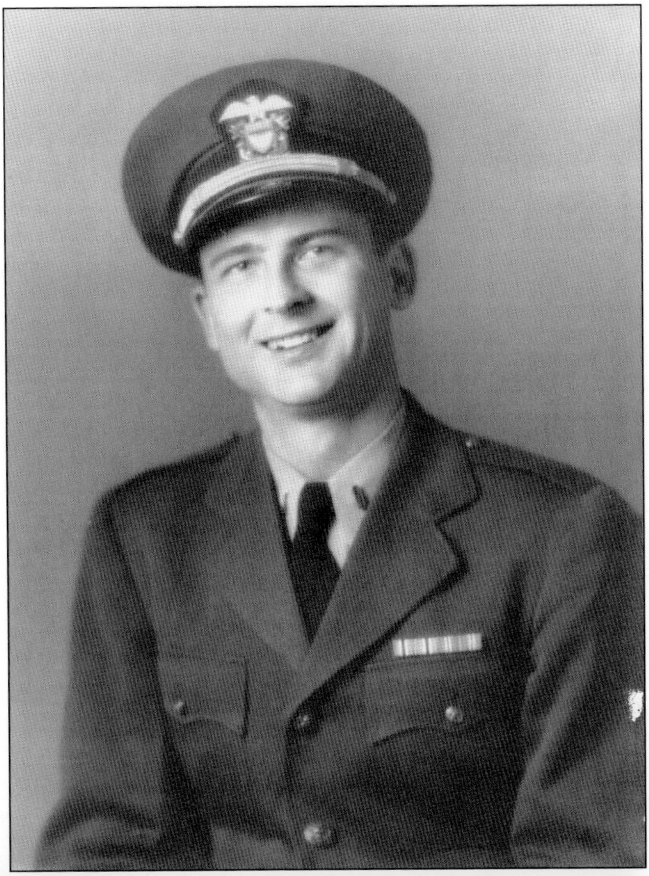

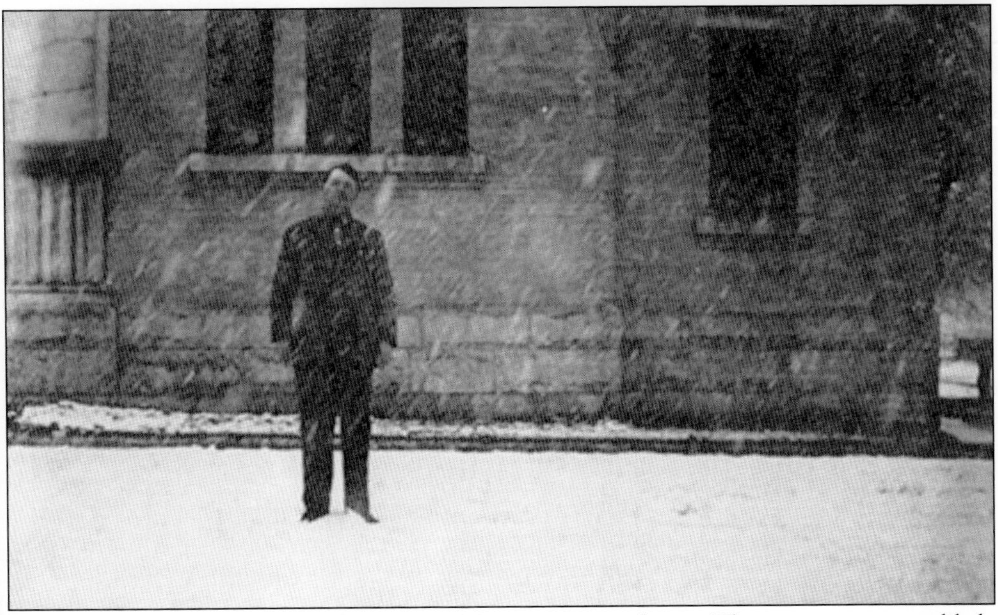

Judge William Luther Pratt stands in front of the county courthouse. This picture was most likely taken in 1899 during a snowstorm. (Courtesy of Dalton and Anne Murphy.)

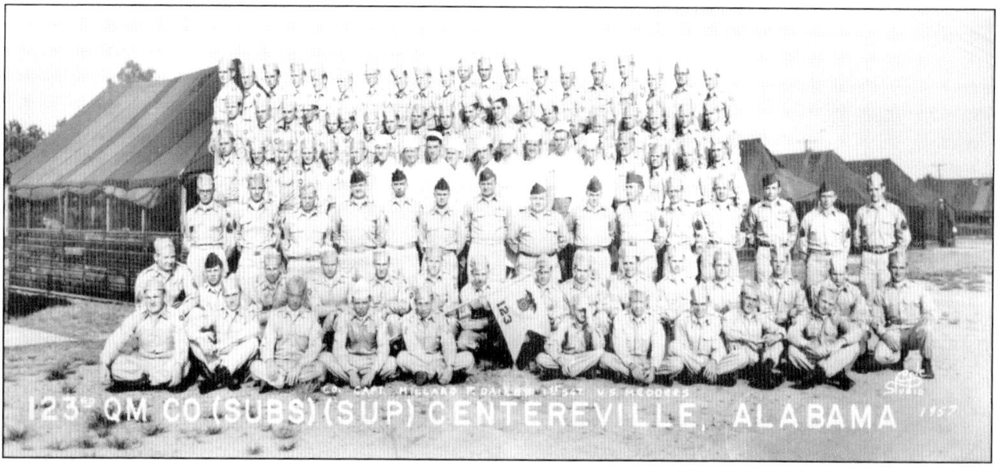

This is the 123rd Quartermaster Company of the Centreville National Guard, which served under Capt. Millard F. Dailey and 1st Sgt. V. S. Medders, in 1957. (Courtesy of Ruth Dailey.)

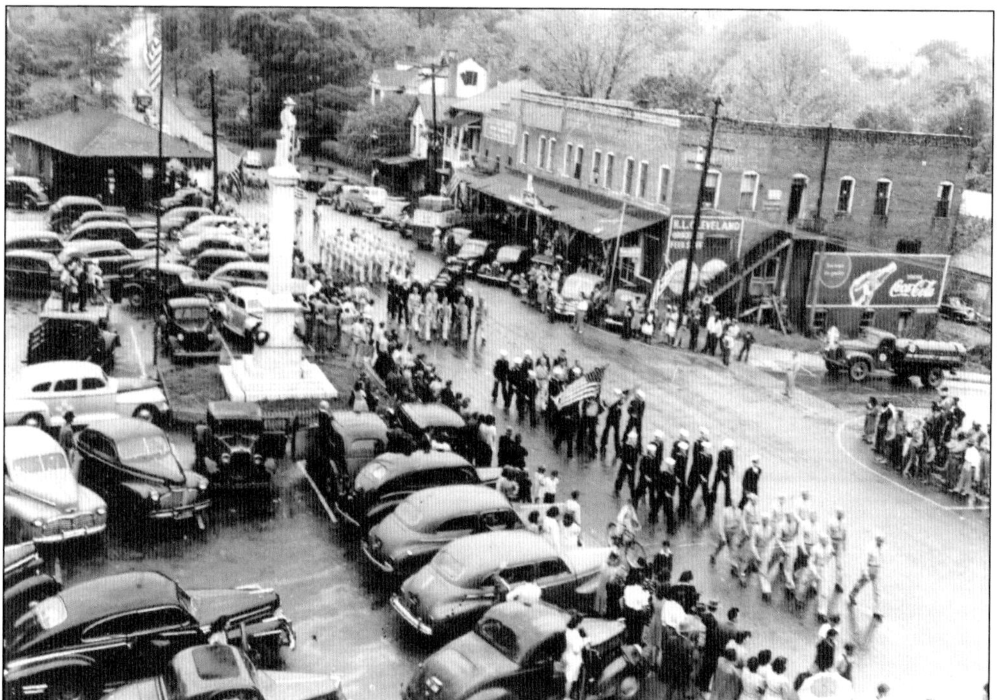

Sgt. Ross F. Gray (1920–1945) was enlisted in the U.S. Marine Corps when he was sent to Iwo Jima two days into his service. Gray, along with his platoon, fell back during a difficult situation when faced with strong automatic weapons fire. Gray made his way back up a hill with a satchel of charges, prepared to take out the machine-gun positions. His heroic action saved lives, and several enemy machine-gun employments were taken out. He was awarded the Congressional Medal of Honor for his actions, but Gray was killed in action on Iwo Jima just six days after the battle that won him the medal. This was a parade in his honor when Gray's father accepted his award. (Courtesy of Jim Oakley Jr.)

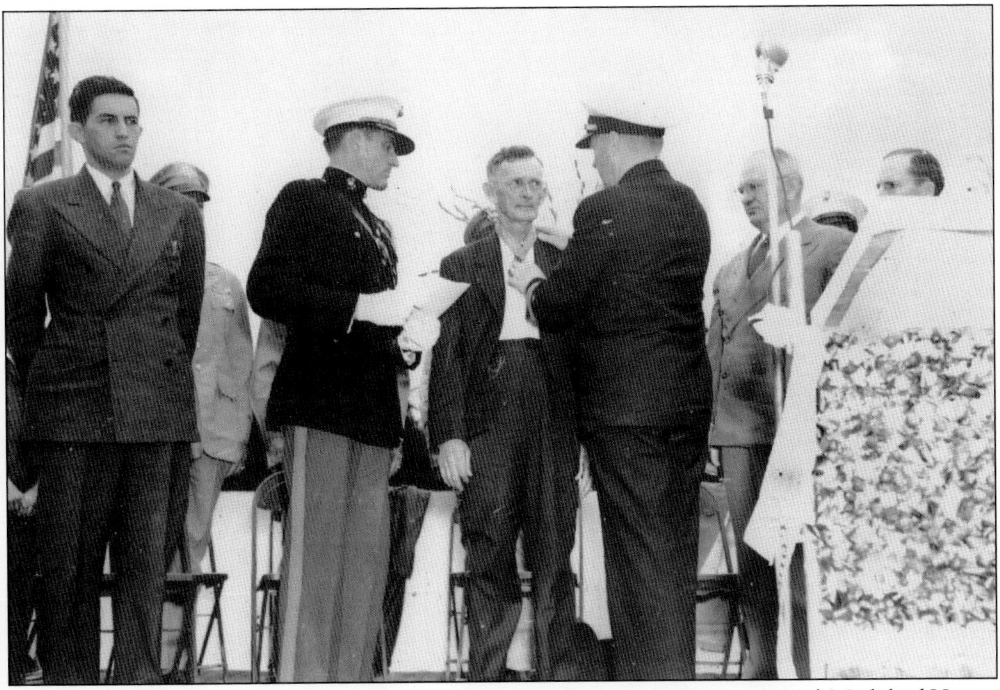

Ross F. Gray's father, Benjamin F. Gray, was awarded his son's Congressional Medal of Honor in a service on the Bibb County High School football field on April 16, 1946. (Courtesy of Jim Oakley Jr.)

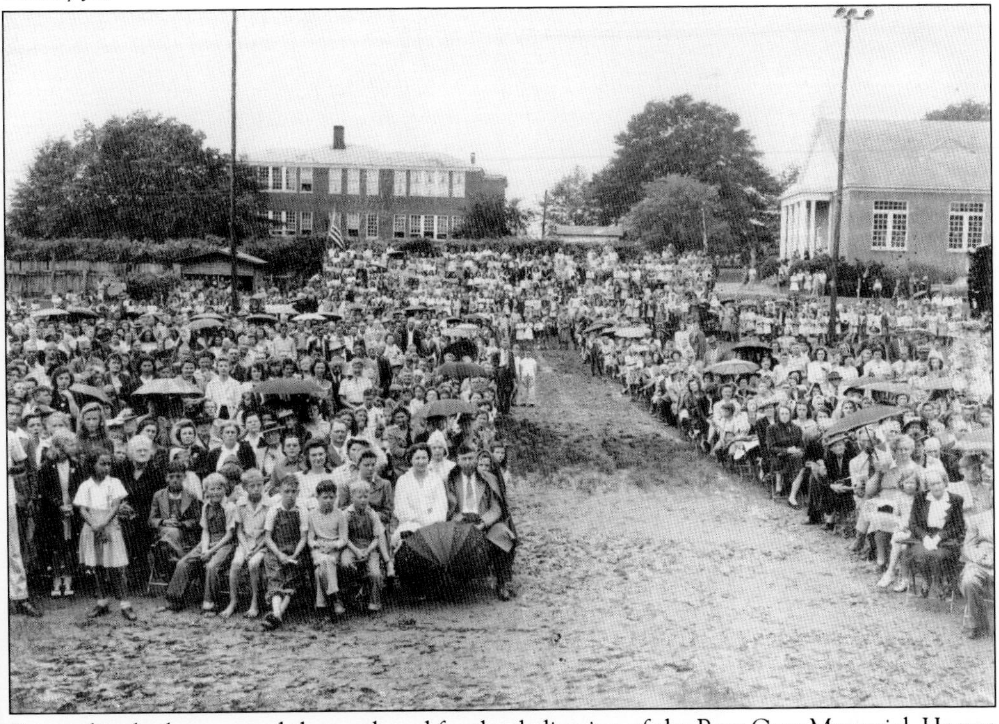

Pictured is the large crowd that gathered for the dedication of the Ross Gray Memorial. He was one of Bibb County's genuine heroes. (Courtesy of Jim Oakley Jr.)

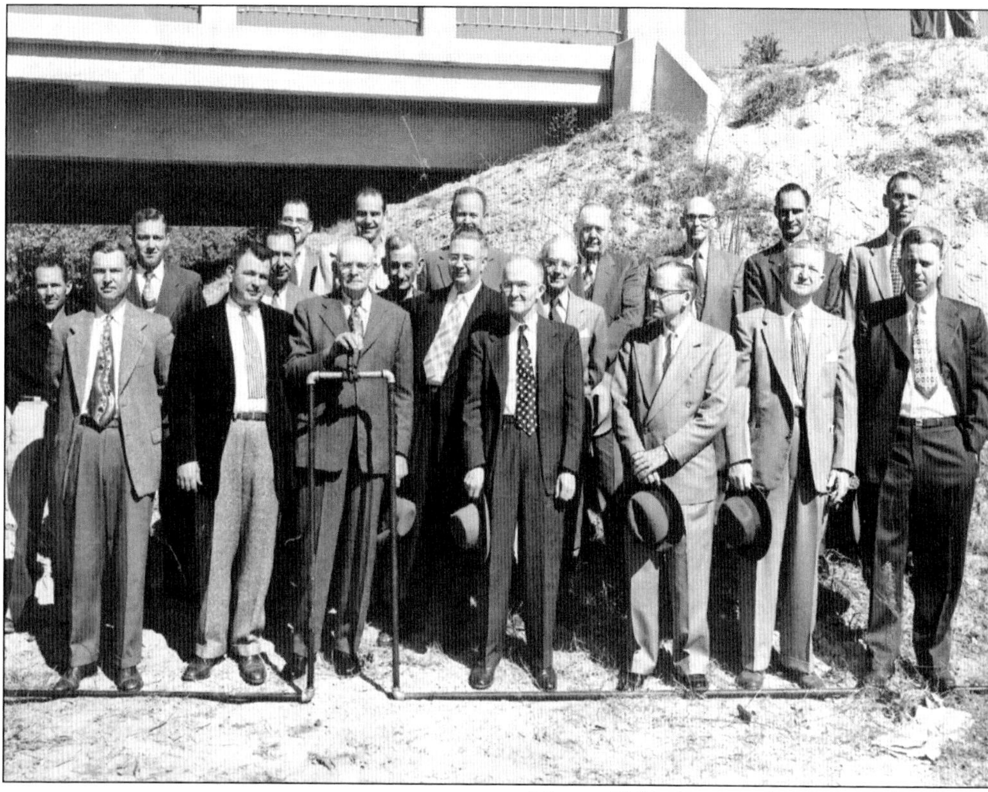

This c. 1953 photograph captures the day natural gas service to Centreville was turned on. Pictured are Brent-Centreville officials at a connection at the Cahaba River Bridge. Some Alabama Gas officials are also included in the image. (Photograph by Jim Oakley Jr., courtesy of Kay Dailey Foster.)

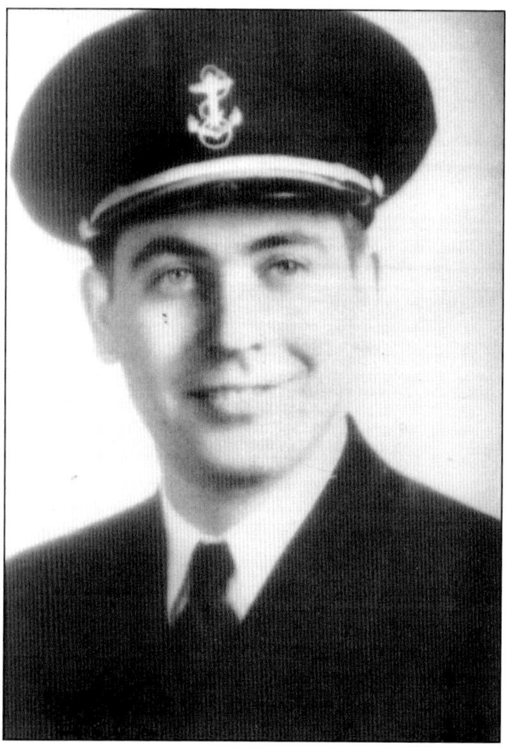

Dr. Alsey Clements Pratt Jr. (1918–1968) married Eileen Mae Engleman. He was a member of the U.S. Navy in 1943. Dr. Pratt performed his internship at the Farragut Naval Hospital, and after the war ended, he returned to Bibb County to begin his practice. He was an original staff member of the Bibb County Hospital. (Courtesy of John R. "Bobby" Pratt.)

Eight

Outdoor Bibb and Disasters

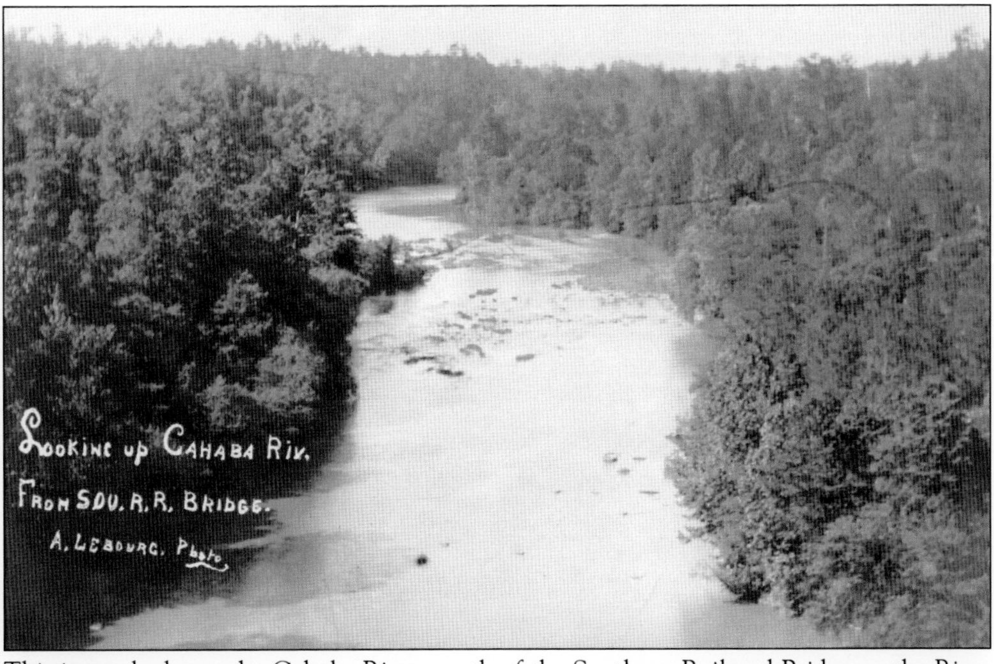

This image looks up the Cahaba River, north of the Southern Railroad Bridge, or the River Trestle as it is known by the locals. The Cahaba River is the longest free-flowing river in Alabama and is home to more than 100 types of fish, including several rare species such as the Alabama Sturgeon, Cahaba Shiner, Crystal Darter, Freckled Darter, Goldline Darter, and Frecklebelly Madtom. (Courtesy of Beverly Beasley.)

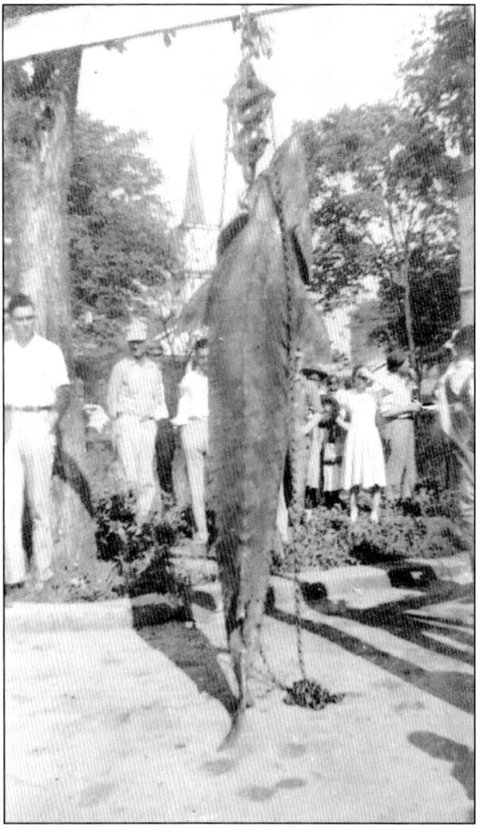

This large sturgeon was caught in the Cahaba River in May 1941 near the present-day location of the Bibb County High School gym. The fish weighed approximately 300 pounds, which made it necessary to use a local log truck to remove the fish from the river. (Photograph by Roberta Oakley, courtesy of John R. "Bobby" Pratt.)

The Weeks family is seen here boating on a lake near their home in Sand Mountain. (Courtesy of Beverly Weeks Beasley.)

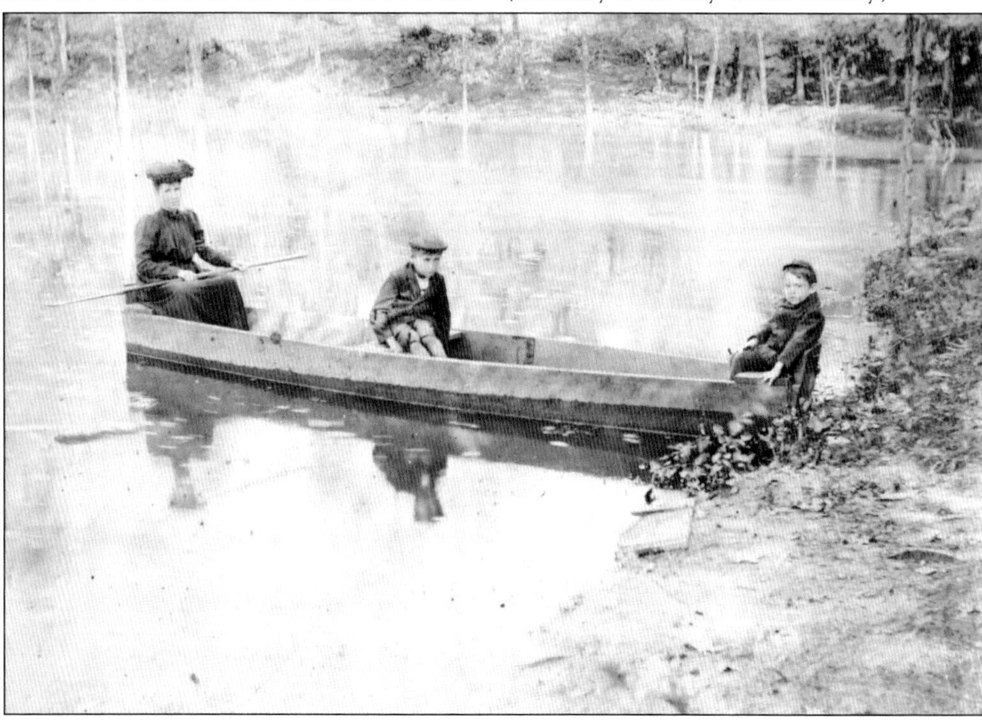

Cahaba lilies are seen on the Cahaba River at Piper in 1934. These lovely river flowers are found only in Alabama, Georgia, and South Carolina and can grow to be 3 feet tall. Legend has it that the rare and beautiful lily was brought here from the Nile River. (Courtesy of Paula Fancher.)

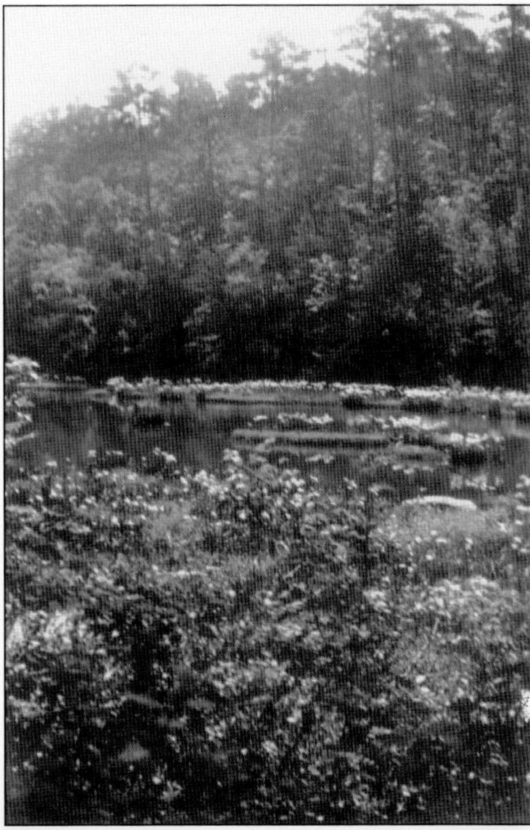

This artesian well was once located near Bethel Baptist Church in Brent and was used by many local folks for gathering fresh springwater. This spring is no longer in use. (Courtesy of Mary Louise Jones Crider.)

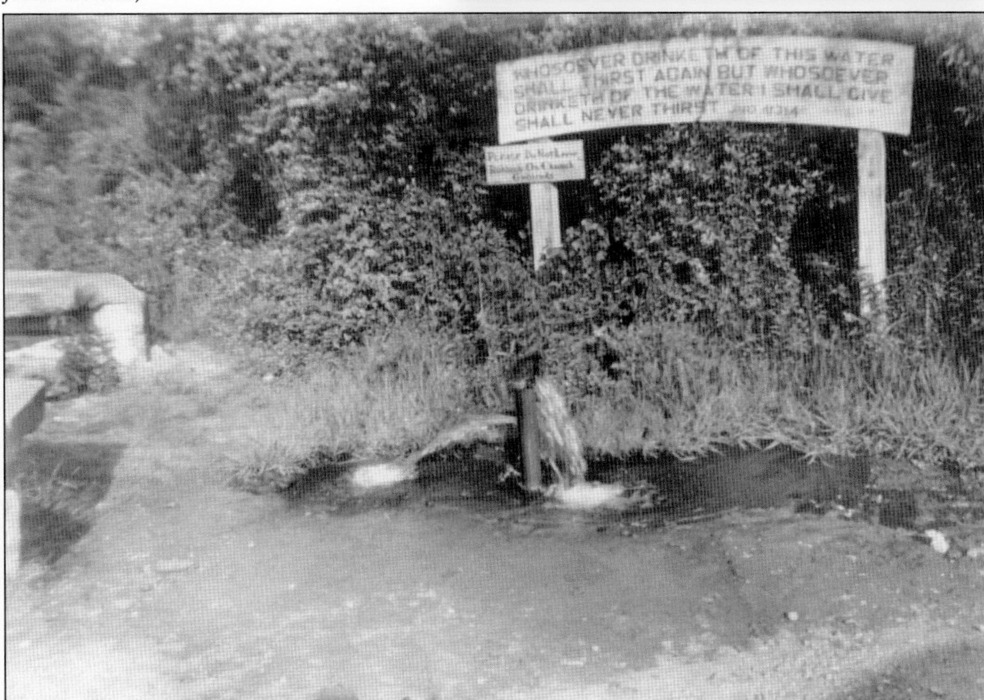

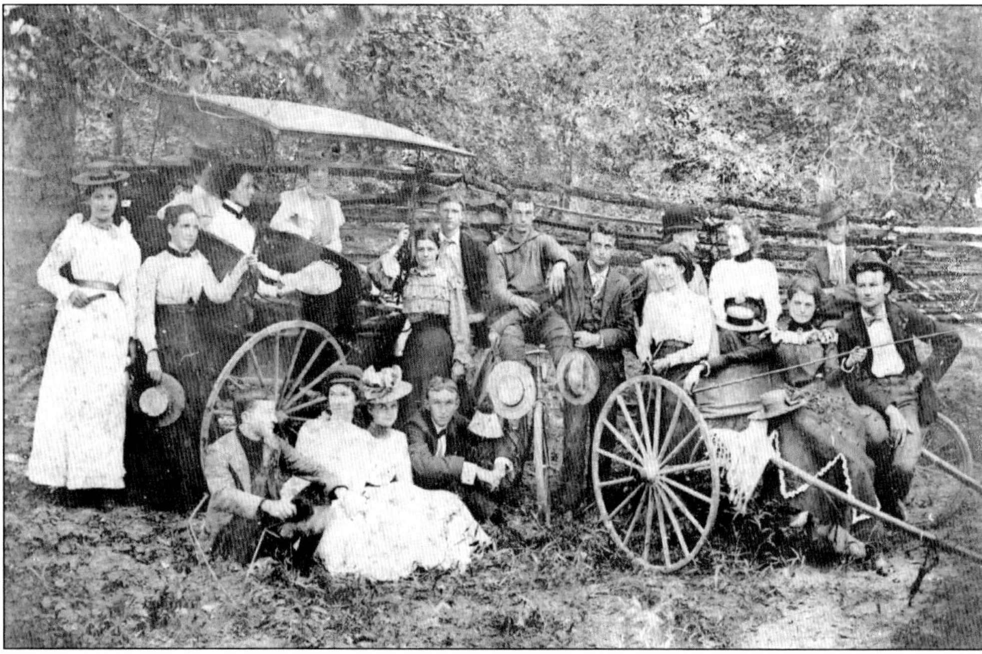

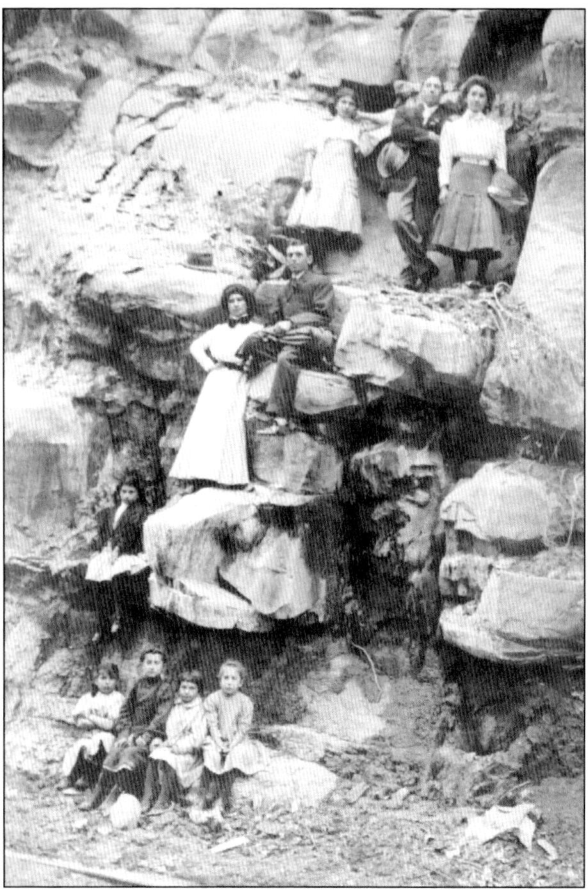

Having a picture taken was a special event, so everyone here is dressed in his or her Sunday best. While the names of the people and the exact location for the photograph is unknown, this picture was found in the Avery/Murphy house located on Cedar Street in Centreville. (Courtesy of Dalton and Anne Murphy.)

This Blocton mining family poses for John T. Weeks beside the railroad tracks. While the identity of this family is unknown, it is perhaps a foreman's or mine owner's clan considering the attire. (Courtesy of Beverly Beasley.)

A lumber company that was named the Twin Pines Lumber Company was most likely named after the unusual formation shown in this photograph. The company was located in south Bibb County near the town of Maplesville. (Courtesy of Beverly Weeks Beasley.)

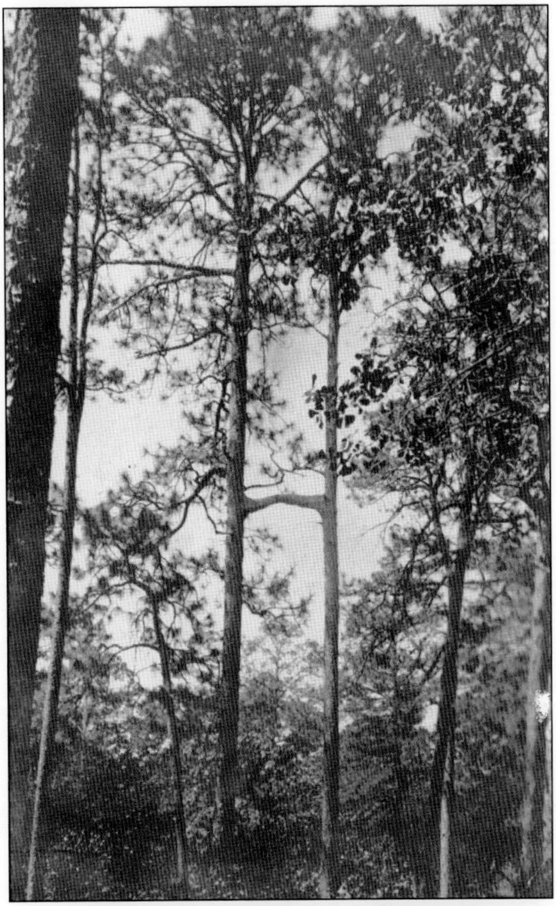

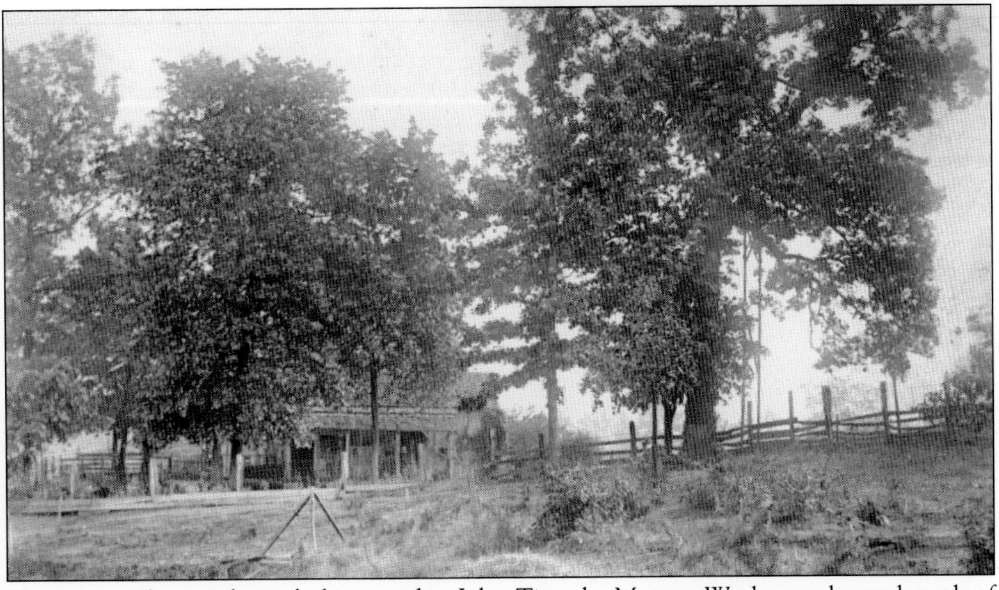

The country home of noted photographer John Timothy Morgan Weeks was located south of Lawley in the Sand Mountain community. (Courtesy of Beverly Weeks Beasley.)

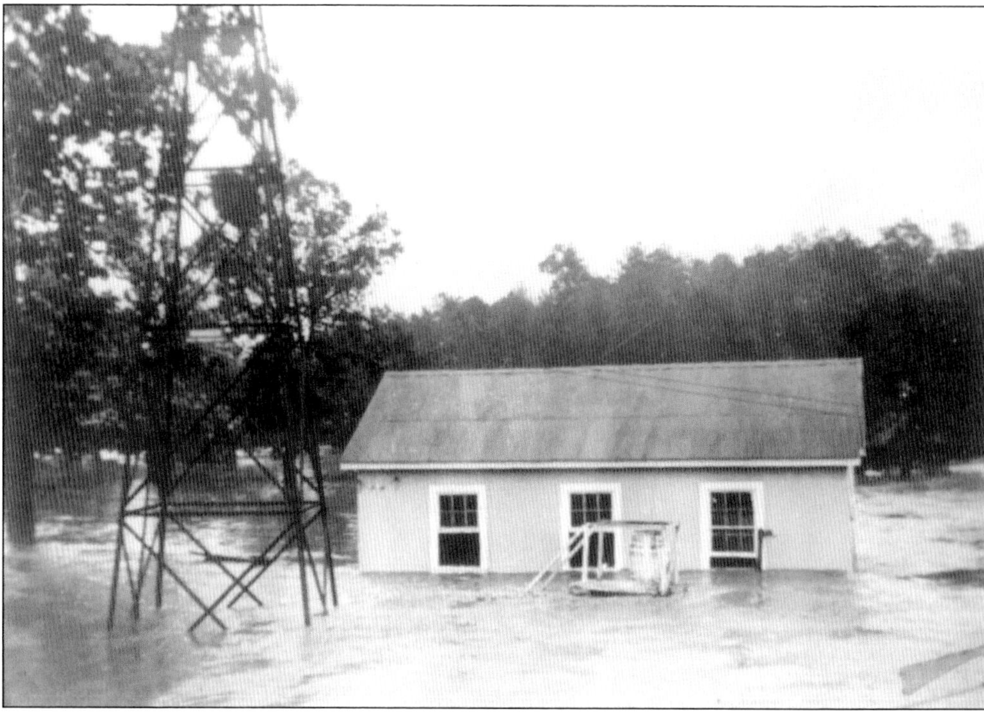

In July 1916, the town of Blocton was flooded by the waters of Caffee Creek. In this picture, the TCI Water Works building has nearly been covered by the floodwaters. (Photograph by Lelia Turner, courtesy of Paula Fancher.)

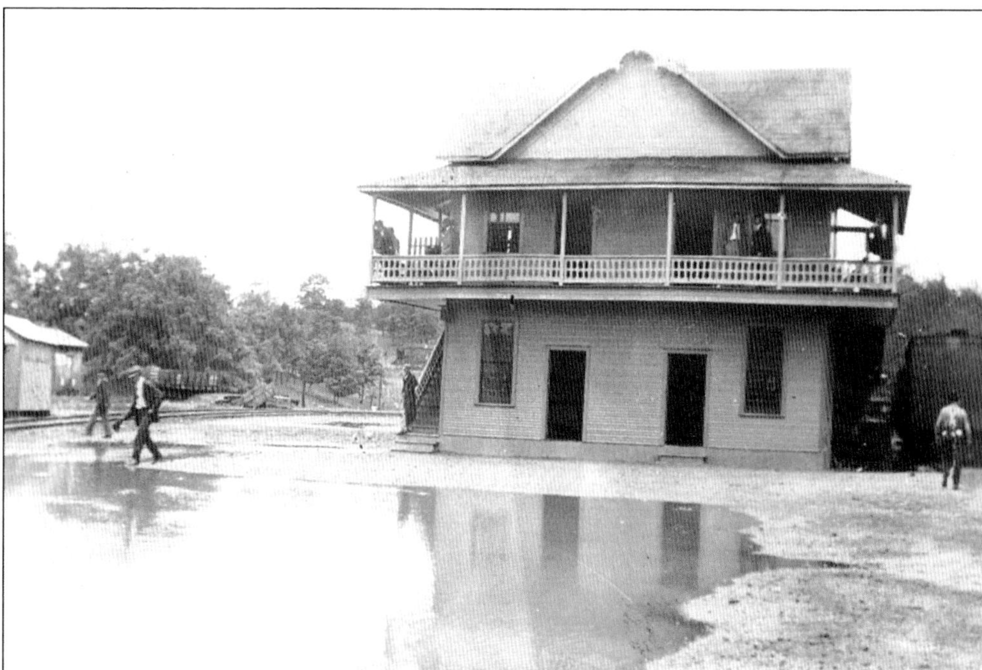

The Blocton Depot served the southern L&N, Alabama Great Southern (AGS), and Mississippi and Ohio (M&O) Railroads after the flood of 1916. (Courtesy of Paula Fancher.)

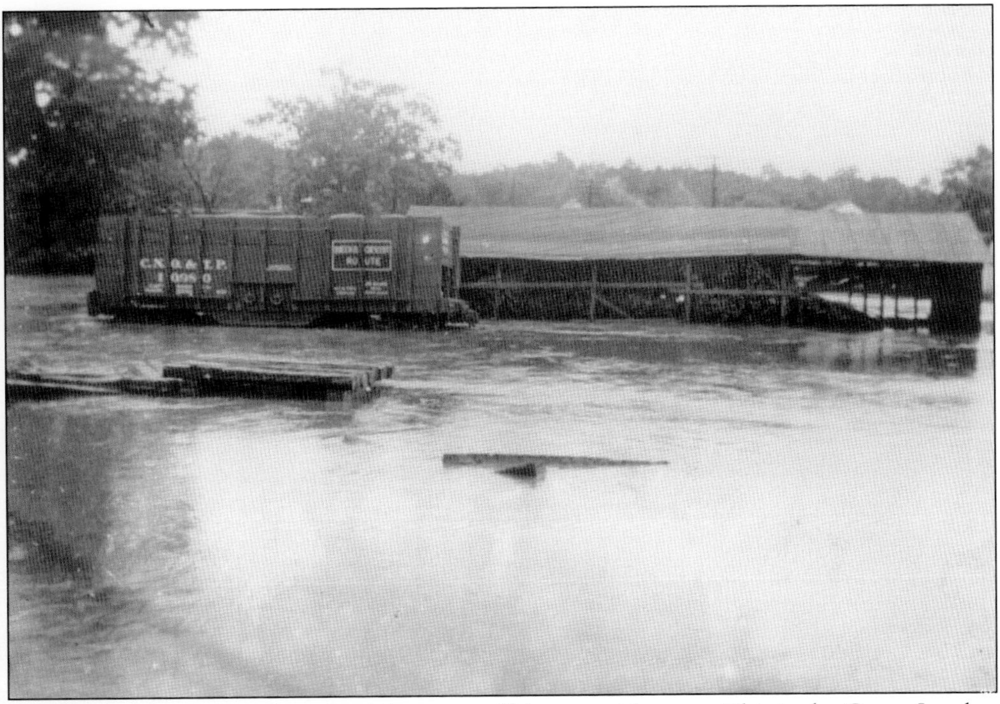

The flood of 1916 covered much of the town of Blocton with water. This is the Green Lumber Company between the M&O tracks and the southern track going to the No. 9 Mine. (Courtesy of Paula Fancher.)

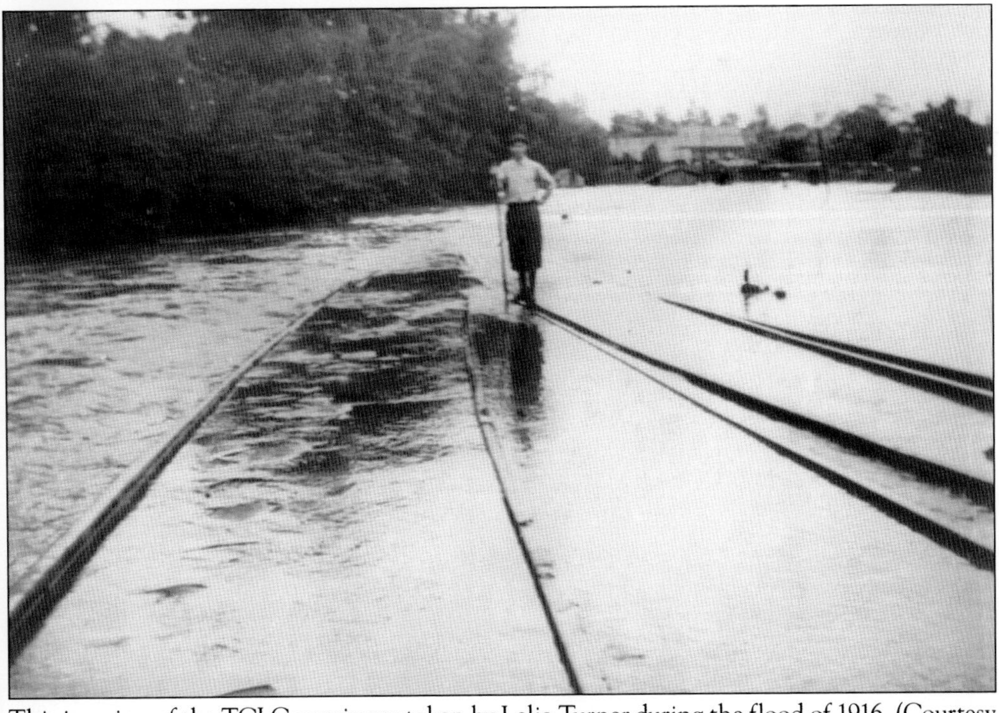

This is a view of the TCI Commissary taken by Lelia Turner during the flood of 1916. (Courtesy of Paula Fancher.)

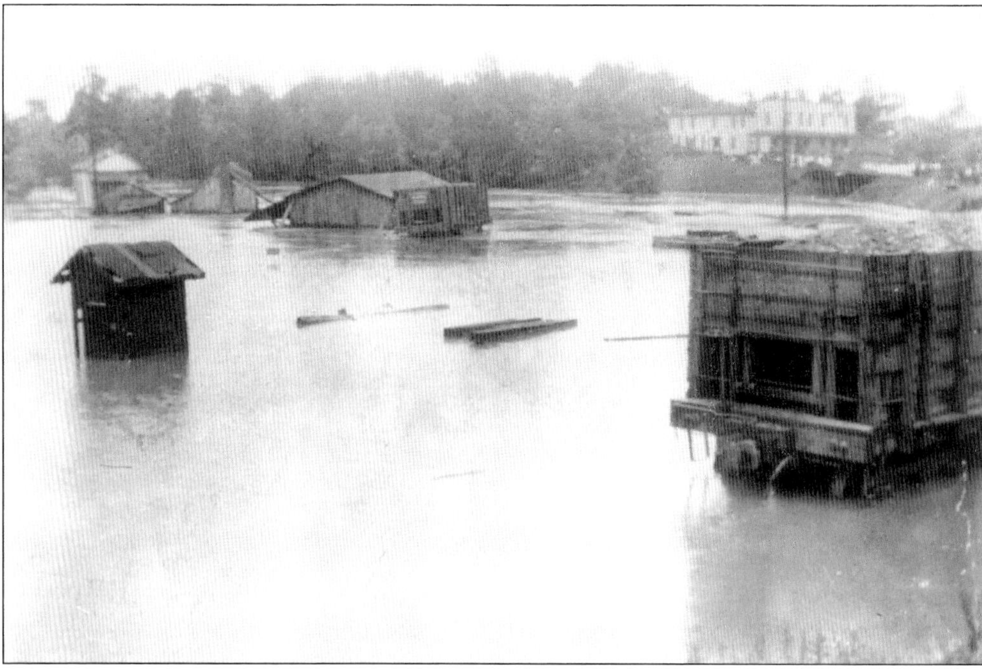

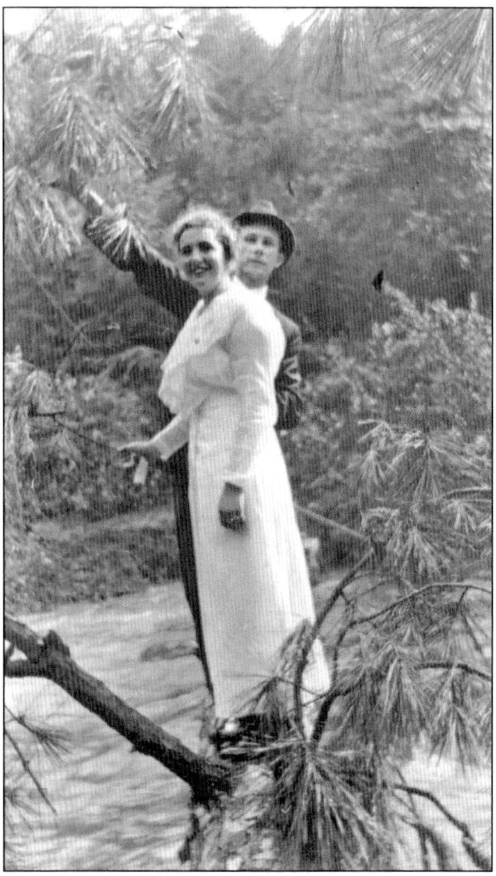

This is a flood picture of the railroad tracks and a railroad car. The TCI Commissary is visible in the upper right corner. (Courtesy of Paula Fancher.)

Nancy Virginia Turner and Oscar Winfield are seen standing on a tree branch during the flood of July 1916, which damaged much of the town of Blocton. (Courtesy of Paula Fancher.)

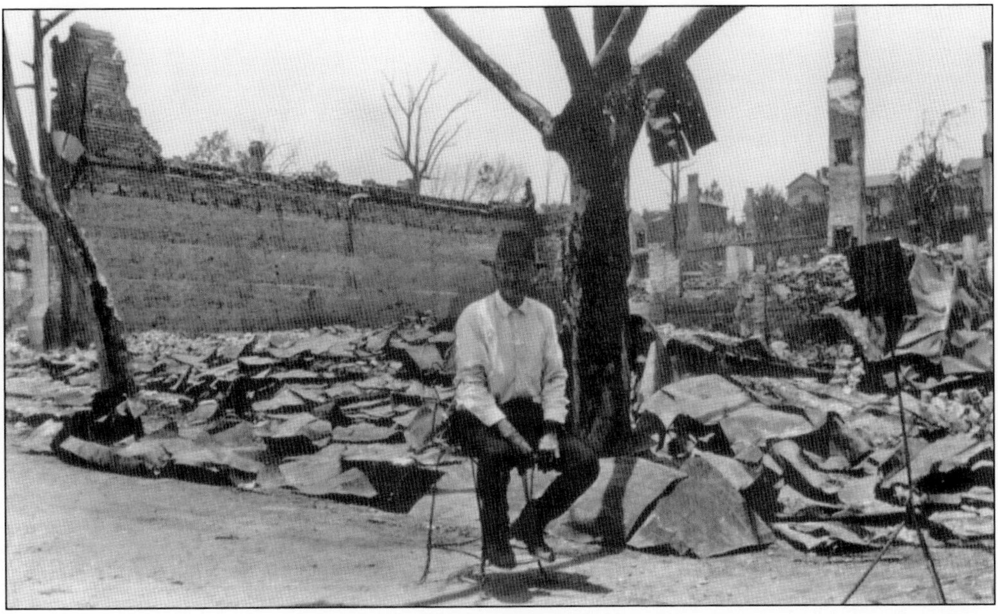

This photograph shows a Mr. Lucas in front of the Harvey's Drug Store that burned in West Blocton in 1927. (Courtesy of Paula Fancher.)

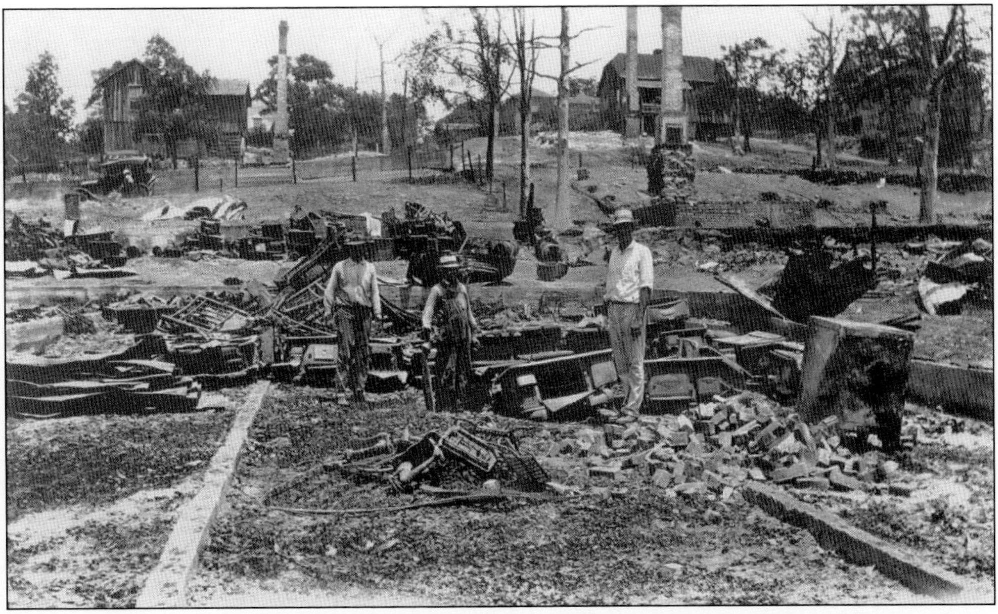

This photograph, taken on July 12, 1927, by Lelia (Coleman) Parker of West Blocton, shows several unidentified men at the Manring Hotel and neighboring homes, which later burned. (Courtesy of Paula Fancher.)

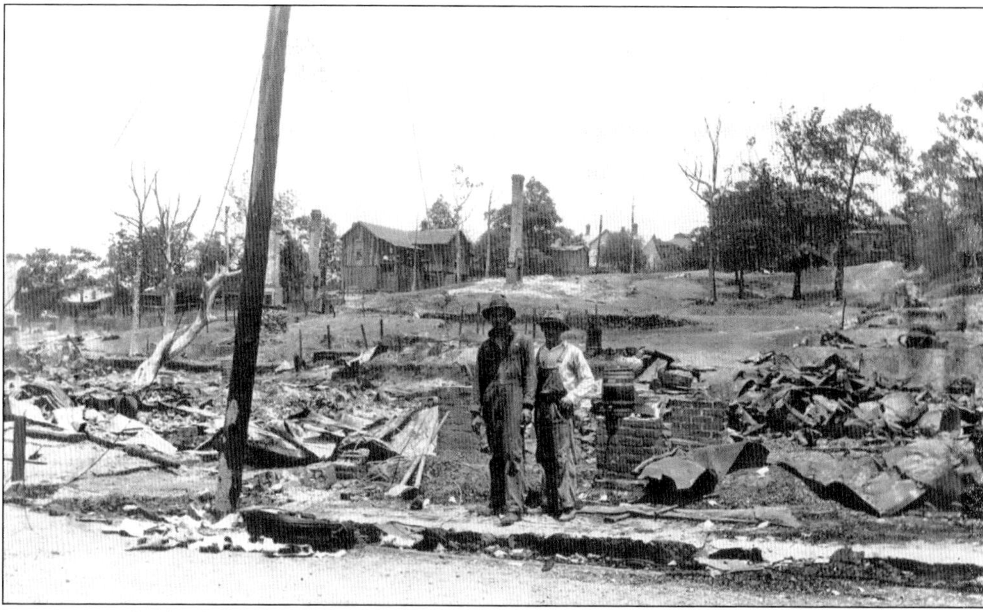

Written on the back of this 1927 photograph is: "The Manring Hotel, several stores and houses burned here." The men are unidentified. This devastating fire was a setback for West Blocton, but the determined citizens vowed to rebuild stronger and better homes and buildings. (Photograph by Lelia Parker, courtesy of Paula Fancher.)

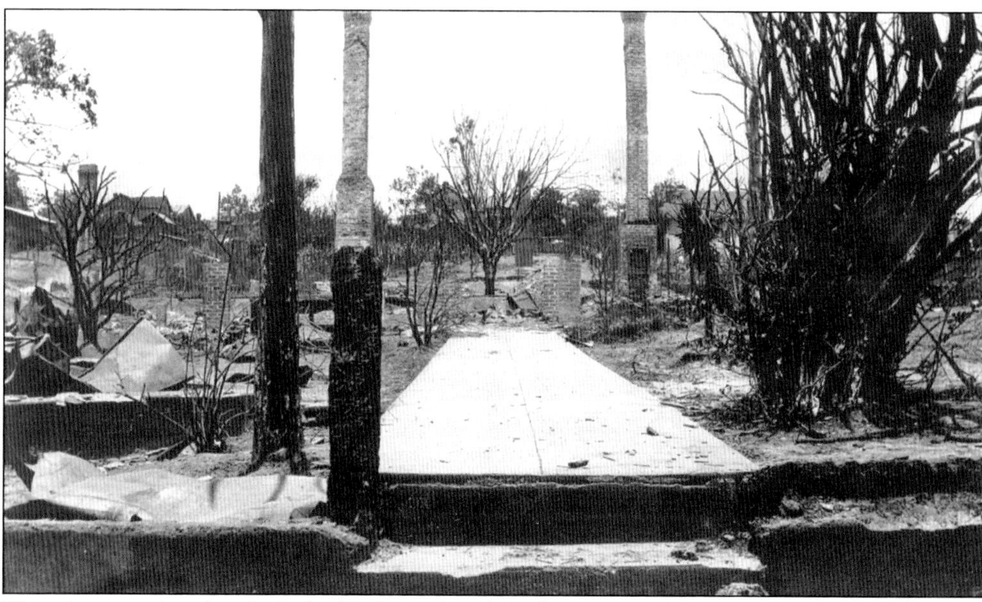

This photograph, taken by Lelia (Coleman) Parker, shows West Blocton. Written on the back is: "The Douthit Hotel burned here." (Courtesy of Paula Fancher.)

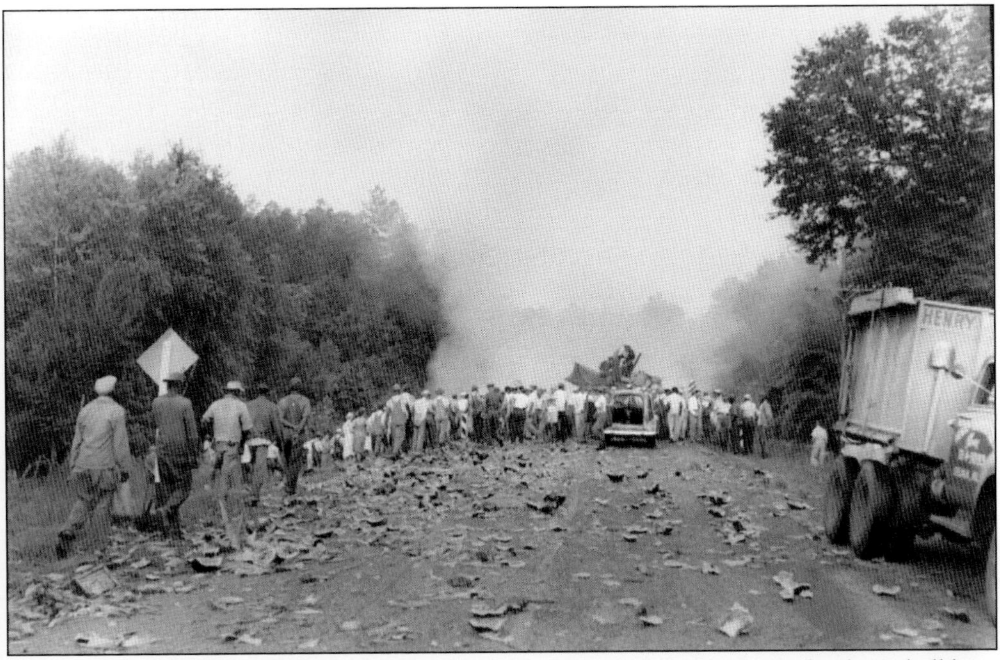

This wreck on the Eoline Bridge resulted in three lives lost when an 18-wheeler hauling a bulldozer met a car on the narrow structure and the bulldozer blade caught the side of the car, flipping it over the side. The rescue was hindered by the toxic fumes from the creosote piling, which caught fire. Jim Oakley, who worked for the *Centreville Press* at the time, remembers the horrible sight and sounds that he witnessed after he arrived on the scene. (Courtesy of Jim Oakley.)

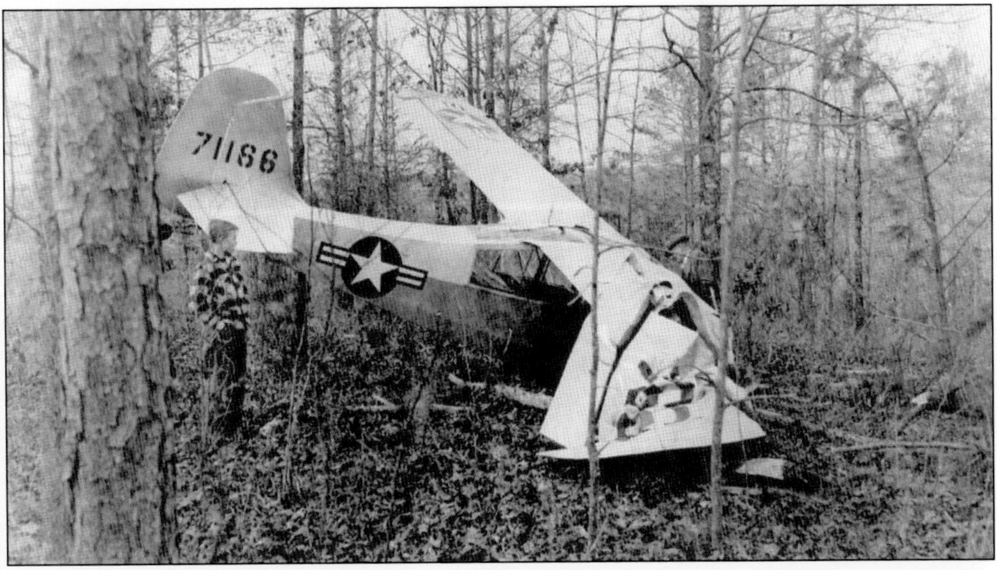

This airplane crash occurred in West Blocton. Two jet pilot trainees were flying a practice exercise from Craig Air Force Base when the two airplanes bumped wings, causing one to malfunction. A number of people saw the smoking airplane as it flew over the courthouse with the other one close behind. A school bus driver saw the airplane go down and called for help. When the military police came, they closed off the area but not before Jim Oakley took pictures of the accident. The pilot was killed in the crash, but his identity is unknown. (Courtesy of Jim Oakley.)

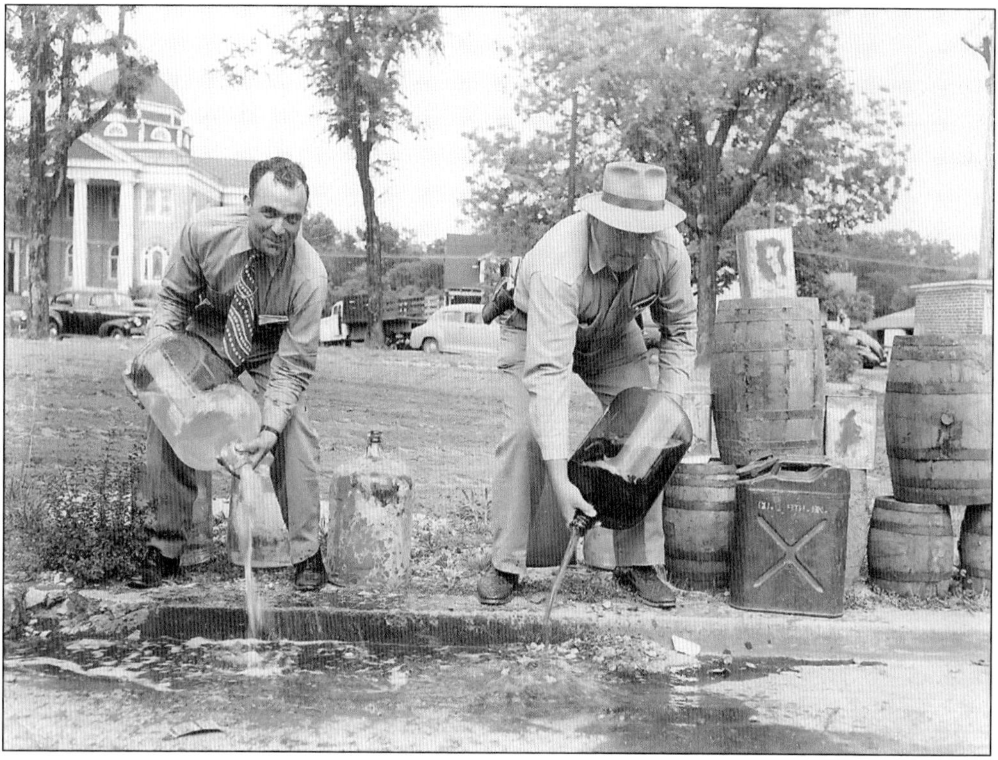

Bibb County has always been a dry county. In days past, it was not unusual to see lawmen with great quantities of homemade liquor to be poured out on the streets of downtown Centreville. These law enforcement officers are Sheriff Jimmy Johnson (left, father of future sheriff Harry Johnson) and deputy Pilgreen. (Courtesy of Kendal Johnson.)

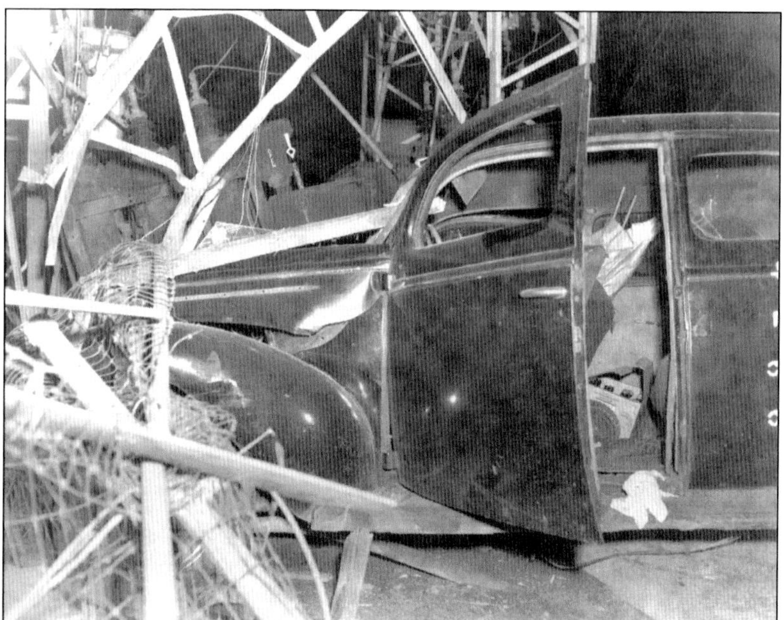

The Alabama Power Substation in Four Points was hit by a drunk driver, and the occupants of the vehicle were trapped inside for some time while workers removed power lines. Rumor has it that after the accident they gave up drinking. (Courtesy of Jim Oakley.)

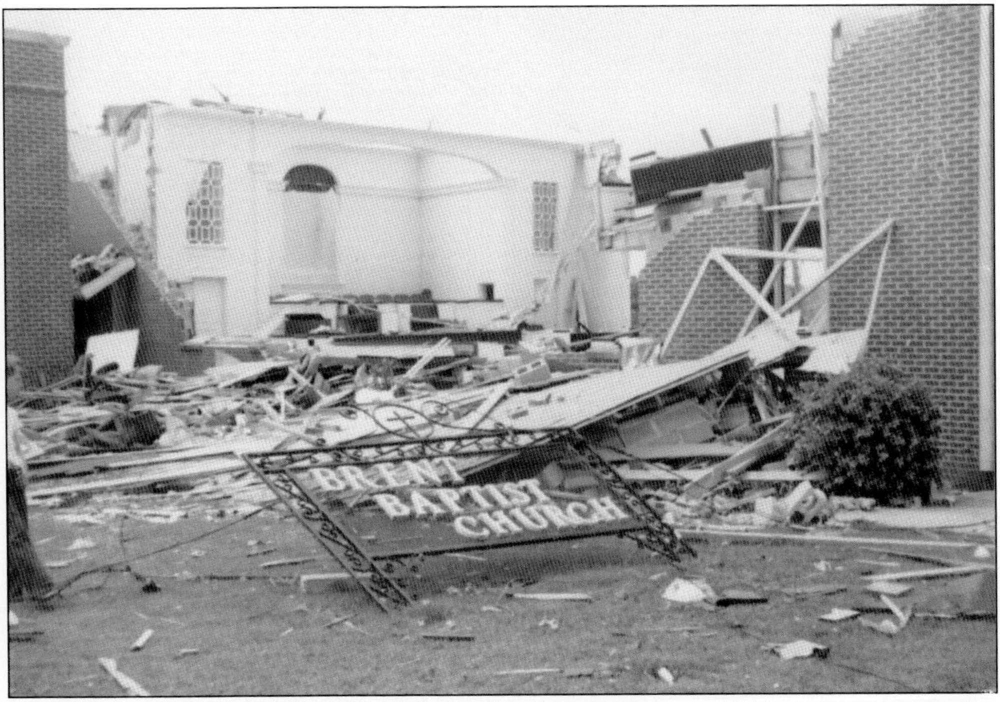

On a Sunday afternoon in May 1973, while the church congregations of Bibb County were meeting for worship, storms built up nearby until a tornado was formed and struck the downtown area. This is a photograph of Brent Baptist Church taken in the aftermath of the storm. One life was lost in this church, and several serious injuries were incurred. (Courtesy of Brent Baptist Church.)

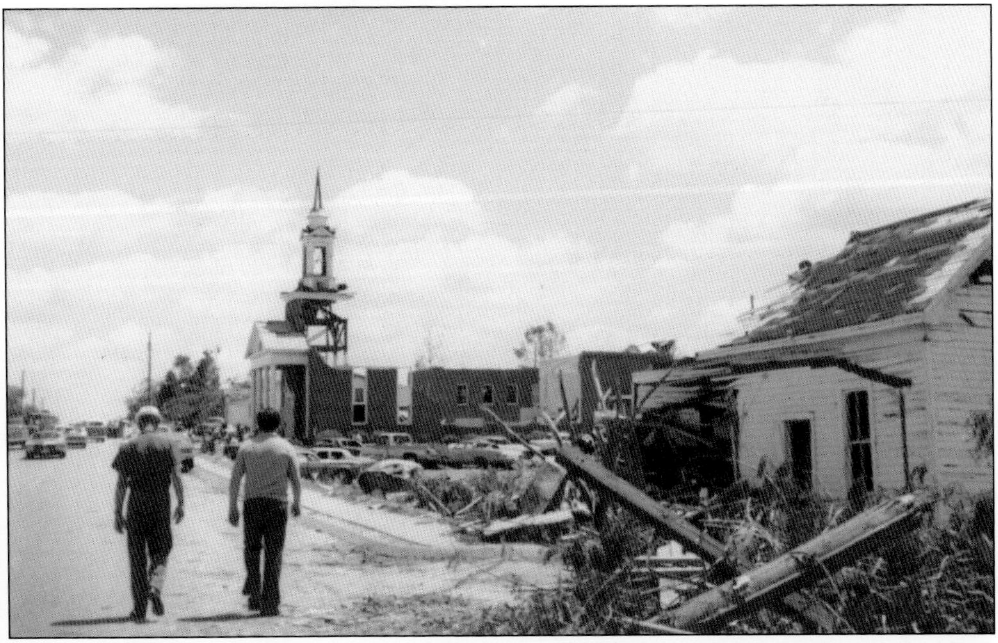

This scene looks north on Main Street in Brent after the devastation of the 1973 tornado, which almost totally destroyed the city. Still standing on the right side of the street is the Brent Baptist Church steeple. (Courtesy of Brent Baptist Church.)

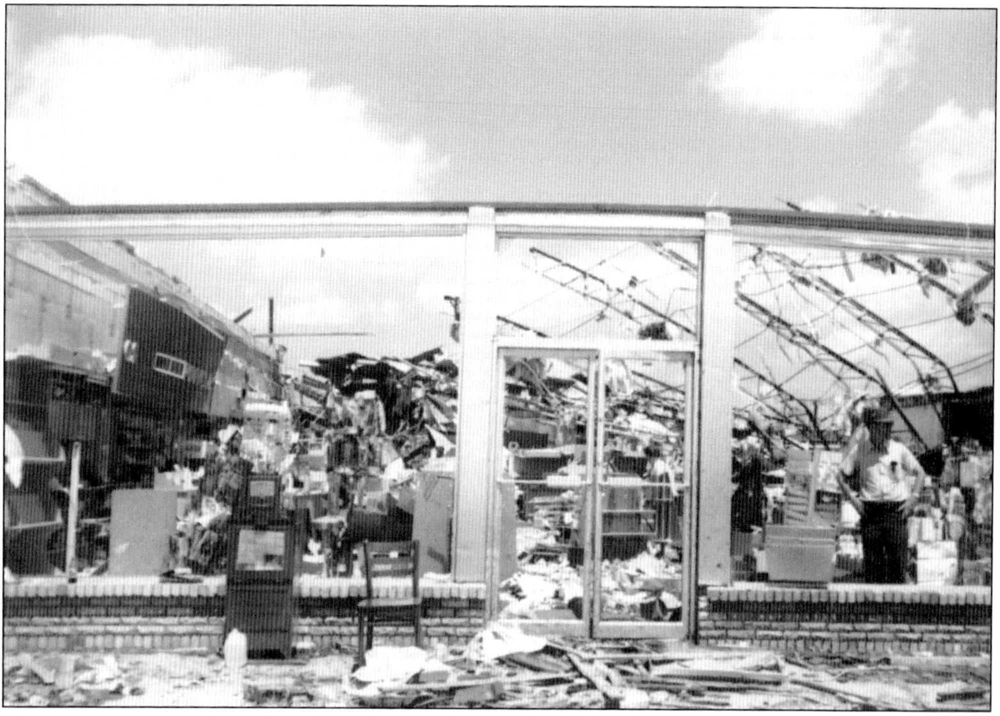

This is one of the many storefronts destroyed by the tornado, which struck Brent in May 1973. (Courtesy of Brent Baptist Church.)

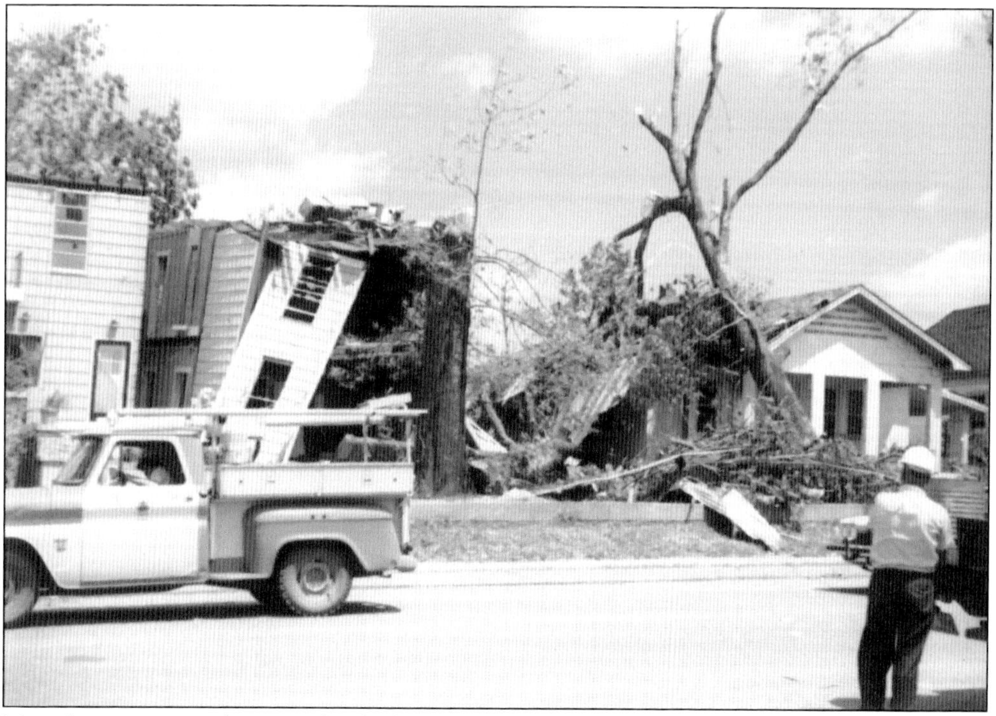

Many homes were either completely destroyed or badly damaged in May 1973 when a tornado struck the town of Brent. (Courtesy of Brent Baptist Church.)

Nine

Modern-Day Bibb

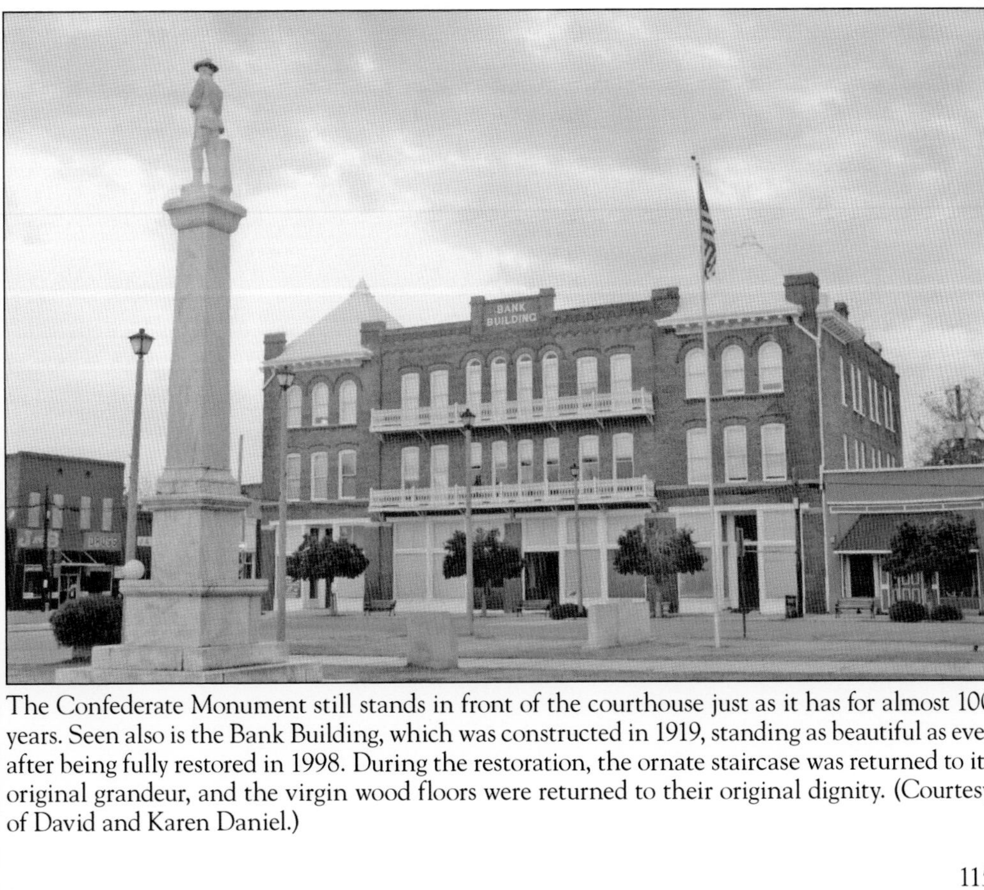

The Confederate Monument still stands in front of the courthouse just as it has for almost 100 years. Seen also is the Bank Building, which was constructed in 1919, standing as beautiful as ever after being fully restored in 1998. During the restoration, the ornate staircase was returned to its original grandeur, and the virgin wood floors were returned to their original dignity. (Courtesy of David and Karen Daniel.)

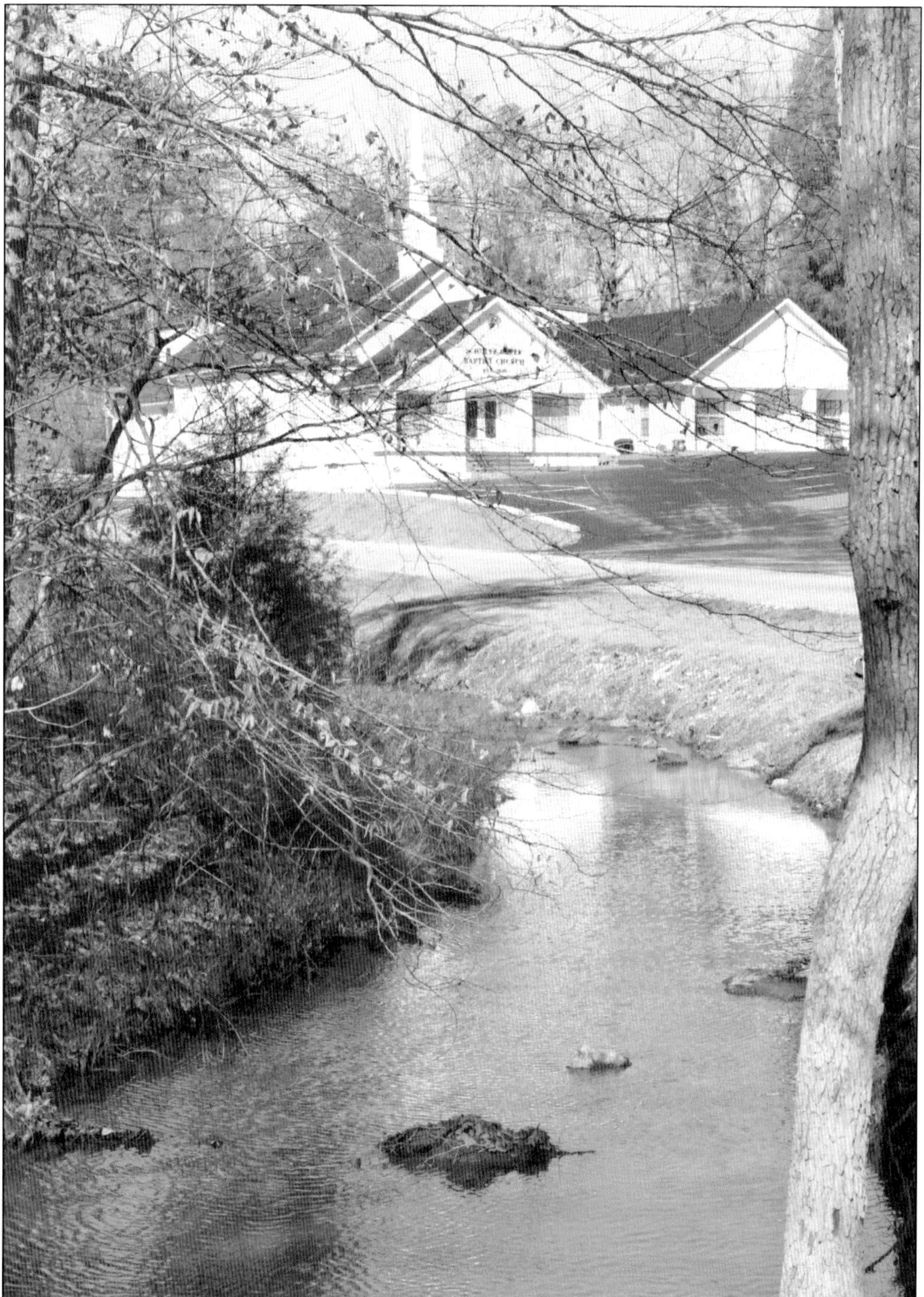

The Schultz Creek Baptist Church is centrally located in Bibb County beside its pristine namesake spring that flows into the Little Schultz Creek and eventually into the Cahaba River. The church is active today and has new additions just to the rear of the original sanctuary. (Courtesy of David and Karen Daniel.)

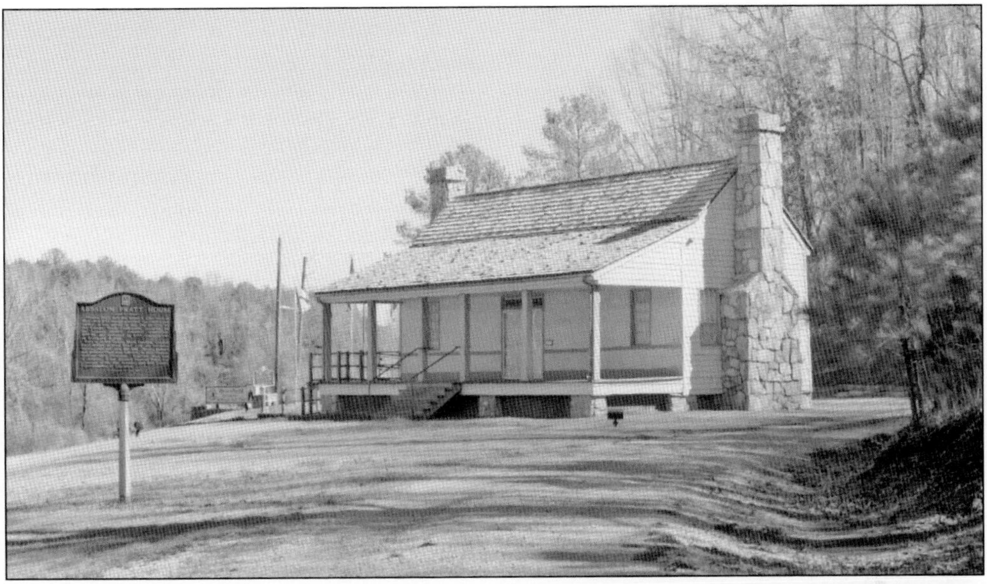

The Absalom Pratt House, which was built 8 miles west of Brierfield in 1835, was moved to a site at the entrance to Brierfield Historic Ironworks Park in 1994. It was restored by the Cahaba Trace Commission and the Alabama Historic Ironworks Commission and dedicated in 1998. Absalom Pratt was the father of Richard Hopkins Pratt, who was a principal of the Six Mile Academy and the Bibb County superintendent of education. (Courtesy of David and Karen Daniel.)

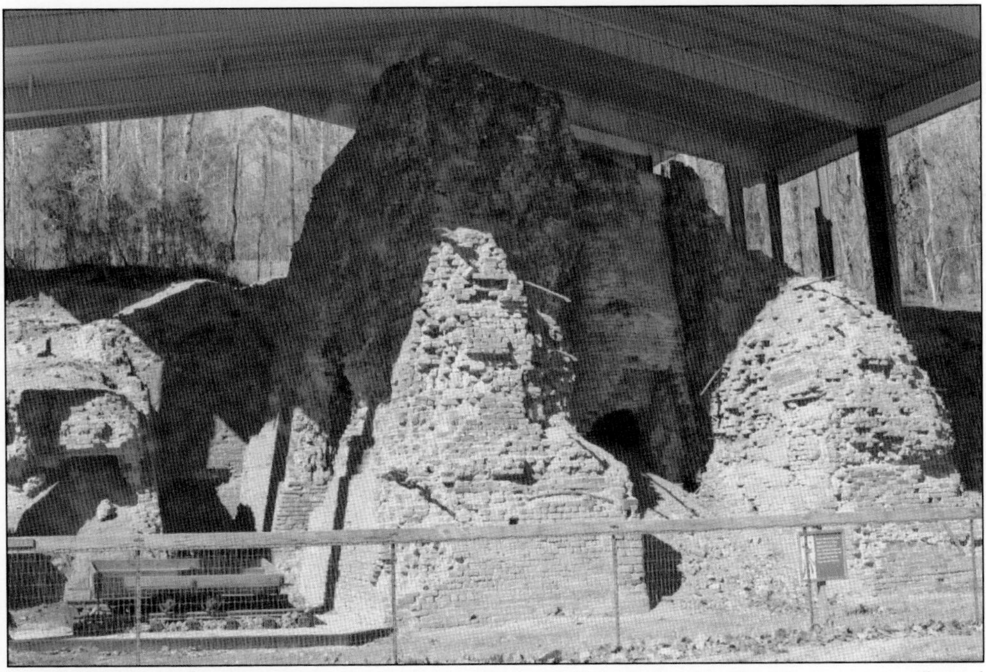

The Bibb County Iron Company built a furnace here in 1862. From this blast furnace once flowed "the toughest and most suitable iron for making guns above any other iron in the South," according to the Brierfield Ironworks Park Web site. In March 1865, the Union army's 10th Missouri Cavalry burned the Brierfield Ironworks. Today it is in the Brierfield Ironworks Historical State Park and one of Bibb County's many historic treasures. (Courtesy of David and Karen Daniel.)

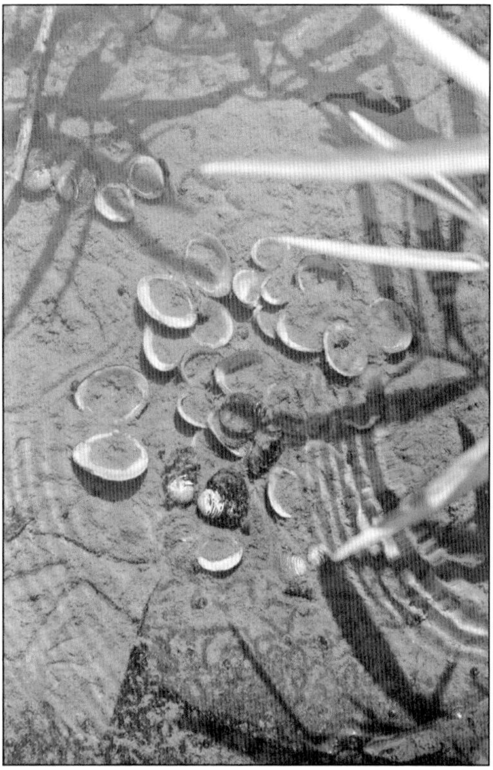

The Cahaba River is home to 27 species of freshwater mussels, including some with colorful names such as Alabama Rainbow, Butterfly, Monkey Face, and the Three-Horned Wartyback. In the past, there were more than 40 species, but they are gradually dying out, which is why the Cahaba River Society constantly monitors the quality of the Cahaba River and its watershed. (Courtesy of David and Karen Daniel.)

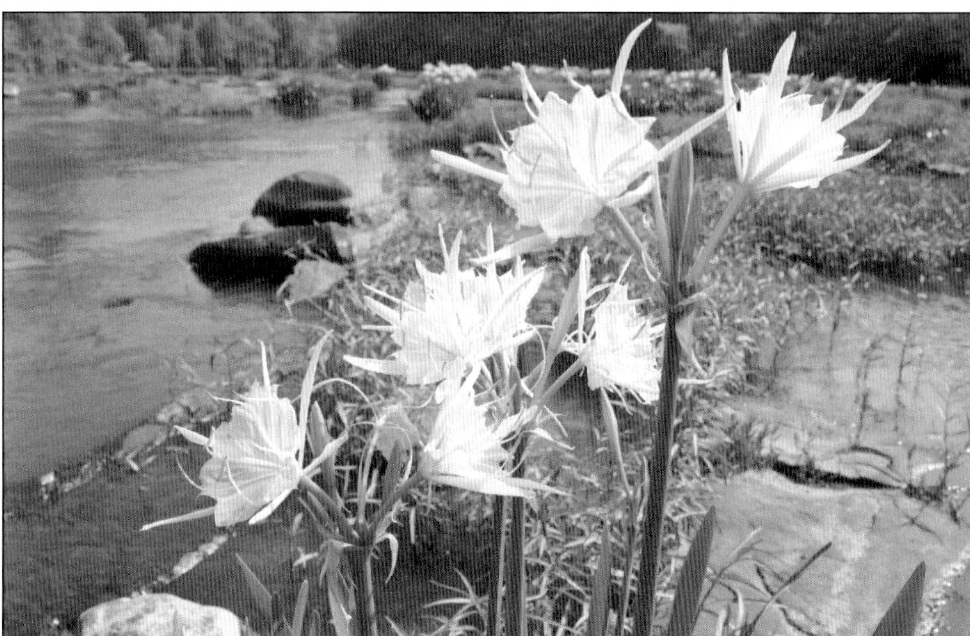

Known by several names, including Hymenocallis Coronaria, Cahaba Lily, and Shoals Lily, this flower is a member of the Amaryllis family, or the spider-lily. Bibb County is known for this breathtaking lily that grows in the rocky shoals of the Cahaba River and is celebrated every year in West Blocton during the Cahaba Lily Festival. (Courtesy of David and Karen Daniel.)

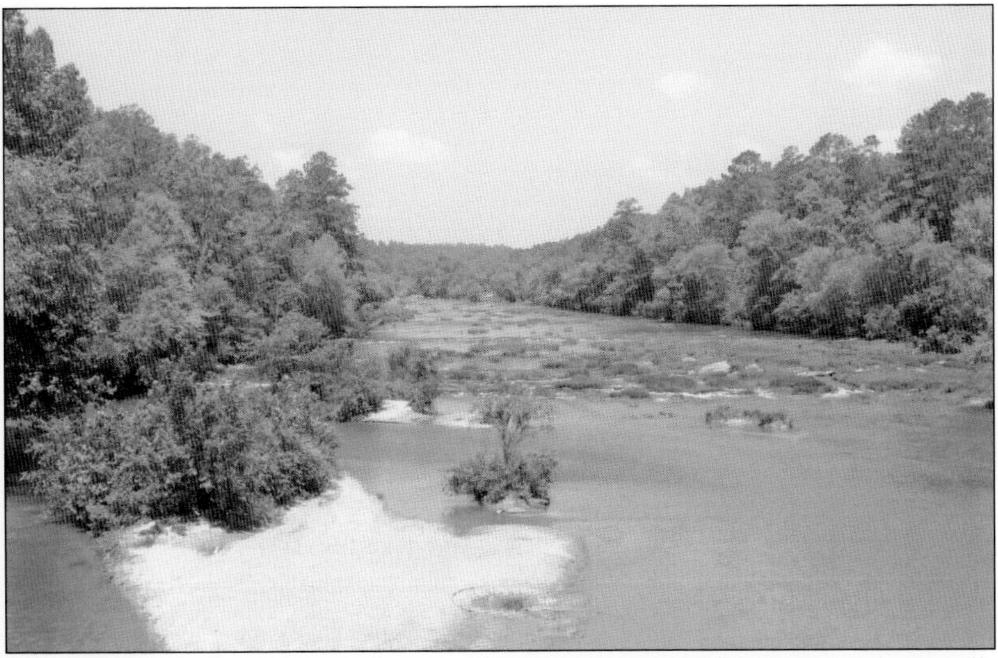

The Cahaba River flows 191 miles from St. Clair County through Bibb County and eventually ends in Dallas County, where it flows into the Alabama River. The Cahaba River is a haven for canoeing, kayaking, fishing, bird-watching, photography, hiking, and camping. (Courtesy of David and Karen Daniel.)

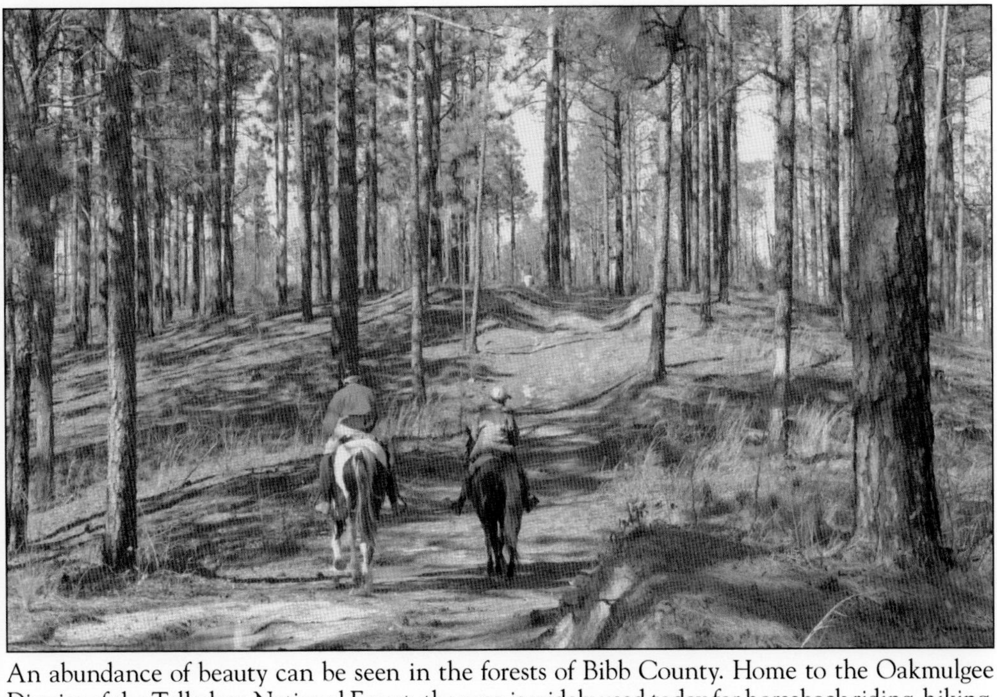

An abundance of beauty can be seen in the forests of Bibb County. Home to the Oakmulgee District of the Talladega National Forest, the area is widely used today for horseback riding, hiking, hunting, and primitive camping to enjoy the preservation of God's natural beauty. (Courtesy of David and Karen Daniel.)

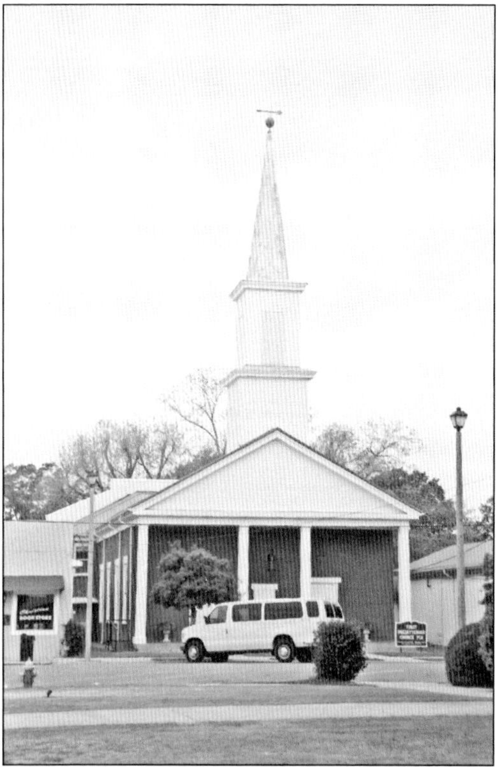

The modern-day version of the Centreville First Presbyterian Church looks much like the church when it was first built. The church was modernized in the 1950s, and in the early 1990s a fellowship center was added. The current minister is Timothy Bonds, who lives in the church manse with his family on Valley Street. The church is listed on the National Register of Historic Places in Bibb County and has a rich history in Centreville, starting with its founding fathers. (Courtesy of David and Karen Daniel.)

This aerial photograph of the Centreville Historic Town Square was taken in 2004. The photograph was taken by Megan Sonnier while she was being flown by pilot Micah Daniel. Copies were available for sale at many local businesses. (Courtesy of David and Karen Daniel.)

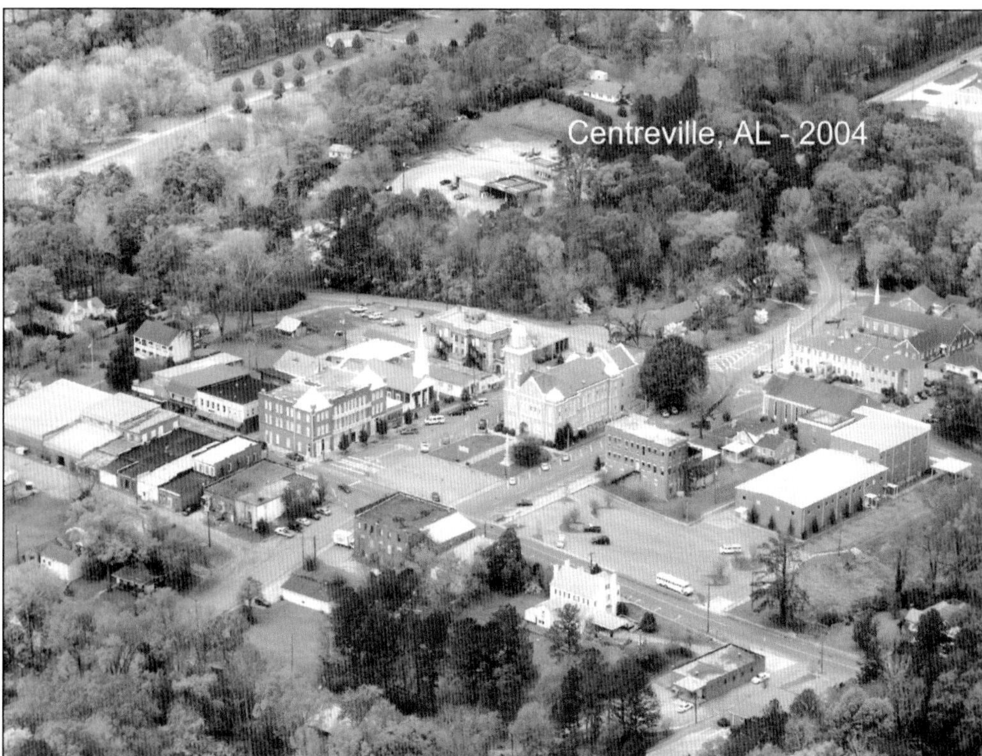

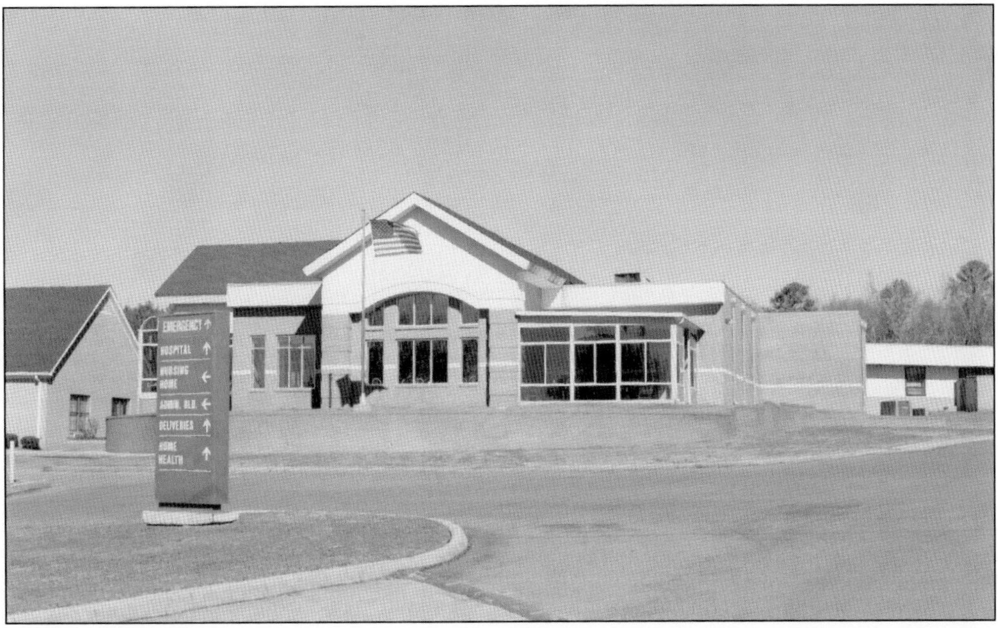

Bibb County is proud of its concern for the health and well-being of the community. The Bibb County Medical Center has grown over the years to include not only a hospital, emergency room, nursing home, cafeteria, apartments, and homes for the elderly, but also a staff of doctors and nurses who work in a number of offices surrounding the facility. (Courtesy of David and Karen Daniel.)

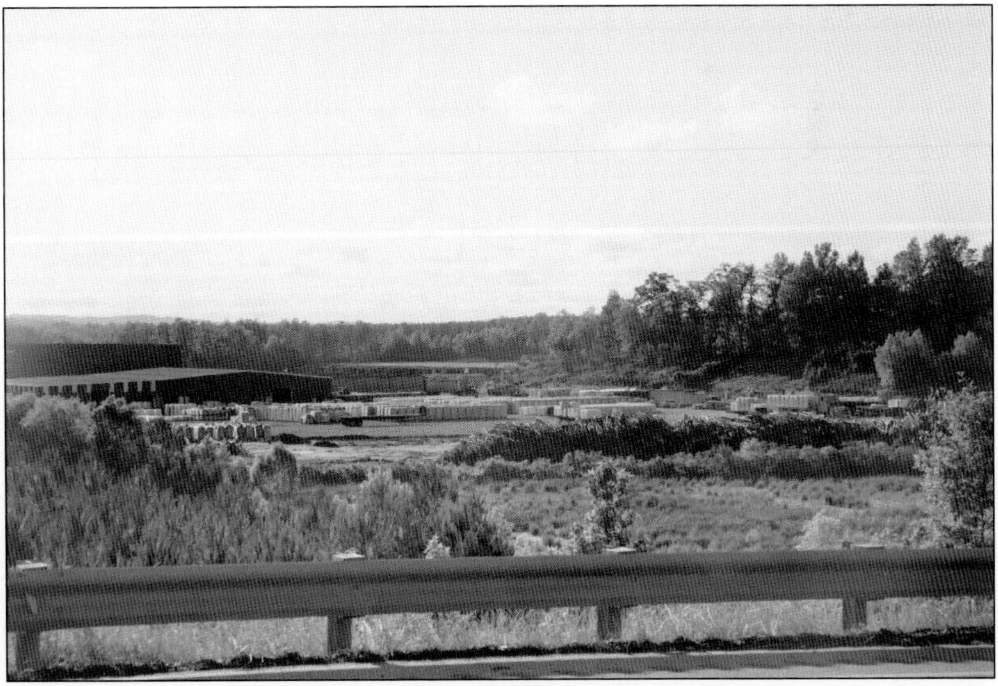

The lumber business thrives today at plants around the county, as seen in this photograph of the Sims Bark Company, which packages by-products from other mills and is sold throughout the country for landscaping needs. (Courtesy of David and Karen Daniel.)

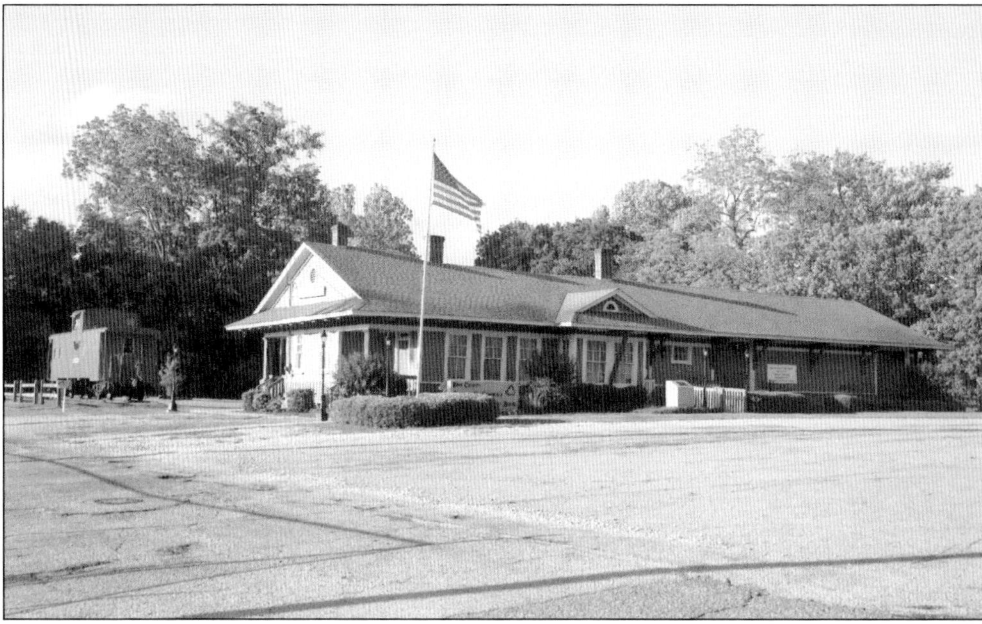

The Bibb County Chamber of Commerce is housed in a restored railroad depot that once sat on the railway that passed through Centreville. The depot was scheduled to be destroyed but instead was donated to the chamber. With the help of many local businessmen, including longtime chamber member Cecil Crews, the depot was moved to its present location and was restored with the help of time and donations. (Courtesy of David and Karen Daniel.)

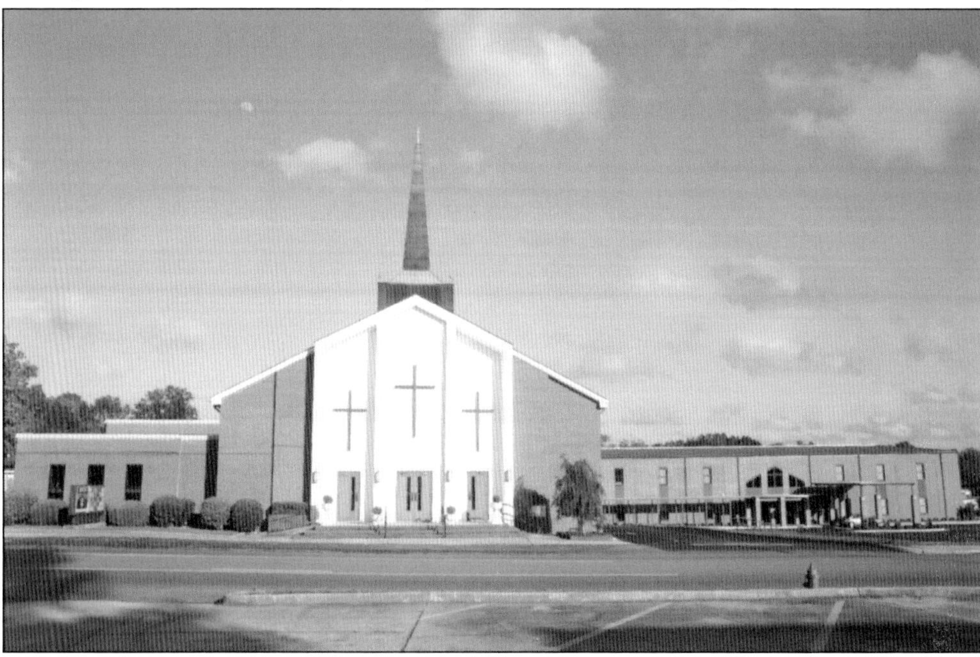

The Brent Baptist Church, which was rebuilt after the devastating tornado of 1973, continues to grow. This growth resulted in the addition of a fellowship hall to the rear of the church and a family life center named after longtime pastor and friend Robert Johnston and his wife, Jean. (Courtesy of David and Karen Daniel.)

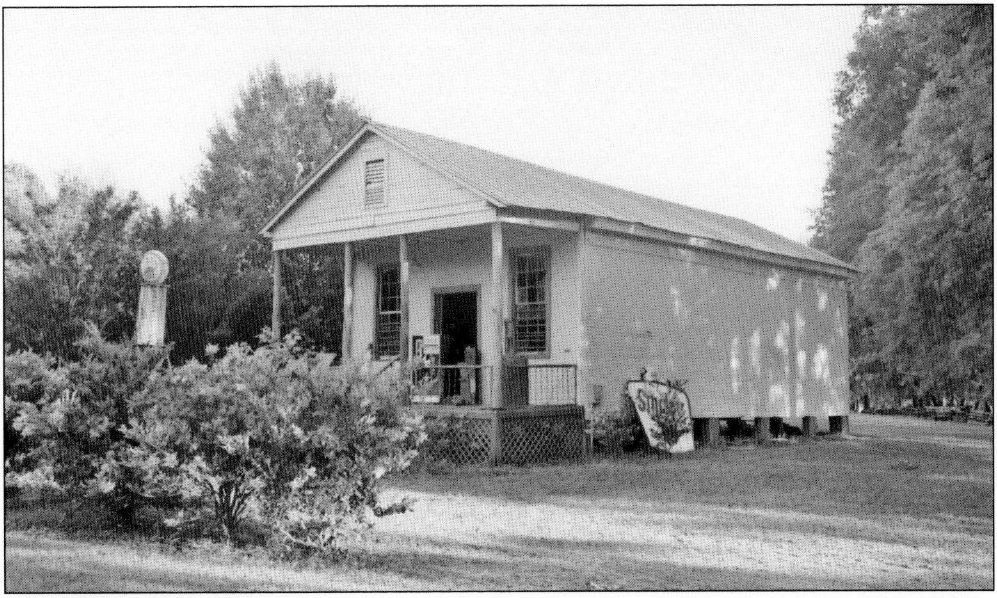

The Cahaba River Historical Park was developed by Cecil Crews and is shared with the neighborhood to enjoy the beautiful Cahaba River. This country store once stood on the home lot of Doc Cleveland in Trio and was used as post office, general store, and magistrate court. (Courtesy of David and Karen Daniel.)

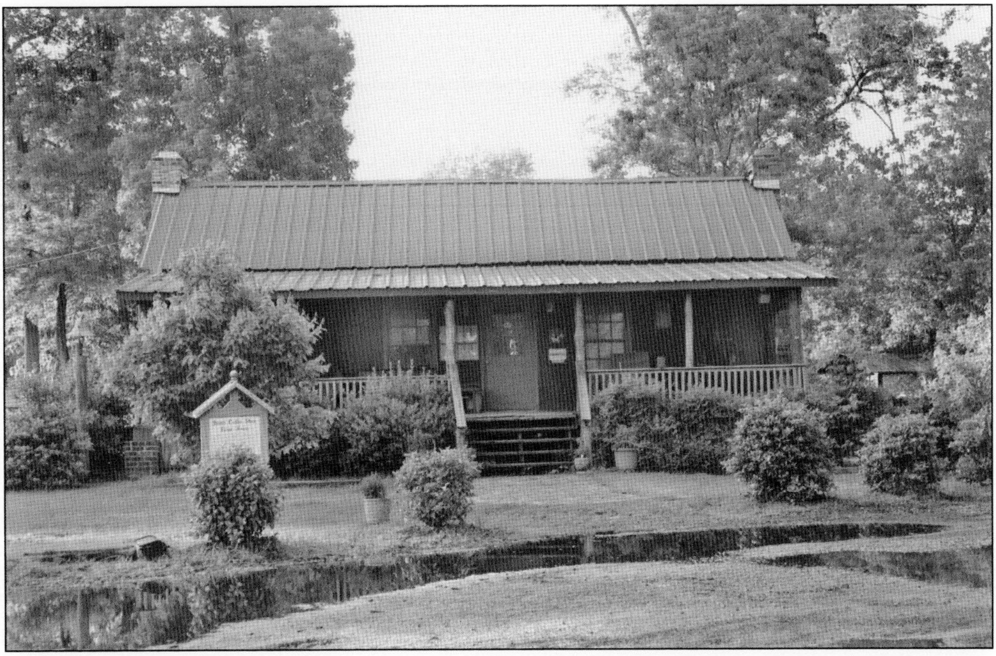

The James Carlos Stone Farm House was originally built in Gary Springs in the Rocky community as an African American church. It was built by the Fuqua and Evans Lumber Company for its employees around 1890. The lumber company later moved, and the church disbanded. The empty church building was then inhabited by the Stone family, who added to it and lived there until 1944. The building was donated to the Cahaba River Historical Park in 2000, and it is now used for special events and as a tourist attraction. (Courtesy of David and Karen Daniel.)

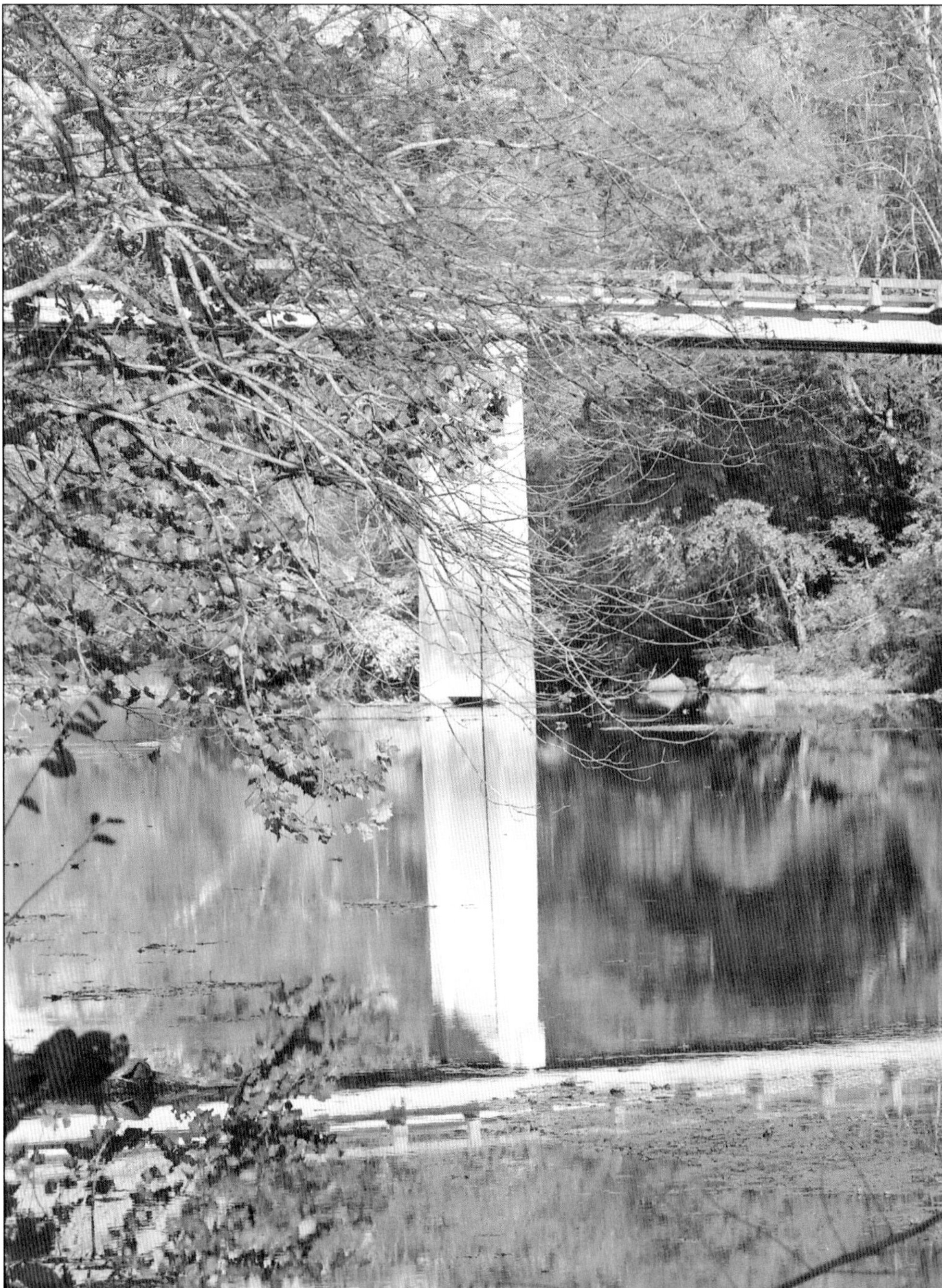

The Cahaba National Wildlife Refuge was established in 2002 and currently has 2,997 acres. It is located north of the confluence of the Little Cahaba and Cahaba Rivers north of the Piper Bridge in Bibb County, 5 miles east of West Blocton. The Friends of the Refuge was organized to provide support for the refuge in respect to protection, preservation, and restoration. (Courtesy of Friends of the Refuge.)

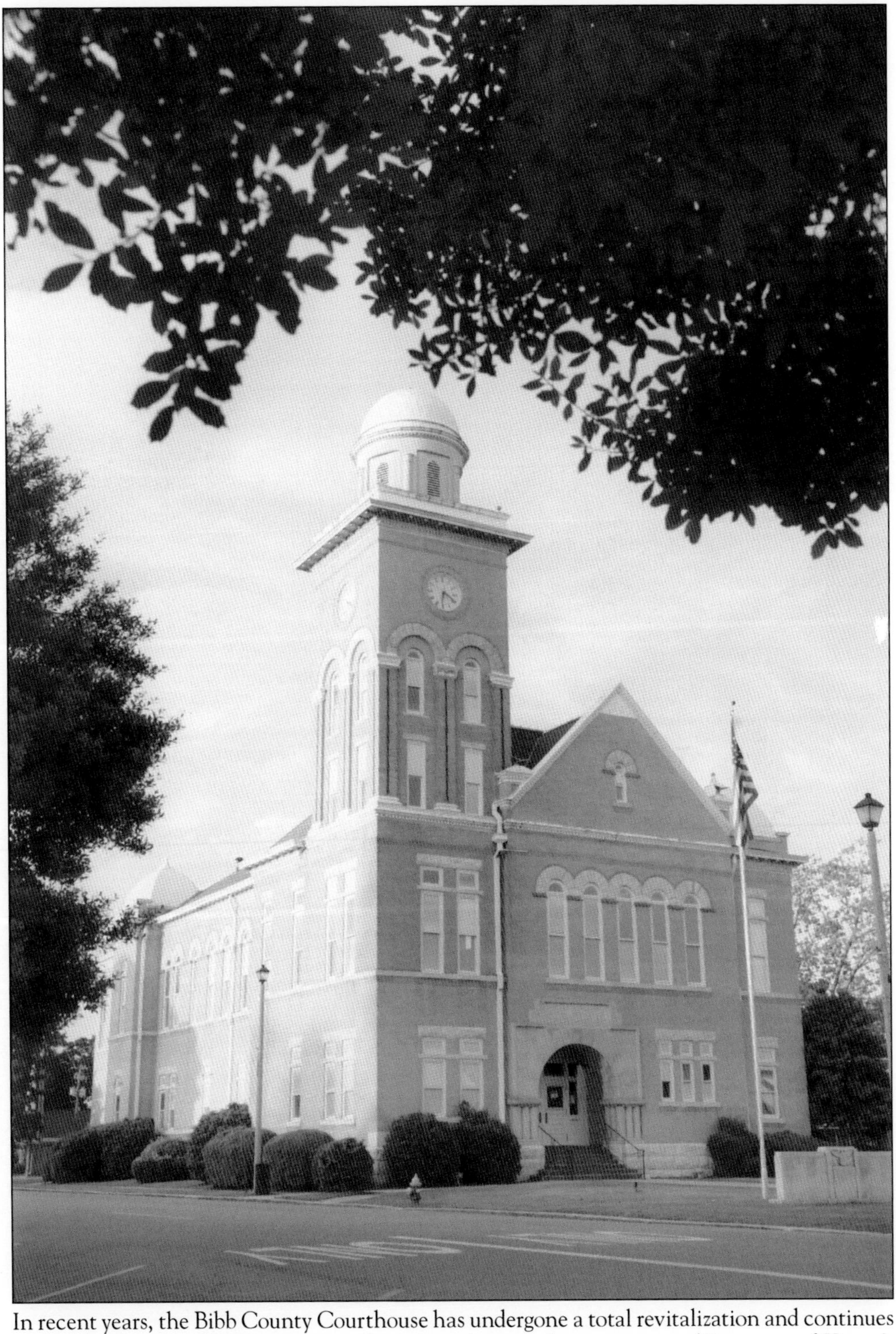

In recent years, the Bibb County Courthouse has undergone a total revitalization and continues its originally intended function as the county's seat of government. (Courtesy of Karen's Photography, Centreville.)

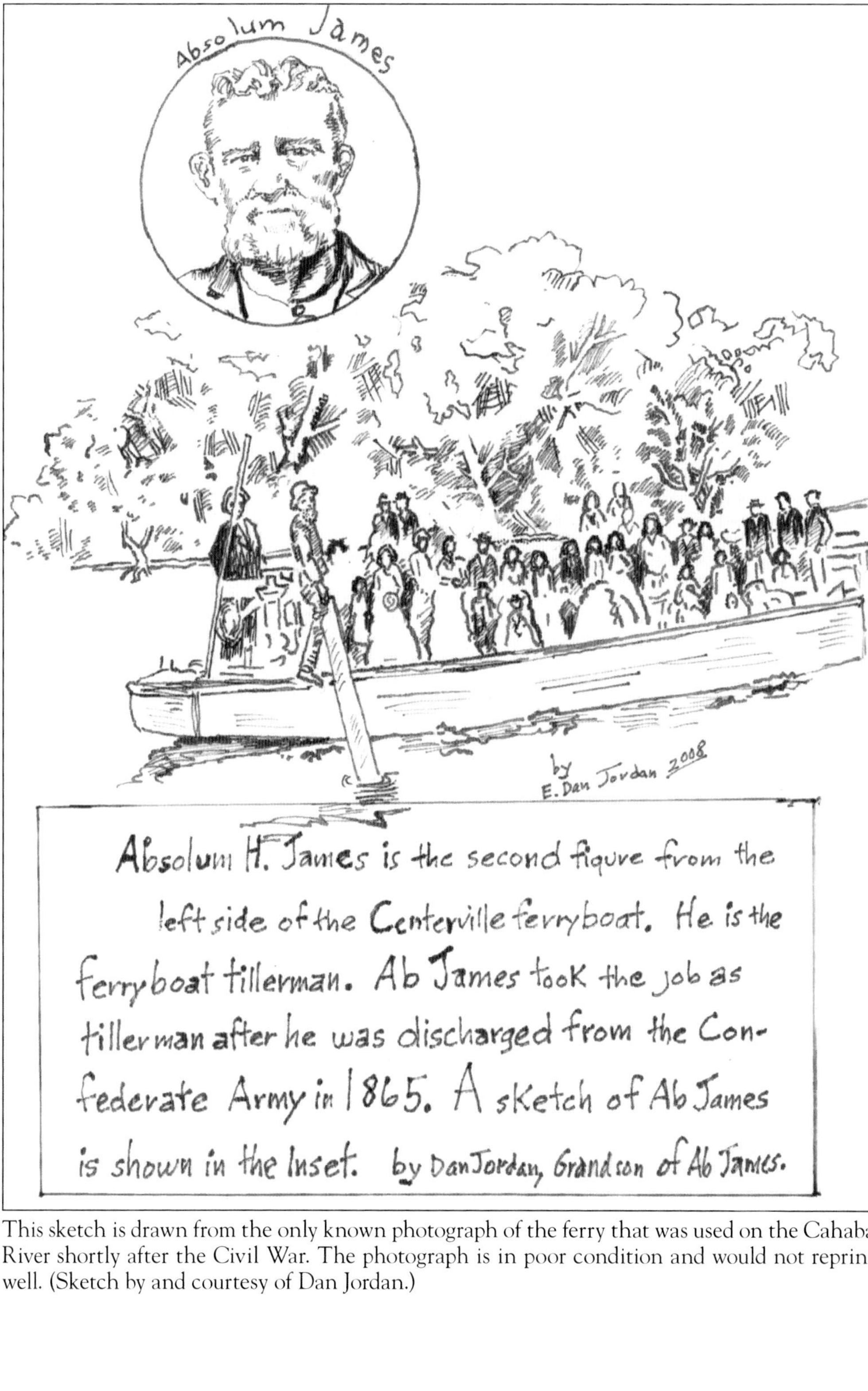

This sketch is drawn from the only known photograph of the ferry that was used on the Cahaba River shortly after the Civil War. The photograph is in poor condition and would not reprint well. (Sketch by and courtesy of Dan Jordan.)

BIBLIOGRAPHY

Adams, Charles Edward. Blocton: *The History of an Alabama Coal Mining Town*. Brierfield, AL: Cahaba Trace Commission, 2001.

Atchison, Ray M. and G. Benton Towry. *Richard Hopkins Pratt and the Six Mile Academy*. Birmingham, AL: Banner Press, 1965.

Cahaba River Society. *A Gift for Generations—Cahaba*. Birmingham, AL: Birmingham Printing and Publishing Company, 1997.

Davidson, Henry Damon. *Inching Along*. Nashville: National Publication Company, 1944.

Daws, Elia Griffin. *1860 Census Bibb County, Alabama*. Centreville, AL: self-published, 1984.

Ellison, Rhoda Coleman. *Place Names of Bibb County Alabama: Abercrombie to ZuZu*. Brierfield, AL: Cahaba Trace Commission, 1993.

———. *Bibb County, Alabama: The First Hundred Years, 1818–1918*. Tuscaloosa, AL: University of Alabama Press, 1984.

Bibb County Heritage Book Committee, Heritage Publishing Consultants And Don Mills, Inc. *The Heritage of Bibb County, Alabama*. Clanton, AL: Walsworth Publishing Company, Inc., 1998.

Langston, Fern. *Echoes of Six Mile*. Six Mile, AL: self-published, 1981.

McCord, Howard F. *Baptists of Bibb County*. Bibb County, AL: self-published, 1979.

Walker, James H. *The Struggle and the Joy: An American Coal Town, Piper, Alabama*: Birmingham, AL: Birmingham Public Library Press, 1993.

Williams, Peggy Henderson. *Memories of Randolph, Bibb County, Alabama*. Birmingham, AL: Banner Press, 2006.

www.bibbchamber.org

www.brierfieldironworks.com

www.cahabariversociety.org

www.cahabafriends.org

www.tannehill.org

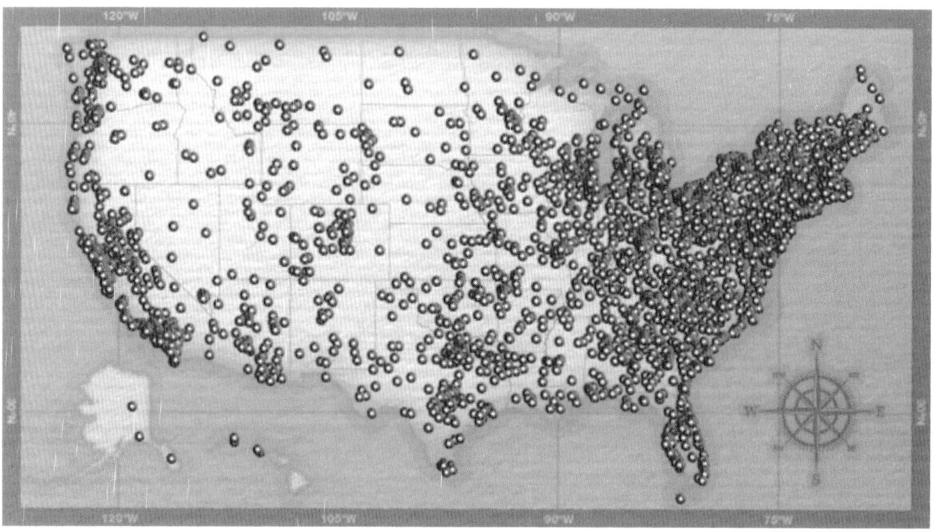